Study Commentary on Exodus

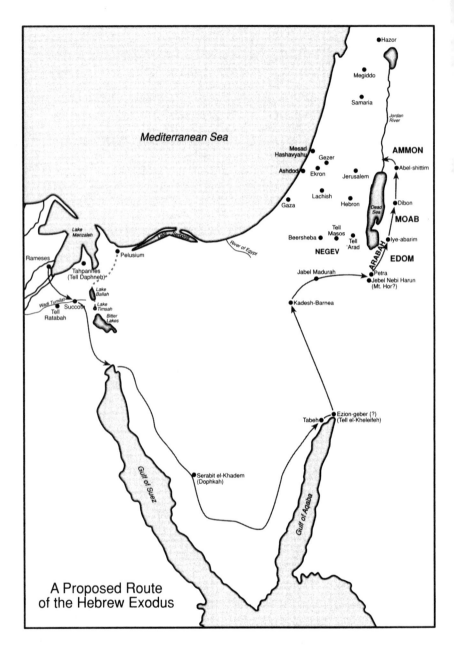

A Proposed Route
of the Hebrew Exodus

Reproduced from the book *Ancient Egypt and the Old
Testament* by courtesy of Baker Book House Co.

A Study Commentary on
Exodus

John D. Currid

 EVANGELICAL PRESS

EVANGELICAL PRESS
Faverdale North Industrial Estate, Darlington, DL3 0PH, England

Evangelical Press USA
P. O. Box 84, Auburn, MA 01501, USA

e-mail: sales@evangelical-press.org

web: www.evangelical-press.org

First published 2000

British Library Cataloguing in Publication Data available

ISBN 0 85234 437 6

Printed and bound in Great Britain by Creative Print & Design Wales, Ebbw Vale.

To Nancy
my companion in the wilderness

Contents

List of abbreviations

ABD	D. N. Freedman, ed., *Anchor Bible Dictionary* (6 vols, 1992)
AJT	*Asian Journal of Theology*
ANET	J. B. Pritchard, ed., *Ancient Near Eastern Texts Relating to the Old Testament* (3rd ed., 1969).
ARE	J. H. Breasted, ed., *Ancient Records of Egypt* (5 vols, 1906)
AUSS	*Andrews University Seminary Studies*
AW	*Ancient World*
BA	*Biblical Archaeologist*
BAMS	*Bulletin of the American Meteorological Society*
BAR	*Biblical Archaeology Review*
BASOR	*Bulletin of the American Schools of Oriental Research*
BDB	F. Brown, S. R. Driver and C. A. Briggs, *A Hebrew and English Lexicon of the Old Testament* (1907)
BH	*Buried History*
BHS	*Biblica Hebraica Stuttgartensia*
BR	*Bible Review*
BS	*Bibliotheca Sacra*
BZ	*Biblische Zeitschrift*
CBQ	*Catholic Biblical Quarterly*
EAJT	*East Asia Journal of Theology*
ETL	*Ephemerides Theologicae Lovianensis*
GTJ	*Grace Theological Journal*
HAR	*Hebrew Annual Review*
HS	*Hebrew Studies*
HTR	*Harvard Theological Review*
IEJ	*Israel Exploration Journal*

JANES	*Journal of the Ancient Near Eastern Society of Columbia University*
JAOS	*Journal of the American Oriental Society*
JBL	*Journal of Biblical Literature*
JBQ	*Jewish Bible Quarterly*
JEA	*Journal of Egyptian Archaeology*
JETS	*Journal of the Evangelical Theological Society*
JNES	*Journal of Near Eastern Studies*
JNSL	*Journal of Northwest Semitic Languages*
JQR	*Jewish Quarterly Review*
JSNT	*Journal for the Study of the New Testament*
JSOT	*Journal for the Study of the Old Testament*
JSSEA	*Journal of the Society for the Study of Egyptian Antiquities*
JTS	*Journal of Theological Studies*
LXX	*Septuagint, Greek Old Testament*
MT	*Masoretic Text of Hebrew Bible*
NG	*National Geographic*
NIDOTTE	W. A. Van Gemeren, ed., *The New International Dictionary of Old Testament Theology and Exegesis* (5 vols, 1997)
PEQ	*Palestine Exploration Quarterly*
PSB	*The Princeton Seminary Bulletin*
RB	*Revue Biblique*
RQ	*Restoration Quarterly*
SJOT	*Scandinavian Journal of the Old Testament*
SJT	*Scottish Journal of Theology*
SR	*Studies in Religion*
SVT	*Supplements to Vetus Testamentum*
TB	*Tyndale Bulletin*
TDOT	G. I. Botterweck and H. Ringgren, eds, *Theological Dictionary of the Old Testament* (1974-)
TJ	*Trinity Journal*
TT	*Theology Today*
UBHJ	*University of Birmingham Historical Journal*
VT	*Vetus Testamentum*
WTJ	*Westminster Theological Journal*
ZAW	*Zeitschrift für die alttestamentliche Wissenschafft*

Preface

In the dedication to his commentary on the book of Romans, John Calvin writes the following to Simon Grynaeus: 'We both thought that the chief excellency of an expounder consists in *lucid brevity*. And, indeed, since it is almost his only work to lay open the mind of the writer whom he undertakes to explain, the degree in which he leads away his readers from it, in that degree he goes astray from his purpose, and in a manner wanders from his own boundaries. Hence we expressed a hope, that from the number of those who strive at this day to advance the interest of theology by this kind of labour, someone would be found, who would study plainness, and endeavour to avoid the evil of tiring his readers with prolixity.'[1]

The Reformer's statement regarding the writing of commentaries reflects my sentiments exactly. An exegetically based commentary is not to be a verbose disquisition that relies on diffuseness, circumlocution and pleonasm as the *modus operandi* of its fundamental expository foundation. The analytical dissertation ought to be perspicuous and laconic, depending on logical acuteness and avoiding involuted language, copious verbiage and rambling. In other words, it should be clear and concise. Less is more.

I have tried to take to heart Calvin's words. I strive in this commentary to mine the riches of the text without being exhaustive or exhausting. In this day when lengthy commentaries abound, there is nothing more formidable for the pastor or biblically literate layman than attempting to struggle through page after page of technical data. It is gut-wrenching. Therefore, my desire has been to rub both sides of the coin; that is, to present in-depth exegesis in a simple, direct manner. I do not know if I have succeeded, but it has been worth it every verse of the way.

This work is a commentary on the *text* of the book of Exodus. I do not spend much time discussing source criticism and other such matters. As a graduate student I did studies in those areas *ad nauseam* and, frankly, I did not find them all that helpful. Some readers, I am sure, will be disappointed that I do not do more with fields such as redaction criticism. For that, I apologize in advance. I truly believe that we need to spend much more time on the text as we have received it (as it has been faithfully preserved by the Holy Spirit). Therefore, I give only a few very basic and general studies before the commentary begins and, then, the bulk of the material is an exposition of the text.

I have written this text for the church. I especially hope that pastors will use it for sermon preparation, and others for Bible study preparation and personal study. It may be difficult going for some, but I hope they take the challenge and really dig into the text. May God use this commentary for his own glory and for the sanctification of his church!

Many people helped in the production of this commentary. I wish to thank the many students at Reformed Theological Seminary (Jackson) who took classes from me in the book of Exodus. You truly stimulated much of my thought. I also appreciate the numerous church groups who heard Exodus material from me over and over again. Especially notable are First Presbyterian Church in Jackson, MS and Providence Presbyterian Church in Clinton, MS. Thank you for not letting me get too technical!

Much credit is due to the board and administration of Reformed Theological Seminary for granting me a sabbatical to complete this first volume (and to begin the second volume). I am grateful especially to Luder Whitlock and Allen Curry for their continued support. Jill Champagne read the manuscript and made some good comments. Ken

Elliott, the head librarian at RTS, and his staff were a great help; and I appreciate the use of an office in the library.

When David Clark of Evangelical Press first approached me about writing a commentary on the book of Exodus, I was overwhelmed by even the thought of it. I was jealous of my New Testament colleagues who pen commentaries on five- and six-chapter books. But forty chapters! In any event, David has been a great encouragement and a friend. Thank you.

Unless otherwise noted, the entire translation is mine. And if there are any errors in the book, be they in English or a foreign tongue, they are mine.

Finally, this book would never have got off the ground without the solid, and often wonderful, support of my family. My children, Elizabeth and David, have heard the stories of Exodus until they could stand it no longer. I think they could have written this commentary. My wife, Nancy, has been a continual source of encouragement. She has never let me down. And that is why this commentary is dedicated to her.

John Currid

Introductory matters

Genesis 3:15 as thematic for the book of Exodus

'And I will put/set enmity between you and the woman and between your seed and her seed and he shall crush you [on the] head and you shall crush him [on the] heel' (Gen. 3:15).

The fall of mankind has occurred immediately before this passage. The man and woman have tumbled into sin, and God is now proclaiming a new order to the universe. In the immediate context God is speaking directly to the serpent and formally cursing him because of his deed of deception.

The entire section, verses 14-19, is prophetic. The prophecy, however, is not announced through a human agent or intermediary, but directly by Yahweh. God is the first prophet. And in this first vision, the Lord describes in general terms the forthcoming history of humanity. Because of its grand predictiveness, some theologians call verse 15 the *'proto-evangelion'*, that is, the first gospel message.

The verse begins with the statement, **'I will put/set enmity ...'** The noun **'enmity'** is emphasized because it appears as the first word in the sentence in the original Hebrew. The term 'enmity' obviously means that one party 'is an enemy to' the other. The noun form occurs five times in the Old Testament, and in each of those cases it signifies hostile intent, of such severity that it can lead to murder (see Ezek. 25:15; 35:5; Num. 35:21-22). We must understand that the new order announced in Genesis 3 includes extreme hatred, animosity and the desire for murder.

It should not be forgotten that it is God who is setting up this new order. He is in control, acting in his providence and managing history unto his own ends. History is being played out according to his desire, will and plan.

The first part of the conflict will be between the serpent (the **'you'** in verse 15) and the woman. The serpent is mentioned first because that is to whom God is directly speaking.

Serpent ('you') $\longleftrightarrow$ Woman

Part of the conflict has already occurred at the beginning of Genesis 3 in which the serpent plays a major role in the fall of mankind into sin. It is interesting that Jesus equates Satan's activity in the fall of mankind not merely with deception and lying, but also sees it as an act of murder (which ties back into the meaning of the word 'enmity'): 'You are of your father the devil, and you want to do the desires of your father. He was a murderer from the beginning, and does not stand in the truth, because there is no truth in him. Whenever he speaks a lie, he speaks from his own nature; for he is a liar, and the father of lies' (John 8:44).

The second stage of the conflict is between **'your seed'** and **'her seed'**. The Hebrew term for 'seed' is commonly used of lineage/descent. The Greek Old Testament, the Septuagint, normally renders the word as *sperma*, which reflects the idea of posterity.[1] Thus we see:

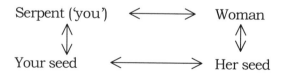

It is critical to understand that this is not referring to physical lineage but to spiritual descent. Satan, or the serpent, cannot bear children. He is a fallen angel, and nowhere in Scripture is there any evidence that he had the power of physical reproduction (cf. Mark 12:25). It is rather a spiritual idea, in which one can be a child of Satan by will, heart and intent. Remember that Jesus said to the Pharisees that 'You are of your father the devil ...' (John 8:44). The believer, or seed of the woman, by way of contrast says, 'Our Father who art in heaven...' (Matt. 6:9).

The idea of the two seeds, or seed theology, has immediate consequences in the book of Genesis. In chapter 4, Cain, who 'was of the evil one' (1 John 3:12), murders his brother Abel, who 'was righteous' (Heb. 11:4). And the basic theme of animosity and conflict can be traced throughout the history of mankind. In John's Apocalypse, the apostle describes the animosity of the two seeds even to the end of time: 'And when the dragon saw that he was thrown down to the earth, he persecuted the woman who gave birth to the male child. And the two wings of the great eagle were given to the woman, in order that she might fly into the wilderness to her place, where she was nourished for a time and times and half a time, from the presence of the serpent. And the serpent poured water like a river out of his mouth after the woman, so that he might cause her to be swept away with the flood. And the earth helped the woman, and the earth opened its mouth and drank up the river which the dragon poured out of his mouth. And the dragon was enraged with the woman, and went off to make war with the rest of her *seed*, who keep the commandments of God and hold to the testimony of Jesus' (Rev. 12:13-17).

The conflict will reach its climax in a battle between two individuals. The final stage is as follows:

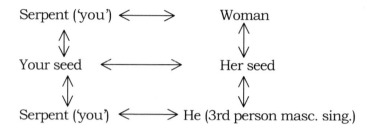

In this final clause, the serpent is not mentioned first but the one referred to as **'he'** is — that is to demonstrate the latter's primacy and pre-eminence in the conflict. In addition, it should be noted that the blow to the serpent is to the head — a mortal, deadly wound. The other combatant's wound is merely to the heel, one that is certainly not fatal.

Genesis 3:15 is Messianic. And the identity of the said descendant is clear from genealogies such as Luke 3 in which the line of Jesus is traced back to Adam and Eve — Jesus is in the direct lineage from the woman. Jesus is simply the 'he' of Genesis 3:15. It is significant in confirming this truth that immediately after the genealogy in Luke 3 we read how Jesus is led into battle with Satan in the wilderness temptation. It is a raging war that finds its climax at the cross where the Messiah lands a mortal blow to the serpent. In consequence, contained in the curse on the serpent in Genesis 3 is the prophecy that God will send a Redeemer to crush the enemy. Jesus is the seed who descended from Eve and went to do battle against Satan.

The remainder of Scripture is an unfolding of the prophecy of Genesis 3:15. Redemption is promised in this one verse, and the Bible traces the development of that redemptive theme. The place of the book of Exodus in the seed conflict is crucial. No longer is the enmity limited to two people — i.e., Cain and Abel, Jacob and Esau, etc. — but now it is enlarged to include two peoples or nations: the covenant people of Israel in opposition to the people of Egypt who are outside the covenant. Thus, in the book of Exodus, we see the clash reaching phenomenal proportions. We thus see a mere glimpse of the extent of the seed conflict — that is, its universal nature.

Authorship of Exodus

It is not my intention to discuss all the ins and outs of source criticism of the book of Exodus and, in general, of the Torah. That is way beyond the scope of this commentary. My principal purpose is to comment upon the text that is before us. In addition, the intricacies of source criticism have been the subject of many recent treatments. If the reader is interested in this topic, those works ought to be consulted.[2]

Even with that caveat in mind, I would like to add two arguments that help support the idea that Exodus is a coherent, unified literary piece. The discussion will take place on two levels. The first proposition is of a general nature dealing with the basic thematic thrust of the document; the second case is more detailed, paying attention to some of the finer points of the work's contents.

1. The life of Moses as a paradigm of the exodus

The early life of Moses serves as a prototype of the exodus event. What I mean by that statement is that the general and major events of Moses' life while in Egypt and in Midian model and prefigure the salient circumstances in the life of the emerging nation of Israel. Consider the following points of correspondence:

Moses

Israel

I. *Exodus 2:1-2.* Born a slave in Egypt; under oppression and persecution; victim of murder attempt.

II. *Exodus 2:3-10.* Undergoes water ordeal and is delivered.

III. *Exodus 2:11-22.* Escapes to Midian.

IV. *Exodus 3.* Theophany of the burning bush at Mount Sinai.

V. *Exodus 4:1-17.* Moses is unfaithful and doubting but God responds miraculously.

I. *Exodus 1:8-22.* Born slaves in Egypt; under cruel bondage; Pharaoh attempts to murder the males (1:22).

II. *Exodus 14-15.* Israel goes through a water ordeal at the Red Sea and is delivered.

III. *Exodus 16-18* Israel escapes to Midian.

IV. *Exodus 19ff.* Theophany and revelation at Mount Sinai.

V. *Remainder of Torah.* Israel responds by being unfaithful but God gives miracles.

On the basis of these parallel features, and their chronological similarity, it is evident that the early history of the man Moses is a microcosm of the early history of the people of Israel.

Some of these major points of correspondence also contain startling parallels in the details of the individual stories. For example, in the episode of the women at the well (Exod. 2:15-22), the daughters of Jethro are maltreated and tyrannized by shepherds who drive them from the watering spot. Moses subsequently rescues/delivers them from the cruel oppressors. He then stays in the wilderness and lives as 'an alien in a foreign land' in the wilderness of Midian and Sinai. The striking thematic similarities between this story and the deliverance of Israel out of Egypt are obvious.

Even the vocabulary and the language used to convey the two events resemble one another. The Hebrew word for 'rescue' in Exodus 2:17 is one of the principal terms used of the redemption of Israel out of Egypt: e.g., Exodus 14:30 states that 'The Lord saved/rescued Israel from the hand of the Egyptians.' In 2:19 a second word for 'rescue' is employed by the author — it is a synonym of the word used in 2:17. The women say, 'An Egyptian man rescued us from the hand of the shepherds.' That clause is almost identical to what the Exodus author says about God who 'rescued you from the hand of the Egyptians and from the hand of Pharaoh' (18:10). These linguistic affinities confirm the fact that the story of the rescue of Jethro's daughters is a paradigm of the deliverance of Israel out of Egypt.

What this has to say about the authorship of the book of Exodus is simple enough. The over-arching, interwoven themes attest to the book being a coherent piece of work written at a particular time. The literary structure is unified and homogeneous. It is not a simple (or complex, for that matter) cut-and-paste job.

2. The author as historian

The Egyptologist Donald B. Redford comments that 'There is little Egyptian colouring in the Exodus account, almost wholly toponymic in nature; but the Egyptologist would soon sense that it is anachronistic.'[3] Redford certainly is not the first to question the reliability of the Egyptian material in the Bible. T. Eric Peet, writing during the 1920s, says, 'The main fact which strikes the Egyptologist is that there is nothing whatsoever in [the biblical accounts with Egyptian colourings] which suggests the Hyksos period, or indeed any particular period at all. It is all the sort of vague general knowledge.'[4] That perspective dominates biblical scholarship today.

I would vigorously disagree with that interpretation. The account accurately depicts the age and historical period of the Exodus. For example, the story of the serpent confrontation in Exodus 7:8-13 is 'saturated with elements of Egyptian religious and cultural background. Only an author well versed in Egyptian tradition could have composed this poignant piece that reeks of Egypt. And he quite subtly used that knowledge to polemicize against Egyptian practices and thereby demonstrate the truth of the Hebrew religion. He did that not only by employing linguistic parallels, but also by constructing his account of the story as a critique of Egyptian customs. That a passage this short contains such a skilful and profound argument stands as a memorial to the literary genius of the biblical writer.'[5]

The writer of Exodus employed many examples that played off his knowledge of Egyptian culture and religion. The use of the rod or staff by Moses and Aaron in their encounter with Pharaoh and his court is one such instance.[6] The episodes of the hardening of Pharaoh's heart are also exemplary. The Egyptian cultural setting is simply there. That is to say, 'The qualities and temper of the episode[s] direct us to Egypt and nowhere else. In addition, [such] account[s] do not appear to be anachronistic, but [they] properly reflect ancient Egyptian customs, particularly those in vogue during the New Kingdom period. The biblical author constructed [such] poignant and profound piece[s] as a critique of contemporary Egyptian dogma and practice and as a demonstration of the truth and power of Yahweh.'[7]

The reader ought to consult recent literature that confirms the precision and veracity of the biblical records of the exodus event.[8] All the evidence points to one incontrovertible fact: the author of the book of Exodus was well acquainted with the land of Egypt and with the wilderness areas of Sinai, Moab and Edom. And this is not a mere general knowledge but it extends to the very smallest of details. That truth will become evident to the reader by studying this commentary.

Regarding the identity of the author much has been written. Sailhamer comments, 'Jewish tradition and the NT have attributed it to Moses (cf. John 5:46). Though many modern biblical scholars doubt the possibility of

Mosaic authorship for most of the book, there is little evidence within the book itself to warrant such scepticism.[9] Indeed, the book of Acts tells us that 'Moses was educated in all the learning of the Egyptians, and he was a man of power in words and deeds' (7:22).

The date of the exodus

Determination of the time and span of the exodus event is a complex and thorny problem. Many, if not most, scholars place the exodus in the mid-thirteenth century B.C.[10] Archaeological research and textual materials lend great support to that setting in time. Historical evidence is weighty in both Egypt and Palestine. I will briefly outline the evidence from both regions.

1. Egypt

At the outset we should recognize that the Hebrews as a people are not directly mentioned on Egyptian monuments or texts from any of the periods proposed for the sojourn.[11] That really is not all that surprising since the exodus event was disastrous for Egypt. Egyptian texts are notoriously propagandistic and pro-Egyptian. Thus, we are left to search for conditions in Egypt that would be right for such a sojourn and escape.

The general nature of Egypt in the thirteenth century B.C. fits well with what we read in the book of Exodus. Firstly, in the fourteenth and thirteenth centuries B.C. there were massive building projects in Egypt that required a huge workforce. Some of this construction occurred in the Nile Delta area abutting the land of Goshen, the residence of the Hebrews. The building in the north began under Haremhab (1319-1307 B.C.), the last pharaoh of the eighteenth dynasty, and it continued at a greater pace under the kings of the nineteenth dynasty (1307-1196 B.C.).

Probably the greatest of these builders was Rameses II (1290-1224 B.C.). Kitchen describes that pharaoh's activity in the Delta region: 'But one of his first acts was to proclaim the founding of a new capital city — Pi-Ramesse, "Domain of Rameses" — around his father's summer palace on the north of Avaris. This, the "Delta Residence" of the Ramesside kings, was the Ra'amses of Exodus 1:11. It was laid out on the grand scale. Great stone temples of the gods arose at each of the four cardinal points... The great royal palace was of brick with stone-framed doorways, its staterooms brilliant with glazed tile decoration. The brick houses and villas of royal princes and high officials clustered nearby. Offices, barracks, stores and warehousing...'[12]

Excavations at the site of Tell el-Dab'a have confirmed that it is the site of Rameses. Just north of the site, excavations have revealed a tile factory that produced glazed tiles for ornamentation. The names of pharaohs, including Rameses II, have been found on some of the tiles.[13]

Prior to the time of Haremhab little building took place in the Nile Delta area north of Bubastis (Tell Basta).

The first certain reference to Israel from Egyptian monuments (or from anywhere for that matter) is the Israel stele from the very end of the thirteenth century B.C.[14] It dates to the reign of Pharaoh Merneptah (1224-1214 B.C.). One should also consider the reliefs at Karnak that may picture Israelites defeated in Merneptah's campaign in Canaan.[15]

In addition, as Sarna comments, '... commencing about 1550 B.C. and for the next few hundred years, energetic and powerful Egyptian monarchs maintained a tight grip on Canaan.'[16] It is not until the thirteenth century B.C. that Egypt truly began to lose its control over its province of Canaan. This was a period of great upheaval in the Middle East with the invasion of the Sea Peoples and Libyans on the coast of Palestine. The latter century would have been very conducive to Israel's escape from Egypt and conquest of Canaan.

A lot of other evidence may be brought to bear on the question. I refer the reader to a recent work by J. Hoffmeier.[17]

2. Palestine

In the thirteenth century B.C., there occurs a great increase in the number of settlements in the hill-country areas of Canaan. Scholars greatly differ over the reason or cause for such a large increase in settlement. Four basic positions are held today. I will only briefly describe them. For extended discussions see the recent literature on the subject.[18]

Peaceful migration theory

This position originated with M. Noth and A. Alt.[19] It argues that the increase of settlement in Palestine was due to a gradual infiltration of Hebrews into Palestine and a gradual subsistence shift from semi-nomadism to agriculture. Thus there was no invasion, only a peaceful penetration from outside to inside Palestine.

Internal political upheaval

First proposed by G. Mendenhall in 1962, this theory claims that there was no outside penetration of the Hebrews into Palestine. Rather, there occurred a withdrawal by a faction of Palestinian society, namely, the peasantry. This peasantry later came to develop into the Hebrews.[20] The catalyst for their moving out of the Canaanite cities was a revolt, or at least a dissatisfaction with the ruling peoples.

Rural Canaanites

Recently Finkelstein has argued that there was no infiltration from outside the land, nor was there a revolution
from inside. Rather, he believes the change may simply be
a shift in the subsistence patterns of the Canaanites.
These Canaanites gave up their urban environment and
moved out to pastoral villages. Much later, these Canaanites became Israelites.

Conquest

This traditional view supports the idea that the Hebrews
invaded Palestine *en masse* in a three-pronged conquest
campaign, destroyed cities and settled in a number of
areas (primarily in the highlands). Confirmation of this
position is given by the thirteenth-century destruction
layers discovered at Bethel, Lachish and Hazor. Generally,
this reconstruction coincides with the biblical record.

An analysis of the archaeological remains of the Late
Bronze Age in Palestine in comparison with the Iron Age
(beginning c. 1200 B.C.) indicates a distinct cultural break
between the two periods. Those who hold to the exodus
occurring in the thirteenth century B.C. would argue that
it is due to the entrance of the Israelites into the land and
their conquest of it.

While the thirteenth-century date for the exodus event
has some strong support, it is not without its problems.
First and foremost is how to deal with certain biblical texts
that appear to ascribe the date to a much earlier period.
The major dilemma is I Kings 6:1, which says, 'Now it
came about in the four hundred and eightieth year after
the sons of Israel came out of the land of Egypt, in the
fourth year of Solomon's reign over Israel, in the month of
Ziv, which is the second month, that he began to build the
house of the Lord.' Since the date of the temple construction under Solomon can reasonably be dated to the middle
of the tenth century B.C., then the exodus would have

taken place some time during the second half of the fifteenth century B.C. A second passage, Judges 11:26, has also been used to argue for an early date for the exodus story.

Dillard and Longman comment: 'As we work our way back from this text to the time of the Exodus, we must admit that the evidence is not as compelling as the I Kings passage, since we are not as sure about Jephthah's date as we are about Solomon's. A close study of the chronological notices in the book of Judges allows the interpreter to arrive at an approximate date for Jephthah's time period. The end result is that the Judges passage collaborates the I Kings passage in placing the Exodus in the fifteenth century B.C.'[21]

Also problematic is the fact that there is no concrete evidence by which to connect the Israelites to the destruction of Bethel, Hazor and Lachish. Furthermore, the lack of evidence of such destruction at a number of sites mentioned in the Bible (e.g., Jericho) must in some way be explained.

Because of such issues, some scholars want to date the exodus and conquest in the fifteenth century B.C. Probably the best treatment of this schema is by Bimson.[22] Following closely upon his heels is Bryant Wood, who examined the unpublished excavation materials of Kathleen Kenyon at Jericho. He concluded that Jericho had indeed been destroyed by the invading Israelites: 'Despite the fact that the area where the wall once stood is gone there is evidence, incredible as it may seem, that this wall came tumbling down and in the words of the Biblical account in Joshua "fell down flat". The pottery stratigraphic considerations, scarab data, and a Carbon-14 date all point to a destruction of the city around Late Bronze I, about 1400 B.C.'[23] Bimson's and Wood's findings, however, have not met with great acceptance in the scholarly community.[24]

The main problems with the early date are as follows: Firstly, the Bible does not record the 'Egyptian domination in Canaan, a domination that lasted from LB I to Iron I, as excavations and texts such as the Amarna letters make clear. How is it that the Bible can place the conquest in 1410 B.C., but suffer from amnesia about Egyptian domination in Canaan from 1410 to about 1140 B.C.?'[25] Secondly, acceptance of the early date requires a radical restructuring of ancient chronology. Proponents move the generally accepted date of the beginning of the Late Bronze Age from about 1550 B.C. down to about 1420 B.C. (the time of the proposed exodus).[26] Such a shift does not seem to be warranted by the archaeological record.

For now, the date of the exodus and the conquest must remain an open question. More evidence is needed. I would agree with Waltke that a definitive verdict cannot be arrived at 'until more data puts the date of the conquest beyond reasonable doubt. If that be true, either date is an acceptable working hypothesis, and neither date should be held dogmatically.'[27]

Route of the exodus

Another issue of great contention regarding the exodus event is the course and direction of Israel's departure from Egypt and escape to Canaan. Nahum Sarna comments that 'It is easier to delineate the route that the fleeing Israelites avoided than to chart the course they actually took to their destination, the land of Canaan.'[28] Since I have already dealt with this question in great detail elsewhere, I will merely summarize the basic arguments and conclusions here.[29]

Various proposals have been made by scholars to determine the route of the fleeing Hebrews. Four different thoroughfares have been put forth.[30] The northernmost and shortest route is along the *Via Maris* through northern Sinai. That direction would not have been feasible because it would have placed the Hebrews in harm's way because the primary roads in the region were guarded by a series of Egyptian forts.[31] In addition, the Bible explicitly states that the Israelites did not go that way: 'Now it came about when Pharaoh had let the people go, that God did not lead them by the way of the land of the Philistines, even though it was near; for God said, "Lest the people change their minds when they see war, and they return to Egypt"' (Exod. 13:17). In reality, as will be shown below, the southernmost route is the likeliest path that the Hebrews took during their escape from Egypt.

Numerous accounts detailing Israel's flight are found in the Bible: Exodus 12-19, Numbers 11-12 and Deuteronomy 10. The principal description, however, appears in Numbers 33:1-49. A study of that latter passage defines three increments in the Israelite itinerary: (1) from Egypt to

Mount Sinai (Num. 33:3-8); (2) from Mount Sinai to Edom (Num. 33:9-40); and (3) from the land of Edom to the plains of Moab (Num. 33:40-49). We will briefly discuss each of these stages in order.

The initial phase of the journey is the one in which we are able to identify with certainty many of the sites recorded. The author of Numbers identifies the first departure site of the Hebrews as the Egyptian city of Rameses (vv. 3, 5). Widely accepted today is the belief that Rameses is located at Qantir (Tell el-Dab'a), about seventeen miles south-west of Tanis. Excavations at the site in the last twenty-five years have confirmed that identification.[32] The site of Pithom is apparently at Tell Hisn (Heliopolis) in the southernmost extremity of the delta.

Within Egypt, an Egyptian text from the end of the thirteenth century B.C., called Papyrus Anastasi V, is helpful in determining the Hebrew route. The text tells of two slaves fleeing from Egypt. Three place names are mentioned in their escape: 'I reached the enclosure wall of Tjeku on the third month of the third season ... to the south... When I reached *htm*, they told me that the scout had come from the desert [saying that] they had passed the walled place north of Migdol.'[33] The slaves headed from Tjeku (probably Succoth) south to *htm* (corresponds to biblical Etham) and finally to Migdol, which appears to have been located on the edge of the desert. That order of escape, Succoth-Etham-Migdol, is the same as the Hebrews' departure in Numbers 33:6-7. The Egyptian papyrus raises the possibility that the Israelites fled from Egypt on a common escape route into the wilderness.

Before attempting to cross into the Sinai wilderness, it appears that the Israelites moved to the south — this is likely because the eastern boundary of Egypt was protected by a huge canal that appears to have run from Pelusium on the Mediterranean Sea to Lake Timsah just to the east of the Wadi Tumilat.[34] Another site the Hebrews passed by is Pi-hahiroth. The name appears to be a Hebraized form of the original Akkadian Pi-hiriti, which literally means 'The mouth or opening of the canal'.[35] One may suggest that Pi-hahiroth was an opening or break in the canal system that allowed entrance into the wilderness of the Sinai Peninsula.

From Pi-hahiroth, the Hebrews 'passed through the midst of the sea into the wilderness'. Although many scholars argue that the sea here is not the Red Sea/Gulf of Suez, recent studies have demonstrated that in fact it is.[36]

In the second stage of the travels, from Sinai to the land of Edom, we are able to identify very few sites with any certainty. The Hebrews, however, appear to have travelled south after they crossed through the Red Sea. This southern route was a primary road for Egyptian mining expeditions during the Middle and New Kingdoms (c. the twentieth to the twelfth centuries B.C.).[37] Semites worked in these mines, and perhaps they participated in the Egyptian expeditions to the digs. The Hebrews certainly would have known this route, possibly in a first-hand way.

In a thought-provoking article, Itzhaq Beit-Arieh argues that the Israelites travelled the southern route because 'This region is ecologically better adapted to the sustenance of life' than are the other parts of the Sinai Peninsula. He claims that the south-central Sinai had 'a reasonably adequate water supply and a relatively comfortable climate that makes it possible to maintain a daily lifestyle suitably adapted to the conditions of the desert... It is covered by assorted vegetation consisting of acacia and palm trees and a fairly dense growth of perennial bushes, along with seasonal cover of grasses and weeds suitable for pasturing sheep and goats.' In addition, south-central Sinai was geographically isolated and outside the control of Egyptian sovereignty: 'Ancient Egyptian hegemony never extended into south central Sinai.'[38]

The precise location of Mount Sinai and the location of the Hebrew encampment are unknown. Many suggestions have been presented. However, we will not take time to review them.[39]

The Hebrews probably left Mount Sinai and journeyed to the western shore of the Gulf of Aqaba, and then travelled northwards along the shoreline. The site of Jotbathah, which is recorded in Numbers 33:34, may be located at Tabeh, approximately seven miles south of Tell el-Kheleifeh on the western shore of the Gulf.[40] We do not know precisely where Ezion-Geber was situated, although we are justified in looking for it in the general vicinity of the northern shore of the Gulf of Aqaba.[41] From Ezion-Geber the Hebrews travelled to Kadesh, which is 'in the wilderness of Zin' (Num. 33:36). Kadesh, or Kadesh-Barnea, certainly lies somewhere in the area of the Wadi Qedeis and the Wadi el-'Ain, approximately fifty miles south-west of Beersheba. The Hebrews could not penetrate the land of Canaan from Kadesh-Barnea because of hostile Canaanites (see Num. 20:14 - 21:4). Therefore, they headed eastward into the land of Edom.

The final stage of the journey is from Edom to Moab, from which the Israelites were to cross the Jordan into the promised land. The specific itinerary through Transjordan recorded in Numbers 33 covers Zalmonah to Punon to Oboth to Iye-abarim (Iyim) to Dibon-(gad) to Almon-(diblathaim) to the mountains of Abarim and to the Plains of Moab by the Jordan River as far as Abel-shittim. Krahmalkov has demonstrated that this Transjordanian route was a traditional road used by the Egyptians throughout the Late Bronze Age. He comments, 'In short, the Biblical story of the invasion of Transjordan that set the stage for the conquest of all Palestine is told against a background that is historically accurate. The Israelite invasion route described in Numbers 33:45b-50 was in fact an official, heavily trafficked Egyptian road through the Transjordan in the Late Bronze Age.'[42] Having travelled that route and now encamped next to the Jordan River, the Hebrews plotted their strategy for the invasion of Canaan.

The precise route of the Israelite itinerary must remain tentative because so few sites can be identified with any certainty. However, a general course of travel emerges from the evidence at hand. Leaving the delta region of Egypt, the Hebrews travelled in a southerly direction towards the Gulf of Suez. There they turned east and crossed through a northern portion of the Red Sea. The Israelites then took a south-south-east route along the shore of the Red Sea in the Sinai Peninsula. They proceeded to the northern point of the Gulf of Aqaba and from there travelled the military road to the Plains of Moab and the Jordan river.

Volume I

A clear and present danger

A commentary on Exodus 1-18

1. Suffering in Egypt

Exodus 1:1-22

Introduction (Exodus 1:1-7)

The purpose of the opening paragraph of Exodus is to serve as a bridge between the books of Genesis and Exodus. Verses 1-5 are a summary of where Genesis ended: the twelve sons of Jacob and their families are dwelling in the land of Egypt. Verses 6-7 fill in the centuries between the conclusion of Genesis and the beginning of the story of Moses and the deliverance of the Hebrews from Egypt: the Hebrews have simply been prolific in bearing children. The passage, in other words, demonstrates how the Hebrews have grown from a patriarchal family to a strong and numerous people.

1:1. And these are the names of the sons of Israel who came to Egypt with Jacob, a man with his household:

The biblical author opens the book of Exodus with the word **'and'** (the conjunctive *waw* in Hebrew). The conjunction is not reflected in most English translations. It is, however, important to recognize its existence because it connects the exodus story to the preceding material of Genesis. It shows a natural flow of material which underscores that this is a story in development. The conjunction perhaps also indicates that the two books were once formally tied together.

The clause, **'These are the names of the sons of'**, is a common introductory formula for a genealogy in the book of Genesis (see Gen. 25:13; 36:10,40). Exodus 1:1, in fact, quotes word for word Genesis 46:8, which says, '[And] these are the names of the sons of Israel who entered Egypt.' The author possesses a deep and remarkable familiarity with the book of Genesis. This truth will be driven home repeatedly in the first chapter of Exodus.

The term **'sons of Israel'** has an ironic usage. From now on in the book of Exodus it will be used to refer, not to the sons of Jacob, but rather to all the people of Israel (as a covenanted nation).

Mīṣrāyim, the Hebrew term for Egypt, is a dual form which probably reflects the ancient division of that land into Upper and Lower Egypt. As the following study will show, the biblical writer had an in-depth knowledge of Egypt, its customs, practices and language.

1:2-4. Reuben, Simeon, Levi, and Judah, Issachar, Zebulun, and Benjamin, Dan and Naphtali, Gad and Asher.

The author now lists the sons of Jacob who went to Egypt. Order of birth is not the basis of this genealogy, but it is according to the one who gives birth.[1] The first six sons named were all children of Leah, even though Issachar and Zebulun were the ninth and tenth sons born to Jacob. Benjamin was the second son of Rachel. And, finally, the two pairs of sons belonging to handmaids are mentioned. This register is exactly the same as the one in Genesis 35:23-26. Once again, the biblical writer demonstrates reliance upon a preceding Genesis account.

Jacob's sons were the ancestors of the tribes of Israel. But the sons did not travel to Egypt alone; according to verse 1, they came **'each with his family'**. The descendants of Jacob have begun to increase in number.

1:5. And all the people that came from the loins of Jacob were seventy persons, and Joseph was in Egypt.

The number of seventy persons having descended from Jacob is first found in Genesis 46:26-27. Included in this figure are only those who came directly from his seed (literally, **'one who came forth out of his loins'**); daughters-in-law and others are not numbered among the seventy. Thus the number of people who accompanied Jacob to Egypt must have amounted to hundreds, at least. The tribes of the Hebrews were in the process of propagation and growth.

The Hebrew readers would have immediately noticed that in verses 2-4 only eleven tribes are listed. So the writer now explains that Joseph did not enter the land with Jacob because he **'was already in Egypt'**. And so the progenitors for all twelve tribes of Israel are accounted for.

1:6-7. And Joseph and all his brothers and all that generation died. And the children of Israel were fruitful and they swarmed and they increased and they became very, very strong. And the land was filled with them.

This passage serves to bring the reader up to date. All the sons of Jacob and all the people living at the time have since died. But the Hebrews have been very active in reproduction. Egypt is simply overflowing with them. The author is attempting to move from a history centred on an individual (i.e., Abraham) or a family/clan (i.e., Jacob's sons), as found in Genesis, to a history that will now focus on a people (eventually a nation).

The extent of procreation among them is underscored by the phrase: **'They became exceedingly numerous'** (NIV). The original Hebrew employs the repetition of the adverb **'very'** *(m''ōd, m''ōd)* to reflect an absolute superlative sense.

All five verbs in verse 7 mirror the language of creation. The writer again takes the reader back to Genesis and, in particular, to the cultural mandate of Genesis 1:28 and 9:7. He does this to demonstrate that the Hebrews in Egypt were fulfilling the command to be fruitful, multiply and fill the earth. In this respect, they were being exceedingly blessed by God.

This great increase was also a fulfilment of God's promise to Abraham that God would multiply his descendants as the stars of heaven and the sand on the seashore (see Gen. 22:17; cf., especially, Acts 7:17-18). God kept his promise to Abraham even though it was many centuries after the promise was first given. God does his work according to his own timetable.

Application

The book of Exodus cannot be understood in a vacuum. It is merely one piece of the unfolding of God's revelational history. The preceding context of the book of Genesis is critical to a proper understanding of Exodus. The reader must spend time in Genesis to be equipped to interpret Exodus. A case in point is the Genesis creation language used in verses 6-7. The Israelites, as the people of God, fulfil the mandate God had originally given to Adam, and later to Noah, to be fruitful and multiply and fill the earth. It seems clear that at this point the Hebrews have become the sons of God, and they are now blessed by him and are under his protection. That type of insight will richly bless the believer who diligently digs into the context surrounding Exodus.

It is also important for us to recognize that the history of Israel during the exodus period is to be viewed as a lesson to all believers. Paul says as much in 1 Corinthians 10:11: 'These things happened to them as examples and were written down as warnings for us, on whom the fulfilment of the age has come.' So Christians need to pay heed to the Scriptures before us and to learn that God deals with his people in the same ways throughout history. He is the same yesterday, today and for ever.

The seed of the serpent oppresses Israel (Exodus 1:8-14)

Egypt responded to Israel's growth by oppression. The biblical author is attempting to impress upon the reader the horrible condition of God's people: they had taskmasters over them who afflicted them with severity and rigour. The overseers were intent on breaking the Hebrews' spirit; they sought to ruin their health, to shorten their days, to lessen their numbers and to leave them without hope. It demonstrates Pharaoh's desire to stamp out the name of Israel so that the people would have no remembrance on earth. As evil Cain extinguished his righteous brother Abel, so did Egypt try to destroy Israel. The ungodly seed of the serpent acts the same way in all ages.

1:8. And a new king arose over Egypt who did not know Joseph.

A **'new king'** does not necessarily mean the next ruler after the pharaoh of the Joseph story. The text says that this new king **'did not know Joseph'**. The verb 'to know' frequently bears the idea of intimate and personal knowledge. Thus, it is not that the new pharaoh had not heard of Joseph, but that he had no personal acquaintance with him. The immediate successor to the pharaoh of the Joseph story certainly would have had some contact with Joseph. It is unlikely that this new king would have been the immediate successor anyway since the Hebrews were in Egypt for over four centuries (see Exod. 12:40). It is also possible that the new pharaoh may have been a foreign invader who knew nothing of Joseph.

1:9-10. And he said to his people, 'Behold, the people of the children of Israel are many and more numerous than we [are]. Come, let us deal shrewdly with them, lest they increase and when war approaches they are added to our enemies, and fight against us, and go up from the land.'

According to the King of Egypt, there was a nagging problem facing the Egyptians: the Hebrews had increased so greatly that they posed a serious threat to Egyptian sovereignty in the land. The word **'Behold,'** is often used to emphasize the immediacy of a situation. The Israelites were simply a clear and present danger.[2]

The verb translated **'approaches'** is a plural in the Hebrew. Its subject, **'war'**, thus has a collective meaning — that is, it includes all aspects and events of war. A similar collective use of war is found in 1 Kings 5:3.[3]

In verses 10-12, the Israelites are referred to in the third person masculine singular. Thus, the beginning of verse 10 literally reads, **'Come, we must deal shrewdly with *him* or *he* will become...'** This use of the singular form may indicate the forming of the Hebrews into a single group, the beginnings of a nation and a covenanted people before God.

1:11. And they set taskmasters over them in order to afflict them with their burdens. And they built cities of storage for Pharaoh: Pithom and Rameses.

Pharaoh responds to the threat by enslaving the Hebrews and forcing them to build the store cities of Pithom and Rameses. Note that Pharaoh afflicts the Hebrews with **'burdens'** — that is, a compulsory, burdensome toil. The same word is used of the corvée, or forced labour, in the reigns of Solomon and Rehoboam (1 Kings 11:28). Under those kings this was an enforced work institution much hated by the Israelites to the point at which they assassinated the superintendent, one Adoniram (1 Kings 12:18). The Hebrew word for 'burdens' is later used in Messianic passages about the work of the coming Redeemer: he will be one who will bear the people's burdens, toils and labours (see Isa. 53:4,11).

The location of **'Pithom and Rameses'** is a matter of debate. It is likely that Rameses is to be identified with Tell el-Dab'a in the eastern Nile Delta and Pithom may be situated at Tell el Hisn in the southernmost extreme of the Delta. The arguments for and against these proposals are quite detailed and complex and, therefore, I refer the reader elsewhere.[4]

The title **'Pharaoh'** derives from the Egyptian *pr,* 'house, palace'. It did not originally refer to the Egyptian king but to his residence. Not until the middle of the Eighteenth Dynasty (*c.* 1550-1070 B.C.) was it employed as an appellation of the ruler.

I would suggest that there is perhaps an allusion to the story of Babel, recounted in Genesis 11, in verses 10-14. In Exodus 1:10, Pharaoh says, **'Come, let us...'** Those are the same introductory words that were used by the men of Babel who conspired to erect a city (Gen. 11:4). In Exodus 1:11-14, the Egyptians are pictured building cities out of bricks and mortar just like the people at Babel. What is the point of the correspondence? The ungodly act in the same way throughout history: they build edifices to their own glory and honour. The fact that one of the cities is called 'Rameses', presumably after the name of the reigning pharaoh, confirms that conclusion.

1:12-13. But as they afflicted them, so they increased and so they broke out [in great numbers]. And so the Egyptians loathed the children of Israel. And they caused the children of Israel to work rigorously.

Pharaoh's plan to destroy Israel did not work because the schemes of the Egyptians were turned back on themselves. The very way in which they sought to diminish the Hebrews actually caused them to increase. Here is a profound scriptural principle displayed in many parts of biblical history, such as during the early church period. At that time the church grew rapidly on account of great persecution.

The Hebrew word translated **'broke out'** carries the idea of breaking out, or bursting forth from the womb (cf. Gen. 38:29). Such an increase appears to be a partial fulfilment of God's promise to Jacob that his descendants would 'break out' in great numbers across the land (Gen. 28:14; 30:30).

The multiplication of the Hebrews occurred to such a degree that the Egyptians **'loathed'** them. The Hebrew word has an active thrust (it is a Qal stem) and comes from a root meaning 'loathing, hatred, abhorrence'. Here is a responsive attitude of animosity on the part of the Egyptians because their intentions came to nothing while Israel prospered.

The word translated **'rigorously'** is rare in the Old Testament. However, it is used in the book of Leviticus where the Hebrews were told that they were not to treat their slaves in the manner of the Egyptians (Lev. 25:43,46,53). That would be too cruel.

1:14. And they made their lives bitter in hard work, in mortar and in bricks and in all labour in the field. They caused them to work rigorously in all their labours.

The type of labour that Pharaoh imposed on Israel was severe and **'hard'**. The latter word is later used in the book of Exodus when God **'hardens'** Pharaoh's heart (see Exod. 7:3). Because the Egyptian king made Israel's labour hard, God made his heart hard.

Application

Peter told the early church, 'Do not be surprised at the painful trial you are suffering, as though something strange were happening to you' (1 Peter 4:12). Persecution is the way that the unbelieving world treats the church. Let us not be naïve in this matter. And if we do not see it at first hand in our own personal experience, it is because of God's restraining, gracious hand. Even then, the hatred is there, festering and ready to pounce. We would be foolish to think otherwise.

Yet God will bless his church in times of adversity, as he blessed his church in Exodus. As Matthew Henry commented, 'Christianity spread most when it was persecuted: the blood of the martyrs was the seed of the church.'

Pharaoh's second attempt to destroy Israel (Exodus 1:15-21)

The seed of the serpent does not cease his assaults on the people of God. Pharaoh has been thwarted in his first attempt to extinguish Israel: the Hebrews simply increased greatly in numbers despite Egyptian persecution. Now Pharaoh orders male infanticide to be performed on Hebrew children by their midwives. Make no mistake about it: this butchery is an attempt to annihilate Israel from the face of the earth.

1:15-16. And the King of Egypt spoke to the Hebrew midwives, [of whom] the name of one [was] Shiphrah and the name of the second Puah. And he said, 'When you help in the birth of the Hebrew women and you look upon the birthstool, if it is a son, then you shall kill him; but if it is a girl, then she will live.'

Pharaoh commands the Hebrew midwives to destroy any new-born Hebrew males. There is ambiguity regarding the nationality of these women because the clause may be translated either **'Hebrew midwives'** or **'midwives of the Hebrews'**. However, the names of both the midwives are Hebrew, or at least Semitic, and clearly not Egyptian.[5] So it seems that the king is sovereignly ordering his slaves to perform a dastardly deed against their own people.

Why were only two midwives summoned by the king's command? Perhaps they were the only midwives in Goshen, although that seems unlikely considering the great increase of the Hebrews. Possibly they were the only two who disobeyed, or their names were the only ones remembered by the author. But it is more likely that **'Shiphrah and Puah'** were the chief midwives, the super-intendents of the midwifery institution.[6]

The etymology of the word **'Hebrew'** is much-debated. Some scholars have attempted to identify it with the *habiru*, a group of people mentioned in documents from the second millennium B.C. The evidence is dubious, however, and the identification highly unlikely. Others argue that it derives from *'br*, which means 'region across, on the other side' (of the Jordan). That term would thus reflect the transient, or semi-nomadic beginnings, of the Hebrew people. The Bible seems to portray the word as deriving from Eber, one of Shem's sons and an ancestor of Abraham (see Gen. 10:21; 11:14,16). There is no reason to doubt that teaching.

Why destroy only the boys? It could be for any, or a combination, of the following reasons: first, males would grow up to be soldiers and would be liable to serve against the Egyptians (Pharaoh's concern in verse 10); secondly, Hebrew women could easily be assimilated into Egyptian society through intermarriage; thirdly, blood-lines and status were continued through male lineage; and, fourthly, it was an attempt on the part of Pharaoh and the seed of the serpent to thwart the promise of a male Redeemer given in Genesis 3:15.

1:17. But the midwives feared God and they did not do as the king of Egypt had spoken to them, but they let the boys live.

The midwives responded with direct disobedience to the civil government. Its command was contradictory to the ways of God. The women feared the Lord more than man. This is reminiscent of the apostles' continuing to preach in spite of the Sanhedrin's strict orders not to do so (Acts 5:28-29). The word for **'feared'** in Hebrew bears the idea of reverence that leads to obedience. One of the major themes of Exodus first appears in this verse: whom are the Hebrews to serve — God or Pharaoh?

The common name for the God of Israel is used here, **'Elōhîm'**. In this verse, however, it has a definite article attached, '*the* God'. Often an appellative form with a definite article attached designates a position of uniqueness. *Elōhîm* is the masculine plural form of *'l*, which means 'strength, might'. When it is used to refer to the God of the Hebrews its associated word-forms are all in the singular; when it designates other gods (as in Exod. 20:3) it takes plural agreement. The plurality of God's name probably reflects the Hebrew practice of the honorific plural, or plural of majesty *(pluralis majestatis)*, in which a singular object is characterized by a quality to such an extent that a plural form is used to designate that object. Others have attempted to argue for the Trinity based upon the plural of *Elōhîm*.

1:18-19. And the King of Egypt called for the midwives, and he said to them, 'Why did you do this thing, and let the boys live?' And the midwives said to Pharaoh, 'Because the Hebrew women are not like the Egyptian women, for they are vigorous; before the midwife comes to them, they give birth.'

The midwives were called to account by the earthly ruler. God did not hide them or miraculously whisk them away; they had to answer to the government for their actions.

How are we to understand the midwives' response to Pharaoh? Many would argue that it was a lie, and the women were being clever to save themselves.[7] There is an unavoidable conflict in God's law: if the midwives did what the king commanded they would be guilty of murder; if not they would only be guilty of lying. Lying is the lesser of two evils.[8] Others say there is no moral dilemma. It is well and good to lie to ungodly governments (but what about the Ninth Commandment?). A third suggestion is the best: there is no reason to doubt the truth of the midwives' statement. It is evident that the Hebrews were under an extraordinary blessing of increase (see verses 7 and 12 above). Maybe the Hebrew women had quick and easy labour. In addition, God may have speeded up their deliveries in order to protect the midwives and his people.

1:20-21. And God was good to the midwives, and the people multiplied and they became very strong. And it came to pass, because the midwives feared God, that he made households for them.

God caused great blessing to come upon the Hebrews because of the midwives' actions. First, the increased persecution by the Egyptians brought about a greater increase of the Hebrew population. God simply blessed Israel with more people. Secondly, God provided families for the midwives. The word for **'households'** is a masculine plural noun that literally means 'houses'. A common sense of this word is as a metonym representing 'household, family', and that is its usage in this verse. The identical expression can be found in 2 Samuel 7:11 and 1 Kings 2:24. The irony here is delicious: the Hebrew midwives save families through disobedience to Pharaoh, so God rewards them with families for their stand against oppression. God's sovereignty is underscored here.

Application

The church today is obligated to obey God before men. So, for example, if a government commanded that no one was allowed to present the gospel to others, Christians in that country would have to disobey because Christ commands us to witness for him (Matt. 28:19-20). Such was the response of the disciples in Acts 5. If a government ordered mandatory abortions for its people,

Christians would have a duty to resist. God will not countenance his people committing murder (Exod. 20:13). This is a general principle for how a Christian is to live: it is to be on the basis of God's Word.

Third attack of the serpent
(Exodus 1:22)

Pharaoh does not give up. He now turns to his own people, the Egyptians, and orders them to destroy the Hebrew male offspring. Each instance of royal oppression has intensified in flagrancy and severity compared with the previous one. First, he enslaves the Israelites, then he orders Hebrew workers to kill their own people, and finally he commands a direct holocaust. Pharaoh issues a mandate that the Egyptians should murder new-born Hebrew males. This is a very blatant case of extinction: the seed of the serpent is to massacre the lineage of the seed of the woman.

1:22. And Pharaoh commanded all his people, saying, 'Every son who is born, you are to cast him into the Nile, but every daughter you are to let live.'

The Hebrew word for **'Nile'** is an Egyptian loan-word. In Egyptian it means 'the river' and, of course, that refers to the Nile. The amount of Egyptian word-borrowing in the early chapters of Exodus is striking and, again, it points to the author's deep intimacy with Egyptian culture.

The Greek Old Testament, the Septuagint, adds the words **'to the Hebrews'** after the clause, **'every son who is born'**. The Greek translators wanted to make certain that the reader knows that no Egyptian infants were included in the butchery.

This slaughter foreshadows a New Testament event recorded in Matthew 2:16, where we read, 'When Herod realized that he had been outwitted by the Magi, he was furious, and he gave orders to kill all the boys in Bethlehem and its vicinity who were two years old and under...' Herod, in the same vein as Pharaoh, attempted to destroy the male lineage of the Hebrews and, in consequence, to kill the coming Redeemer. God, in his great mercy, however, protected both deliverers.

It is ironic that in Exodus 15:1 God hurls the Egyptian army into the Red Sea and, thus, destroys the élite males of Egypt. The word 'cast' in that verse is a synonym of the one used here in Exodus 1:22. The schemes and wiles of the Egyptians turn back on their own heads.

Application

We need to be careful when we think that such savage acts against the church only occurred in ancient days. Recent studies have demonstrated that more Christians have been martyred in the twentieth century than the previous nineteen centuries combined.

Nina Shea comments: 'Millions of Americans pray in their churches each week, oblivious to the fact that Christians in many parts of the world suffer brutal torture, arrest, imprisonment and even death — their homes and communities laid waste — for no other reason than that they are Christians. The shocking, untold story of our time is that more Christians have died this century simply for being Christians than in the first nineteen centuries after the birth of Christ. They have been persecuted and martyred before an unknowing, indifferent world and a largely silent Christian community.'[9] The lesson for us is that the seed of the serpent is alive and well on the planet earth.

2. God raises a deliverer

Exodus 2:1 - 4:31

The birth of Moses (Exodus 2:1-10)

In the first chapter of Exodus the author set the scene of severe persecution of the people of God. The reader antici-pates that God will somehow miraculously intervene in the situation to bring redemption to his people. We are not disappointed, because chapter 2 narrates the birth and preparation of the deliverer of Israel — Moses.[1] There are no surprises here. God is in control, guiding, directing and working out all things for the good of his people. Thus, no matter how the ungodly, the seed of the serpent, attempt to thwart God's plan (chapter 1), they cannot and will not succeed (chapter 2).

2:1-2. And a man came from the house of Levi and he took the daughter of Levi. And the woman conceived and she bore a son. And she saw that he was healthy and she hid him for three months.

A literal reading of the opening verse of this chapter says that a Levite man married **'the daughter of Levi'**. The definiteness of the identity of this woman needs to be recognized because, according to Exodus 6:18-20, this woman was indeed Levi's daughter. It states there that Amram, the grandson of Levi, wedded his aunt, whose name was Jochebed. Jochebed was the daughter of Levi and the woman mentioned in Exodus 2:1. She became the mother of Moses, the deliverer of Israel. Levi was therefore Moses' grandfather and great-grandfather at the same time!

It is significant that Moses was born a Levite. The tribe of Levi was later to be set apart (at Mount Sinai) for the particular work of carrying the holy objects of the tabernacle. They were also set apart as substitutes for the first-born of Israel (Num. 3:40-51). Moses descended from the Kohathite division of the Levites: this group was specially designated at Sinai to carry the holy things upon their shoulders, particularly the ark of the covenant (Num. 7:9). Such a genealogy meant much to the Hebrew reader; it indicated that Moses was being set apart for God's special service, as his tribe would later be set apart.

There is no indication in the text that this child was the first-born son. Later passages tell us that he had an older sister (Exod. 2:4) and an older brother, Aaron (Exod. 7:7). The suggestion has been made that Moses had a different mother from his elder siblings, but that is pure speculation.

In verse 2, Jochebed bears a son. This is quite dramatic because of Pharaoh's recent command to kill all Hebrew male infants. She views the baby and sees that, in a direct translation of the Hebrew, **'He was good'**. What does this mean? It would be a mistake to suppose that it is a moral statement, to the effect that the child was good and not evil. It is also unlikely that it has to do with mere beauty, that he was good to look at (in contrast to a plain-looking child). Rather, it probably means that the child was healthy. He was not going to die in infancy, as so many children did in those days. So Jochebed responds by hiding the child because of his strength.

The verb 'see' followed by the word 'good' is a common idiom of the author of the book of Genesis (see Gen. 1:4,10,12,18,21,25,31; 3:6; 6:2; 40:16; 49:15).[2]

According to Hebrews 11:23, Jochebed 'hid him for three months' because she and her husband had faith in God, and they were not afraid of Pharaoh's command. Even at the risk to their own lives they disobeyed, and they did that without fear.

2:3. And when she was no longer able to hide him, she took for him a papyrus basket, and covered it with tar and with pitch. And she put the boy in it. Then she set it in the reeds along the bank of the Nile.

No doubt, after three months, the healthy child began to cry too loudly and to have some mobility. He would soon draw attention from the authorities, so Jochebed put the baby in **'a papyrus basket'** and abandoned him in the reeds on the shore of the Nile river. The two Hebrew terms used for 'a papyrus basket' are both Egyptian loan-words. The first word, *gōme'*, is Egyptian for 'papyrus', long reeds found in Egyptian waters (the Egyptians used papyrus for writing, and our word 'paper' is a derivative of it). According to Isaiah 18:1-2, the Egyptians employed papyrus boats.

The second term is *tēbāh*, an Egyptian word that signifies 'chest' or 'coffin'. It is used in only one other story in the Old Testament, in the account of the flood, where 'The Lord then said to Noah, "Go into the ark *[tēbāh]*, you and your whole family"' (Gen. 7:1) This is no coincidence; rather, we have here a thematic parallel. Both Noah and Moses undergo water ordeals in which they survive. They then become deliverers for the people of God, the seed of the woman. (It is also worth noting that both Noah and Jochebed covered the 'arks' with **'pitch'** to protect them from destructive elements — see Gen. 6:14).

Where the woman placed the child, **'in the reeds'**, is also a word borrowed from Egyptian.[3] The word *sûp* is later used of the sea which the Hebrews miraculously crossed through (Exod. 13:18).

Why did Jochebed do this? What would have driven her to commit such a desperate act? The text does not tell us. The most we can say is that God put it into her heart so that his plan would proceed and unfold. 'Cast your bread upon the waters, for after many days you will find it again' (Eccles. 11:1).

2:4. And his sister stood at a distance to know what would happen to him.

The mother was not willing to proceed by mere blind faith, but she had her daughter watch the ark to see what would happen to the child. In addition, Jochebed obviously deposited the basket in a location where human (royal?) traffic was frequent. She wanted to ensure that the child would be discovered. What she could not be certain of was whether or not the person who discovered the baby would have compassion on him. That was in the hands of God.

2:5. And the daughter of Pharaoh came down to bathe near the Nile. And her servant girls were walking along the Nile. And she saw the basket in the midst of the reeds. And she sent her maid, and she took it.

If the Pharaoh at this time was Rameses II (see discussion in the introduction), then this was one of his many daughters. It is well known that he engendered over 100 children, including at least sixty daughters. The name of the daughter is not mentioned because it is not important to the theme or development of the story. Much later Apocryphal literature gives her name as Tharmuth (Jubilees 47:5), but there is no reason to accept that tradition.

There is a delicious irony about the sequence of events which begins in this verse. One of Pharaoh's own children delivers a Hebrew child who would later save God's children from bondage to Pharaoh. God thus uses one from

the house of the seed of the serpent to help deliver the seed
of the woman.

2:6. When she opened it, she saw the boy; and, behold, the
child was crying. And she felt sorry for him. And she said,
'This is one of the Hebrew children.'

The Hebrew word for **'felt sorry'** carries the basic meaning
of 'to spare'. So, for example, when the prophet Samuel
orders Saul to destroy the Amalekites in 1 Samuel 15:3, he
says, 'Do not spare them; put to death men and women,
children and infants, cattle and sheep, camels and donkeys.' Frequently, however, it also bears the idea of sparing
a life with compassion (see, for instance, 2 Chron. 36:15;
Mal. 3:17).[4] And that is how we are to understand the
woman's act in verse 6: she displayed great pity for the
child which resulted in her saving his life. Once again we
see the irony of the situation, because her tenderness and
mercy were antithetical to the brutality of her father.

This is not a case of misidentification. Pharaoh's
daughter recognized the child as **'one of the Hebrew
children'**. She then spared him in direct violation of her
father's command. That act of disobedience was no small
thing, since Pharaoh had absolute power over the land of
Egypt and its inhabitants. His word was law. One only
breached it knowing that the severest penalties, often
death, would result. In this regard, Pharaoh's daughter
ought to be considered in parallel with the Hebrew
midwives who also disregarded the 'divine' authority of
Pharaoh.

2:7. And his sister said to the daughter of Pharaoh, 'Shall I
go and call for you a nursing woman from the Hebrew
women, so that she might nurse the child for you?'

Presumably because so many of the Hebrew children had
been destroyed by mandate of Pharaoh, there certainly

would have been numerous **'Hebrew women'** able to suckle a child. That is why the offer of a Hebrew woman to Pharaoh's daughter was not out of place.

There is a repetition of **'for you'** in the verse: **'Shall I go and call *for you* a nursing Hebrew woman so that she will nurse the child *for you*?'** The emphasis of the sister's question is the benefit accorded to the princess. The sister is being wise here, making the princess the centre of attention, and not the child.

2:8. And the daughter of Pharaoh said to her, 'Go!' And the girl went and she called the mother of the boy.

In the original there is no 'Yes' in the princess's response. She merely employs the Hebrew imperative, **'Go!'** That command is instantly followed by a variation of the same verb: **'and she went'**. That grammatical configuration in Hebrew often indicates the immediate fulfilment of a command (see Gen. 12:1-4; 26:16-17; Exod. 4:27). In other words, the girl went quickly to fetch her mother.

2:9. And the daughter of Pharaoh said to her, 'Take this boy and nurse him for me. And I will give you wages.' So the woman took the boy and she nursed him.

The drama now reaches fever pitch as the child is saved and returned to his mother. But now he is under royal protection. And not only that, but Jochebed is even given wages for carrying out her natural task and duty! This appears to be a precursor of how the Hebrews would later plunder the Egyptians (Exod. 12:36).

This event was also important in regard to the child's upbringing. Through his mother's influence the young boy would have been introduced to Hebrew religion and culture. There is nothing in the biblical text to indicate that he did not know his Hebrew heritage. On the contrary, the subsequent story in Exodus 2:11-14 indicates that he was well aware of his ancestry. In any event, this early training in the ways of the Hebrews and their God must have had a great impact on the child who was one day to deliver his people.

The fact that the lad was under the patronage of the princess is underscored by the use of the imperative for both the verbs **'take'** and **'nurse'**: these are royal decrees. Thus the child not only had heavenly royal guardianship, but earthly royal protection as well. God was simply preserving the boy in every aspect.

2:10. And the boy grew, and she brought him to the daughter of Pharaoh. And he became like a son to her. And she called his name Moses. And she said, 'Because I drew him out from the waters.'

We do not learn much about Moses' childhood except that his early years were spent with his Hebrew mother. At some point in his youth he was brought to Pharaoh's daughter and he was considered **'her son'**. She named the child **'Moses'**, which derives from the Hebrew verb *māshāh*, that means 'to draw out'. However, it is also a common Egyptian word, meaning 'son of'. Many Egyptian names employ it in conjunction with other words: Thut-mosis (son of Thut) and Ahmosis (son of Ah), for example. In the name 'Moses', however, the genitive has no object. He is simply 'the son of'. This is probably a pun by the biblical writer to emphasize the point that Moses was not a son of Egypt, but rather a son of Israel. His later rejection of Egypt and her ways confirms that he disowned all allegiance to her (see Heb. 11:24-25).

In Stephen's speech in the book of Acts, we read that 'Pharaoh's daughter took him and brought him up as her own son. Moses was educated in all the wisdom of the Egyptians and was powerful in speech and action' (Acts 7:21-22). Here is the reason why God placed Moses in the Egyptian court. It was a period of preparation. God was equipping Moses to do battle with the Egyptians. At that time, Egypt was the greatest kingdom on earth and had the most advanced education of the time: astronomy, mathematics, medicine, and so forth. Moses learnt these things so that he would not be caught unawares when the time of confrontation drew near.

Application

The church should take great encouragement from this story. As with ancient Israel, the work of Satan and his followers will never destroy the church. No matter how bleak things appear, no matter how great the persecution, God will not allow his church to perish. As Jesus promised, 'The gates of hell will not overcome it' (Matt. 16:18). It will persevere on earth until the end of time, and then continue into eternity in the celestial city.

The appearance of a deliverer in Exodus 2 underscores the doctrine of the providence of God. He is working here, and all things are under his control. Even in the tiniest details of this story the sovereignty of God is evident. None of the events of the birth episode happened by chance, but God was making preparations for the redemption of his people.

God's sovereignty is also seen in the fact that the birth narrative of Moses points to the coming of the ultimate Redeemer, Christ Jesus. Moses is a type of Christ. Like Moses, Jesus is born into a situation of severe persecution against the people of God. The ruler in both stories destroys Hebrew infants in order to prevent the coming of a deliverer. Both redeemers escape the holocausts. And it is ironical that in the case of Jesus, he and his family flee the massacre by going to Egypt (Matt. 2:13). God thus lays down a pattern in the early life of Moses that is repeated and heightened in the life of Christ. Indeed, Jesus delivers his people as Moses delivers his, but how much greater is Christ's redemption! Therefore, Jesus is to be seen as a new and greater Moses.

Moses escapes to Midian (Exodus 2:11-22)

The first recorded act of Moses is now presented. It appears to be a despicable work of murder. The Scriptures here demonstrate that God uses even the most shameful events in the history of mankind to bring about his good purposes. In other words, the Lord employs mankind's sin to execute his plan in creation. He is simply sovereign, and nothing happens in heaven or on earth apart from God's decretive will. The murderous act of Moses and his subsequent flight from Egypt will highlight God's total control of history.

2:11. And it came to pass in those days that Moses grew up, and he went out to his brothers. And he saw their burdens. And he saw an Egyptian man beating a Hebrew man, one of his brothers.

Moses was clearly not detached from his own people. Twice in this verse it is stated that the Hebrews were **'his brothers'**. The verb **'he saw'** is also used twice, and it indicates that Moses was giving attention to the living conditions of his people. The previous story of Pharaoh's daughter finding the baby Moses employed the verb 'to see' (2:5-6), and it reflected the Egyptian woman's compassion on, and pity for, the infant. Perhaps Moses was also sympathizing with his people and showing them mercy.

In the course of observing the general wretched condition of his people, Moses witnessed an incident in which an Egyptian was beating a Hebrew. Some interpreters assume that the Egyptian 'was beating a Hebrew to death'.[5] The Hebrew verb, however, ranges in meaning from hitting to killing. A point in favour of the verb's signifying murderous intent here is its appearance in the very next verse (2:12) when Moses, in fact, kills the Egyptian.

2:12. And he looked this way and that, and he saw that there was no man. So he killed the Egyptian and hid him in the sand.

Some scholars believe that Moses acted in an upright fashion here. They argue that his act of looking **'this way and that'** was to see if anyone else would come to the man's rescue.[6] When no one else helped, they say, Moses stepped in and acted the part of the deliverer. The fact that Moses hid the man in the sand would argue against such an interpretation, however. He was acting surreptitiously. He wanted no one to witness his violent deed. His surprise in verse 14 that people had come to know of the execution he had carried out confirms the latter understanding.

2:13. And he went out on the next day and, behold, two Hebrew men were struggling with one another. And he said to the guilty one, 'Why are you striking your comrade?'

The day following the murder, Moses repeats his activity by setting out to see the condition of his people. The same verb 'to go out' is used as in verse 11. That repetition 'suggests the concern Moses felt for his kinsmen, a concern that overcame any apprehensions he might have had over the consequences such visits might bring upon him'.[7]

When Moses arrives a similar incident greets him. It is a surprise to him, as the clause begins with the Hebrew particle, **'Behold!'** Now Moses sees two Hebrews **'struggling with one another'** (a Niphal verb used to indicate reciprocal action). And he intervenes as he did in the previous story.

Whereas in the earlier incident Moses had killed the Egyptian who had instigated the trouble, here he merely verbally confronts the **'guilty'** antagonist. The word used has the meanings, 'wicked, wrong, criminal'. It is a term often used in legal contexts when pronouncing a person guilty of a crime.

2:14. But he said, 'Who set you as a prince or a judge over us? Are you saying you will kill me as you killed the Egyptian?' And Moses was afraid. And he said, 'Surely the thing has become known.'

Moses' intervention and the taunting response of the Hebrew foreshadow the later relationship between Moses and the entire Israelite nation. Here the man questions Moses' authority — why, Moses is no more than the son of a Hebrew slave! Who is he to lord it over his fellow Hebrews? Acts 7:25 indicates that the people did not recognize that God had put Moses in his court position, or that God had appointed him to deliver the people. The anger and insolence of the people towards Moses are pinpointed in the man's remarks.

The man's second question is accusatory. Who is Moses to try to put a stop to a beating when he himself had killed a man just the day before? The revelation that his murderous deed had become known was a blow to Moses. He begins his statement with an adverb with strong assertive force: **'indeed, surely'**. That term reflects a strongly emotional response on the part of Moses. Apparently he thought his misdeed had gone undetected, but obviously the man he had delivered had spread the word.

2:15. And Pharaoh heard of this matter. And he sought to kill Moses. So Moses fled from before Pharaoh, and he dwelt in the land of Midian. And he sat down next to a well.

Because Moses killed the Egyptian, Pharaoh tries to kill him. This is another pointer to a later event. After the Egyptian first-born are killed during the tenth plague, the Israelites flee to the land of Midian. The Egyptian army follows in an attempt to destroy them.

Moses is again placed in a position of preparation. He will later lead the people of Israel out of Egypt into this very land that he now traverses and where he will soon live. In a subtle manner, God is in control and preparing Moses for future redemption.

'Midian' refers to land under the control of a series of semi-nomadic tribes called Midianites. Centred in the north-western part of the Arabian peninsula, the Midian-ites often controlled parts of the Sinai peninsula, the Negev and the Arabah. The name Midian derives from one of the sons of Abraham by Keturah — a son who had been sent to the east, away from Isaac (Gen. 25:2-6). The Midianites were primarily herdsmen, migrating with their livestock according to the seasons, and they were also involved in international trade (Gen. 37:28). It goes without saying that the culture and lifestyle of Midian were unlike those of Egypt.

Wells were important for shepherds and semi-nomadic peoples. It was quite natural that Moses should be drawn to a well, not only for physical sustenance, but because it was the meeting-place for shepherds and travellers.

2:16. And the priest of Midian had seven daughters. And they came and they drew water and they filled the troughs to give water to their father's flock.

Apparently this desert priest had no sons or, at least, none is mentioned in the story. He did, however, possess an abundance of daughters, as is implied by the number **'seven'**. That figure is frequently used in Scripture to symbolize completeness, or the ideal.

The work of watering animals was a common activity for women in Old Testament times (see Gen. 24:11-19).

The fact that this man is described as a **'priest'** has caused some scholars to theorize that Moses received his basic religious instruction from this Midianite. In support of that position is the fact that Moses received his first revelation from God (Exod. 3) and the Torah (Exodus 20ff.) at Mount Sinai in the area of Midian. Contrasting evidence is more compelling, however. First, it is clear that Moses was instructed in the religion of the Hebrews as a child (see 2:9). Secondly, Exodus 18 indicates that this Midianite was not a priest of the Lord (Yahweh) but a polytheist. He is not convinced of monotheism until 18:11. It is not, then, from this man that Moses learns the religion of the Israelites.

2:17. But the shepherds came and drove them away. So Moses arose and he rescued them. And he gave water to their father's flock.

This act serves as a microcosm of the later exodus deliverance. Here the women are victimized and oppressed by shepherds who drive them away from the water. Moses stands up for the persecuted and rescues them from the oppressors. The word **'rescued'** simply means 'saved', or 'delivered'. The same verb is generally used for the deliverance of the Israelites out of Egypt: 'That day the Lord saved Israel from the hand of the Egyptians' (Exod. 14:30).

The word for **'drove away'** is also employed in the later exodus event when Pharaoh 'drives away' Moses and Aaron from his court (Exod. 10:11) and when Yahweh causes Pharaoh to 'drive away' the Hebrews from the land of Egypt (Exod. 6:1).

The character of the man Moses is underscored here. He is brave, loves justice and does good things. He takes the side of the weak and the oppressed. These traits will serve him well in the later deliverance of the Hebrews.

2:18. Then they came to Reuel their father, and he said, 'Why have you come back quickly today?'

The father's name is **'Reuel'** (cf. Num. 10:29), which perhaps means 'friend of God' or 'shepherd of God'. Elsewhere he is called Jethro (Exod. 3:1; 4:18; etc.). The latter name derives from a stem meaning 'abundance, superiority'. Why is he given two names? Some argue that they refer to two different people, although that is difficult to support textually. Others say they are the result of two separate sources or traditions which were later brought together by a redactor. However, an editor splicing together two conflicting names within a few lines of one another seems an unlikely solution.[8] It is more probable that one of the names was the man's common name, whereas the other was his official, priestly title. Frequently in the Scriptures, high officials have both types of name (see Judg. 6-8; 2 Kings 15:19,29; 23:34 - 24:6; 1 Chron. 3:15; 2 Chron. 21:17; 25:23).

2:19. And they said, 'An Egyptian man rescued us from the hand of the shepherds. And furthermore he drew water for us and watered the flock.'

Why did the daughters conclude that Moses was an Egyptian? It could have been for any number of reasons. Moses' language, or dialect of Semitic, would have given him away; so would his clothing or his being clean-shaven (as the Egyptians were in contrast to Asiatics). In other words, his general appearance and demeanour as one who had lived in the court of Pharaoh for many years would have stood out starkly against the background of a desert, tribal environment.

A different word for **'rescued'** is used here from that in verse 17 — the Hebrew verb *nasal.* The girls said, **'An Egyptian man rescued us from the hand of the shepherds.'** That statement uses almost identical wording to

Exodus 18:10, which tells of the Lord who 'rescued you from the hand of the Egyptians and from the hand of Pharaoh'. This appears to be another point of confirmation that the story of the rescue of the daughters is to be seen as a paradigm for the entire salvation event of the exodus.

There is a repetition of the verb 'to draw' in this verse (an infinitive followed by a verb in the perfect tense). This is for the purpose of emphasis, to show the daughters' surprise at Moses' aid to them.

2:20. And he said to his daughters, 'And where is he? Why did you leave the man? Call to him, that he might eat food.'

The dialogue of the father begins with a *waw* conjunctive in Hebrew, meaning **'and'**. Its purpose is to link his question to the story of the daughters, with the sense being: 'If this is so, why is he not here with you?'[9]

'That he might eat food' is literally **'that he might eat bread'**. The word for 'bread' is a figure of speech called a synecdoche of the part, in which a portion of a thing is put for the whole. Thus 'bread' signifies food in general.

2:21. And Moses agreed to dwell with the man. And he gave Zipporah his daughter to Moses.

The verb translated **'agreed'** has various meanings in the original. It can mean 'to determine, to be pleased, to show willingness, to undertake', but here it clearly demonstrates Moses' acquiescence to Reuel's suggestion — that is, his acceptance of an invitation.[10] And his desire was not merely 'to stay' for a short time with Reuel, but to **'dwell'** with him: that word reflects a long-term situation.

The Midianite priest **'gave Zipporah ... to Moses'** for a wife. The father, of course, held the power to make such decisions in biblical times (see Gen. 29:28; Judg. 1:12; 1 Sam. 17:25; etc.). In the entire ancient Near East, for that matter, the family was universally patriarchal in nature.[11]

The name of Moses' wife, **'Zipporah'** *(Ṣīpōrāh)*, simply means 'bird'.

2:22. And she bore a son. And he called his name Gershom, for he said, 'I have become a stranger in a foreign land.'

Immediately after the mention of the marriage we are told that Zipporah gave birth to a first-born son. Moses calls his name **'Gershom'**, which derives from the Hebrew verb 'to drive away' *(gārāš)*. It is the same verb that was used in 2:17, where the shepherds attempted to drive away Jethro's daughters from the watering-spot. There is also a pun here, because the name Gershom is a composite word in Hebrew that means 'a sojourner/stranger there'. And that is how the biblical author understands its usage, as Moses comments on his naming the child that **'I have become a sojourner/stranger** *[gēr]* **in a foreign land.'** The question is, to what land is Moses making reference? Midian? Egypt? The verb **'become'** does not help us here because in its perfect tense it could be translated past, present, or future. Thus an acceptable translation would also be: 'I *was* a stranger in a foreign land' (i.e., Egypt).

Moses' naming of the child could, in fact, be a greater, spiritual, eternal statement. When the author of the book of Hebrews describes Moses' disowning of Egypt, along with other activities on the part of men of faith, he says that they 'admitted that they were aliens and strangers on earth' (Heb. 11:13). To the point, he claims that Moses 'was looking ahead to his reward' (Heb. 11:26), because 'Here we do not have an enduring city, but we are looking for the city that is to come' (Heb. 13:14).

Application

Two general points of application need to be made here. Firstly, believers are called to understand and take to heart the truth that God's plan for the universe and eternity will come to pass despite sin. Dare we think that in some way our sin will thwart God's decrees from operating in the world? Not even Satan, at his most malevolent and malicious, can hinder the providence of God. Even the very gates of hell are powerless to obstruct God's purposes for the universe. May we hold to that truth dearly.

Secondly, may we grasp the truth that God will use us, like he did Moses, despite our sin. That, of course, does not give us a licence to sin, but God employs frail and weak vessels to proclaim the gospel to a dying world. Christ uses redeemed sinners to proclaim the excellencies of him who has called us out of darkness! God uses his people, despite their feebleness, debility and transgressions, for his glory and his purposes.

God remembers his covenant
(Exodus 2:23-25)

The author now returns to the account of events in Egypt. He wants to inform the reader that God has not forgotten his people there. In fact, not only are the Hebrews remembered by God, but God also recalls the promise of the covenant that he had made with the patriarchs so many centuries before. The Lord is about to fulfil his covenant promises made to Abraham, Isaac and Jacob.

2:23. And it came to pass in those many days that the King of Egypt died. But the children of Israel sighed as a result of the labour. So they cried out. And their cry went up to God because of the bondage.

An interval of time now occurs between the previous story of Moses' rescue of the Midianite women and what is to follow. How long that period was is not directly stated in the text. However, elsewhere in the Scriptures we are given some clues that help in solving the problem. First, the Bible teaches that Moses lived 120 years (Deut. 34:7), and his life may be divided into three forty-year segments. The first part of his life consists of his time in Egypt up to the point when, at 'forty years old, he decided to visit his fellow Israelites' (Acts 7:23; cf. Exod. 2:11). Moses was then forced to flee from Egypt to Midian, where he was to spend the next forty years (Acts 7:30). At the end of that time he returned to Egypt and appeared before Pharaoh at the age of eighty (Exod. 7:7). The final stage of his life was his leadership of Israel through their wilderness wanderings,

which took forty years to complete (Num. 14:33-34).
Consequently, the time interval between Moses' first arrival
in Midian (Exod. 2:15) and this introductory statement in
verse 23 is forty years!

It should be noted that the number forty in the Bible
often symbolizes a period of trials and testings. So, for
example, when the deluge hit the earth in the time of
Noah, it lasted forty days (Gen. 7:17); Goliath's taunting of
Israel occurred every morning and evening for forty days
(1 Sam. 17:16); and when Jesus was tempted by the devil
the Saviour fasted for forty days and nights. Thus the life
of Moses may be summarized as three forty-year segments
of various trials — in Egypt, in Midian and in the
wilderness.

At some time during this period of forty years, the King
of Egypt, the one who tried to kill Moses (Exod. 2:15), died.
This is an important marker for it helps to pave the way for
Moses to return to Egypt. As the Lord later tells the
prophet, 'Go back to Egypt, for all the men who wanted to
kill you are dead' (Exod. 4:19).

And now, even though a new pharaoh rules Egypt, the
Hebrews remain under severe oppression. They respond in
two ways. First, they **'sigh',** or 'groan', because of their
servitude. And Proverbs tells us that 'When the wicked
rule, the people groan' (Prov. 29:2). Secondly, the people
cry out to **'God'.** Note that the name Yahweh is not used
here because it is not revealed until the next chapter. Here
we find the more general name Ĕlōhîm.

2:24. And God heard their groaning, and God remembered
his covenant with Abraham, with Isaac and with Jacob.

The idea that God **'remembered'** his covenant with the
patriarchs is not a matter of mere recall. The Hebrew term
bears the additional idea of a person's acting upon the
remembrance. Thus, the point here is that God not only
remembers his covenant promises to the patriarchs, but
he is now about to act to fulfil those promises.

When God established a covenant with Abraham, one of its foundational promises was the deliverance of the Hebrews from a foreign land. The Lord prophesied to Abraham during the covenant ratification: 'Know for certain that your descendants will be strangers in a country not their own, and they will be enslaved and mistreated four hundred years. But I will punish the nation they serve as slaves, and afterwards they will come out with great possessions' (Gen. 15:13-14). The exodus event is the fulfilment of that covenant promise of salvation that God had given to Abraham so many centuries before.

2:25. So God saw the children of Israel and God knew.

In this summary statement, it says that **'God saw the sons of Israel, and God knew'**. The verb 'to know' in Hebrew bears a greater sense than a simple intellectual knowledge or understanding. It frequently means to have an intimate relationship with someone or something. For example, when the Bible speaks of human intercourse that results in birth it often uses that verb. Genesis 4:1 literally translates as: 'The man knew his wife Eve and she conceived and she gave birth...' God's personal relationship with the righteous is characterized as one of knowing (see Ps. 1:6; Jer. 24:7). The point of this verse is to emphasize that God is not distant from his people, but he knows their labour, sighs and groanings. He was intimate with Israel's situation of oppression.

Application

How comforting to know that God does not forget his people, or the promises he has made to them! He is also near to his people. He maintains a close personal relationship with, and attachment to, them. He truly knows and has an intimacy with what his people endure, whether it be trials, sufferings, or temptations.

The book of Hebrews tells us this is the work of Christ: 'Therefore, he [Jesus] had to be made like his brethren in all things, that he might become a merciful and faithful high priest in things pertaining to God, to make propitiation for the sins of the people. For since he himself was tempted in that which he has suffered, he is able to come to the aid of those who are tempted' (Heb. 2:17-18). And, again, the same author comments: 'For we do not have a high priest who cannot sympathize with our weaknesses, but one who has been tempted in all things as we are, yet without sin. Let us therefore draw near with confidence to the throne of grace, that we may receive mercy and may find grace to help in time of need' (Heb. 4:15-16).

The God of the Bible is not distant, or far-removed, from his church. Deism is not an option for the people of God. He is close to his people, running the universe for their good and for his glory.

Theophany of the burning bush
(Exodus 3:1-22)

Exodus 2 has demonstrated that God has already begun to act upon Israel's dire circumstances by raising a deliverer in Pharaoh's court. That prophet is then forced to flee to Midian for a further period of preparation for the forthcoming deliverance of the Hebrews from Egypt. God's hand is clearly evident, guiding and directing all events to his purposes. The next step in the process of the liberation of Israel now occurs: the call and commissioning of the man Moses. His appointment in chapter 3 may be divided into three parts: the revelation of the burning bush (3:1-6); the call of Moses (3:7-10); and dialogue between God and Moses (3:11-22).[12]

3:1. And Moses was shepherding the flock of Jethro his father-in-law, the priest of Midian. And he led the flock behind the wilderness, and he came to the mountain of God, to Horeb.

We are now introduced to Moses in his desert occupation, that of a shepherd for his father-in-law. He has gone from a position of royalty in Egypt, where he was acknowledged as the son of Pharaoh's daughter, to being a lowly sheepherder. This would have been particularly humbling for Moses because the Egyptians despised herding flocks as an occupation. Joseph comments that 'All shepherds are detestable to the Egyptians' (Gen. 46:34). Thus, Moses, of whom Acts 7:22 says that he 'was educated in all the wisdom of the Egyptians', is snatched from the Egyptian royal court and deposited on the far side of a desert mountain to tend sheep.

To man, who judges primarily on the things of the flesh, Moses appears, at this stage in his life, to be a tragic figure. He has lost his position of power and authority, his fame and his riches. And he is now carrying out the most menial type of work in a barren land! But to God, all earthly authority, power, riches and pride are mere chaff that the wind drives away. For here is a poor shepherd who will one day be the deliverer of Israel. In fact, this lowly work is preparation for the task of shepherding the flock of the Lord.

Moses nears the mountain of **'Horeb'**. Some have attempted to argue that Horeb is not Mount Sinai but another mountain in the same vicinity. Others say it refers to the entire mountain range of which Mount Sinai was a part. It is most likely that it is an alternative name for Mount Sinai and is used interchangeably with it (see 3:12).

3:2. **And the Angel of Yahweh appeared to him in the heart of the fire from the midst of the bush. And he looked, and behold, the bush was burning in fire, but the bush was not being consumed.**

At the mountain of God Moses witnesses an amazing sight: he sees a bush on fire but not being burned up. The writer employs two participles here: **'The bush was burning ... but the bush was not being consumed.'** These participles in Hebrew represent continuous action; that is, the bush was continuing to burn and it was continuing not to be consumed.

The burning bush was truly a great sight, one that the palace of Pharaoh could never have afforded. But what is the significance of the image? Why did God use it in calling Moses? First, it may have been to reflect the circum-stances of God's people at the time. The Hebrews were in the furnace of Egypt but God was not permitting them to be destroyed. Secondly, it may have illustrated the way in which the Lord was soon going to deal with the Hebrews in Egypt: he would purify Israel in Egypt but he would not allow the people to be destroyed. Or, finally, the representation may simply have signified the appearance of God. Fire is often a sign in the book of Exodus of the presence of God among his people (see Exod. 13:21; 14:24; 19:18; and especially 24:17, which says, 'The glory of the Lord looked like a consuming fire'). [13]

But even greater than the sight of the burning bush is the appearance of **'the Angel of Yahweh'** in the flames of the fire of the bush — literally, **'in the heart of the fire'**. Who is this? The angel is identified with God in the passage and speaks as if he is God (3:4). That identification is made elsewhere in Scripture (see Judg. 13:17-22). Some commentators argue that the Angel of the LORD is the Second Person of the Trinity, a pre-incarnate Christ. As John Calvin remarks, 'But let us enquire who this Angel was?… The ancient teachers of the Church have rightly understood [it to be] the Eternal Son of God in respect to his office as Mediator.'

3:3. And Moses said, 'I must, indeed, turn aside and see this great sight — why the bush is not burning up.'

Moses is intrigued by the sight. He decides to **'turn aside'** and to witness the burning bush at closer range. Attached to the verb 'go over/turn aside' is the Hebrew particle *na'* that is used for emphasis. It indicates Moses' strengthening of his resolve to draw near to the spectacle. That particle is often left untranslated in modern versions, but it is quite proper to render it with the word **'indeed'**.

The term **'great sight'** derives directly from the verb 'to see' used in the sentence. It is the basic word in the original for 'sight/appearance/looks'. However, the word is used to indicate the presence of extraordinary phenomena, such as the glory-cloud above the tabernacle (Num. 9:15) and the seraphim (Ezek. 1:14). Thus, the burning bush is to be understood as an unnatural event, a unique happening, that was intended to capture Moses' attention.

3:4. But Yahweh saw that he turned aside to look, and God called to him from the midst of the bush. And he said, 'Moses, Moses.' And he said, 'Here I am.'

In this passage, two Hebrew names for God are employed by the author: **'Yahweh'** (LORD) and **'Elohim'** (God). The use of the two appellations in the same verse would imply that the alleged division of the text according to sources using different divine names is specious.[14] The tetragrammaton, Yahweh, had not yet been revealed to Moses and thus it is Elohim who speaks to him from the bush.

The repetition of Moses' name is for the purpose of emphasis. It serves to caution him as he approaches a holy, sacred place. Such a call in Scripture often indicates that a dialogue with God is about to occur. See, for example, God's calls to Abraham in Genesis 22:11 and to Jacob in Genesis 46:2.

Moses answers the call with **'Here I am'**, or more literally, 'Behold me!' His reply conveys his willingness and eagerness to listen and to obey. It is significant that both Abraham and Jacob responded in exactly the same manner in the verses quoted above.

3:5. And he said, 'Do not come near! Remove your sandals from your feet! Because the place where you are standing is holy ground.'

God's call begins with a negative command: **'Do not come near.'** The negative used here with an imperfect verb tends to reflect a sense of urgency.[15] With this construction God is again warning Moses that he needs to take great care and to pay attention immediately.

The negative prohibition is followed by a positive injunction: **'Take off your sandals.'** The verb here is an imperative. The same command is used elsewhere only in Joshua 5:15, where the captain of the Lord's army enjoins Joshua to remove his footwear. In the ancient Near East and the Old Testament, this act was a sign of humility and reverence before one who is greater.

The text also tells us that Moses is commanded to take off his sandals because he is standing on **'holy ground'**. The word for holy, *qōdĕsh*, is a term meaning 'set apart, uncommon, unique'. The Old Testament teaches that places can be holy only because of the presence of God, the appearance, in a theophany, of the Almighty. So, for example, Mount Sinai was sacred only because of God's presence on top of the mountain. That is different from other ancient Near-Eastern peoples, who believed some places and objects were inherently holy, that is, in and of themselves.[16]

3:6. And he said, 'I am the God of your father, the God of Abraham, the God of Isaac and the God of Jacob.' And Moses covered his face because he was afraid of looking at God.

God now identifies himself. He announces that he is the same God who appeared to the patriarchs and called them to follow him. This declaration of continuity is to recall, or bring to remembrance, the promises God had made to the patriarchs, that he would be in covenant with the Hebrews, and he would deliver them from 'a land that is not theirs, where they will be enslaved and oppressed four hundred years' (Gen. 15:13).

The epithet **'God of your father'** is a common ancient Near-Eastern designation that reflects a special, unique relationship between a person and a deity.[17] Observe that it is the singular, **'father'**, in our passage. After this time, whenever the expression is used it appears almost exclusively in the plural, 'God of your fathers'. The reason for the change is that after this revelation to Moses the formula applies to the relationship between God and all the people of Israel.

Moses responds to God's self-disclosure by hiding his face. That is a typical response on the part of humans in the Bible (Deut. 7:20; Job 13:20) and even of the angelic host (Isa. 6:1-3). Confronted with the presence and holiness of God, the biblical person believed he would be destroyed because of his own lack of holiness (Judg. 13:22).

It is this verse that Jesus quotes in his debate with the Sadducees regarding the validity of resurrection (Mark 12:26). His argument is that the God who appeared to Moses at the bush is the God of the living and not the dead. At the bush, Yahweh claimed to be the God of the patriarchs even though they had been dead for some time. So they must still be living, or have hope in life through resurrection.[18]

3:7. And Yahweh said, 'I have indeed seen the affliction of my people who are in Egypt. And I have heard their cry from before their taskmasters because I know their sufferings.'

God speaks of the present situation of the people of God in Egypt. He declares, **'I have indeed seen'**. In the original the phrase is a construction involving a play on words: the infinitive absolute of 'to see' appears in conjunction with a finite verbal form derived from the same root.[19] A literal translation would be something like 'Seeing, I have seen.' Thus the construction bears a quality of intensification and emphasis. In other words, the idea being relayed is that God is really and truly aware of Israel's circumstances.

God's knowledge of Israel's condition is further revealed by the author's use of a chiastic structure. In the Hebrew it appears this way:

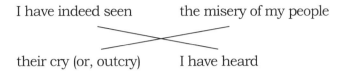

A chiasm is a type of Hebrew parallelism that emphasizes a point through repetition, with inversion of the word order.

The Lord's response to Israel's trying circumstances is, literally, **'I know his pains.'** First, observe that the Hebrews are spoken of in the singular, probably reflecting the covenant oneness of God's people. The word for the pain Israel is suffering is used in the Scriptures of both physical and mental distress. Indeed, the Hebrews are being physically abused because of the difficulty of their work in the fields (1:11), and they have mental, emotional anguish because of oppression and lack of freedom.

God says, **'I know'**. As we have already noted in our comments on Exodus 2:25, the Hebrew verb indicates more than a mere divine cognisance of the Israelites' plight; it reflects an intimate knowledge. For instance, we read that 'Adam knew his wife Eve and she conceived…' (Gen. 4:1). God says of Israel that 'I knew you in the wilderness' (Hosea 13:5). Both of these are examples in which the verb reflects a great intimacy rather than a mere head-knowledge.

3:8. 'And I will come down to deliver them from the hand of the Egyptians and to bring them up from that land to a good and a spacious land, to a land flowing with milk and honey, to the place of the Canaanites and the Hittites and the Amorites and the Perizzites and the Hivites and the Jebusites.'

The Lord now declares that he will intervene and act on behalf of his oppressed people. The verb **'[to] come down'** is a common anthropomorphic expression meaning that God is especially intervening in a situation (see Gen. 11:5 concerning the tower of Babel). God's plan is to deliver the

Hebrews from **'that land'**, i.e., Egypt, and bring them to another **'land'**. This land of promise is described in three ways.

First, it is **'good and spacious'**. Pharaoh had described Goshen, the present residence of the Hebrews, as a good land (Gen. 47:6), but he never called it broad or spacious. Since the time of their initial settlement the Hebrews had increased greatly in numbers and, therefore, the limited space of Goshen probably seemed confining to them by this time. For a semi-nomadic people, the greater the land area, the greater would be the blessing.

Secondly, it is **'a land flowing with milk and honey'**. This is the first time Scripture employs this description of the promised land. It becomes a frequent idiom in the Old Testament (see, for example, Exod. 13:5; 33:3; Lev. 20:24; Num. 13:27; 14:8; 16:13; etc.).[20] Egyptian texts also characterize Palestine as an abundant, productive land. In similar language to the Bible, the *Story of Sinuhe* describes a district of Palestine as '... a good land ... plentiful was its honey ... there was no limit to any cattle'. Ironically, the land of Egypt itself appears to have been well known in antiquity for its supplies of milk and honey.[21]

Thirdly, it is **'the place of the Canaanites ... Hittites ... Amorites ... Perizzites ... Hivites and Jebusites'**. The list of pagan nations is an oft-repeated formula in the Bible. Genesis 15:18-21 provides the first list of the nations occupying the promised land (ten nations). The number of nations in the formula changes from one citation to another, although the reason for this is obscure. The point of the formula is to demonstrate that God will work mightily to remove the pagans and give the land to the Hebrews. They will have to depend upon him. In addition, the fact that six nations currently reside there signifies that the land is spacious enough to provide for the Hebrews.

3:9. 'And now behold the cry of the children of Israel has come to me, and also I have seen the oppression with which the Egyptians are oppressing them.'

The thrust of this verse is the same as that of verse 7. It also bears much emphasis. For instance, the beginning of the verse reads, **'And now behold the cry...'**; the addition of the word **'behold'** serves to stress the activity occurring. The second half of the verse contains a cognate accusative: **'I have seen the oppression [with] which the Egyptians are oppressing them.'** The noun **'oppression'** is a derivative of the verb **'oppressing'**: that grammatical feature also underscores the intensity of the situation.

Because verse 9 is for all intents a repetition of verse 7, it should be understood as an *inclusio*, or a repeated theme which both introduces and concludes the first part of God's speech to Moses and thus encompasses the whole. In other words, the declaration of God's knowledge of Israel's vile circumstances brackets these opening statements of the conversation.

3:10. 'So now, go! And I will send you to Pharaoh, that he might send out my people, the children of Israel, out of Egypt.'

The next section of God's address to Moses explains what the Lord is going to do about Israel's predicament. Here is the crux, or pivot, of the burning-bush episode — the call of Moses. Moses is the one God has designated to deliver Israel from the land of Egypt, from the house of bondage. And he will also lead them to the land of Canaan. God's call to Moses is not in the form of a question, as if Moses had a choice in the matter. It is in the form of a command, a Hebrew imperative: **'So now, go!'** By divine fiat Moses has been chosen to shepherd Israel out of the land of darkness into the wilderness and on to the promised land.

In the original there is a second imperative in this verse which is not reflected in the translation. It literally reads: **'I am sending you to Pharaoh. Bring out...!'** (in the Hiphil stem). Consequently, there is no ambiguity regarding what Moses' task is to be when he returns to Egypt.

3:11. And Moses said to God, 'Who am I, that I should go to Pharaoh, and that I should bring forth the children of Israel out of Egypt?'

This verse reveals Moses' initial reaction to God's call. We might have expected that his response would have been different, more along the lines of other prophets who answered, 'Here I am. Send me!' (Isa. 6:8). But Moses questions God: **'Who am I?'** Many commentators argue that Moses is demonstrating humility here, that in comparison with God's holiness he is nothing and, therefore, totally unsuitable to represent God before Pharaoh.[22] He is proclaiming his unworthiness to lead such a magnificent enterprise.

I am not convinced, however, that humility is the central factor in Moses' questioning of the Lord. As will be seen throughout Exodus 3-4, Moses repeatedly calls into question his mission and his ability to serve as God's instrument of deliverance (see 3:13; 4:1,10,13). It is likely that Moses was suffering from fear because of his previous experiences in Egypt, particularly Pharaoh's edict that Moses should be killed. He was therefore reluctant to accept his call.

Moses' attitude actually conveys a lack of confidence in God. He was viewing himself apart from the Creator, and he realized he could accomplish nothing on his own. He appears not to have grasped the truth that he was not being called to succeed in his own power, but in God's power. And that is why God says to Moses in the following verse, 'I will be with you.'

3:12. And he said, 'Because I will be with you. And this is the sign that I am sending you: when you bring out the people from Egypt, you will serve God upon this mountain.'

God answers Moses' scepticism by saying, **'Because I will be with you**.' The particle translated **'because'** serves to introduce a direct response to a previous situation, which in this case is Moses' fear of attempting to deliver the people from Egypt on his own. God is saying that it is not by the prophet's might that redemption will occur, but only by the divine presence.

The statement, **'I will be'**, is anticipatory of the next section of the story where God reveals his name to be 'I AM THAT I AM', or 'I will be that I will be' (3:14).

The **'sign'** that God gives to Moses has received various interpretations. In other words, what does the word **'this'** refer to? One position states that the sign is the incident of the burning bush itself. Others argue that it is the immediate presence of God with Moses. The problem with both views is the significance of the last clause of the verse, which seems to indicate that the sign is the return of Moses, with the people of God, to the very mountain of the burning bush and their worship of the Almighty there. The sign is thus actually given in Exodus 19 when Israel comes to Mount Sinai.

This latter interpretation is poignant. God provides a physical signpost for Moses that he is doing what the Lord desires. But the sign is not given until after Moses steps out in faith to go to Egypt and to do what God has commanded.

3:13. And Moses said to God, 'Behold, I am going to the children of Israel. And I will say to them, "The God of your fathers has sent me to you." And they will ask me, "What is his name?" What shall I say to them?'

Moses raises a second objection to his call. When he returns to Egypt, the prophet understands that the

Hebrews will want to know the name of the God who sent him. (There is no hint of doubt in Moses' statement, as implied in the way some Bible versions render this verse.) Moses says, **'Behold ... they will ask me...'** And that would have been a natural question in ancient times because the name of a person expressed that person's character, or one attribute of it. So, for example, the name Abel means 'vapour, fleeting', and it reflects his life. Jesus' name means he is the 'one who brings salvation'. This same principle applies to gods in the Bible: different names for a deity express different aspects of that god's character.

The God of the Bible is known by various Hebrew names. For example, the name Elohim probably derives from the basic Hebrew word for 'strength, might'. The unusual feature about it is its plurality, which may reflect the concept of the plural of majesty, or plurality of persons in the Godhead. Another title, Adonai, means 'Lord, Master', and is a common epithet for God in Scripture.

By asking for God's name, Moses shows he does not know it. This does not mean that the name about to be revealed was not known prior to the burning bush incident. It simply indicates that either the name had somehow been lost to the Hebrews in their many centuries of slavery, or that it was not a prominent designation for God before this time.

3:14. And God said to Moses, 'I AM THAT I AM.' And he said, 'Thus you shall say to the children of Israel, "I AM has sent me to you."'

Here God reveals his name to Moses. It is **'YHWH'**, often referred to in modern literature as the tetragrammaton (literally the 'four letters'). The original pronunciation has been lost because orthodox Judaism, from the time of the Second Temple period onwards, refused to pronounce the name. It was considered too sacred or holy. Whenever a Jew saw YHWH written he would replace it in speech with Adonai (see comments above on verse 13).[23]

As mentioned in the exposition of the last verse, the name of a person often reflects an attribute of that person. So it is with the name YHWH (usually now written as 'Yahweh'). It is derived from the simple Hebrew verb 'to be'. God's name means, 'Being, I am who I am.'[24] The name signifies, first of all, that God is self-existent. That is, he determines his own existence and he is independent of anything else for his being. He is autonomous of creation. Secondly, it means that he is immutable or unchanging. He is not in the process of becoming something else. God is the same yesterday, today and for ever. Finally, it implies the eternity of his being. He has always been and he will always be. The name may be summarized in the words of the *Shorter Catechism* (7.004): 'What is God? God is a Spirit, infinite, eternal, and unchangeable, in his being...'

In the New Testament, Jesus' use of the 'I am' sayings helps to convey his claim to deity (see, for example, John 8:52-59; 15:1-5; Mark 14:53-64).

3:15. And God again spoke to Moses: 'Thus you shall say to the sons of Israel, "Yahweh, the God of your fathers, the God of Abraham, the God of Isaac, and the God of Jacob, has sent me to you." This is my name for ever and this is my memorial-name from generation to generation.'

God repeats his answer to Moses from verse 14, but here he adds more detail to his response. The repetition is manifested by the author's use of the word **'also'**, or **'again'**, which is used as a particle of emphasis.

So that there is no mistake on the part of Moses regarding who is speaking to him, God combines the name Yahweh of verse 14 with the previous revelation of verse 6. Yahweh is 'the God of your fathers', and 'the God of your fathers' is 'Yahweh'. Yahweh is the one who called and led Abraham, Isaac and Jacob. There is no polytheism here.

The final sentence is a parallel structure:

| This is | my name | for ever |
| This is | my memorial-name | from generation to generation |

The Hebrew word translated **'memorial-name'** is a parallel and synonym for **'name'** in the Scriptures (e.g. Prov. 10:7). However, it carries a more specific meaning of invocation, proclamation and praise.

The final clause of the verse, **'from generation to generation'**, is a repetition serving as the periphrasis (i.e. use of many words when one word would do) for the superlative. In other words, it signifies 'unto the remotest generations'. The idea of eternality is found here and it is linked to the name Yahweh.

3:16. 'Go and gather the elders of Israel. And you shall say to them, "Yahweh, the God of your fathers, has appeared to me, the God of Abraham, Isaac and Jacob, saying, 'I have surely visited you and have seen what has been done to you in Egypt.'"'

God now issues Moses a direct command. It is the Hebrew imperative: **'Go!'** When he arrives in Egypt, Moses is to **'gather the elders of Israel'** and explain to them that God understands their plight. This is the first time this group is mentioned in Scripture. The elders were the ruling body of Israel, and they are often referred to in the book of Exodus. Very little is known about their composition or detailed function.

Moses is instructed to tell the Hebrew leaders three things: first, the name of the deity who met with him; note that it is a combination of two names for God, Yahweh and Elohim (see comments on 3:15). Secondly, he is to reveal that he has witnessed a theophany, or revelation of this divinity, the burning bush. And, finally, the prophet has a message from God, and it is that God is acutely aware of Israel's oppression.

The words, **'I have surely visited** [or observed] **you and have seen...'**, can be literally rendered, **'Visiting, I have visited...'** Here we have another construction involving word-play in which the infinitive absolute 'to visit' is combined with a finite verb from the same root. It serves as an expression of great emphasis.

3:17. 'And I said, "I will bring you up from the affliction of Egypt to the land of the Canaanites and the Hittites and the Amorites and the Perizzites and the Hivites and the Jebusites to a land flowing with milk and honey."'

See the explanation in the comments on 3:8. It may be added that the term **'affliction'**, also used in verse 7 above, is never used in the Old Testament of deserved misery or oppression. It always relates to people who have been wrongfully mistreated or exploited.[25]

3:18. 'And they will listen to your voice. Then you shall go, you and the elders of Israel, to the King of Egypt, and you shall say to them, "Yahweh, the God of the Hebrews, has met with us. And now let us go three days' journey in the wilderness, and we will sacrifice to Yahweh our God."'

This is the second step Moses is to take in Egypt. After the elders are ready to co-operate, Moses is to accompany them before Pharaoh. It is clear that Moses is not excused from the audience with Pharaoh because God's command uses a personal pronoun to emphasize Moses' attendance: **'Then you shall go, you and the elders of Israel.'** God further directs that all of them **'shall say to them'** (second person plural) that God **'has met with us'**. Apparently this command was not obeyed in the confrontation in Egypt, for the elders nowhere appear in the court of Pharaoh with Moses.

The divine name appears in a different form in this verse, as **'Yahweh, God of the Hebrews'**. The reason it is so formulated is because these words are being spoken to Pharaoh, who would not know the name Yahweh, but he would understand that the Hebrews had their own god. A formulation like 'God of the Hebrews' was a common way in the ancient Near East of identifying the deity/deities of a people.

The Hebrew leaders are to tell Pharaoh that Yahweh **'has met with us'**. The verb used often signifies a meeting that was not prearranged. It is to be used to explain to Pharaoh the unexpectedness and suddenness of the encounter. That is why the Hebrews have not made this request at an earlier time.

How are we to understand this request? God's intentions are ultimately to deliver the Hebrews from Egypt, so is he condoning deceit here? Is this an attempt to fool Pharaoh with divine trickery? Absolutely not. The Hebrews are to go to the Egyptian king with a reasonable and humble request. Pharaoh's denial of such a simple demand exposes his true nature as a wicked, tyrannical ruler. It is to show the Hebrews what they are really up against.

3:19. 'And I know that the King of Egypt will not give you leave to go, and not by a strong hand.'

This verse in Hebrew begins with the independent personal pronoun, **'I'**. The verb form itself sufficiently indicates the first person singular, 'I know'. Thus, the beginning of the sentence is pleonastic (i.e. using more words than are needed), reading, **'I, I know'**. But it is not a case of using redundant words without purpose; grammarians attribute such a structure to the need for emphasis. Because God is God and he is omniscient, there is no question but that Pharaoh will respond in the negative.

The final clause is sometimes translated, 'unless by a strong hand', or 'unless a mighty hand compels him' (NIV), as if God were speaking of his own power that will be needed in the situation (see following verse). However, it actually says, **'and not by a strong hand'**, probably referring to Pharaoh's own power and might. Ancient Egyptian texts characteristically describe the power of Pharaoh in terms of his strong hand, his being the possessor of a strong arm and the one who destroys enemies with his arm.[26] The Exodus account assigns the same qualities to the Hebrew God as he humiliates Pharaoh and Egypt (e.g. 3:20; 6:1; 7:4; 15:16).

Because Pharaoh is proud, arrogant and believes in his own sovereignty, he will not let the people go. And God will not let him do it until the Egyptian king is brought low and humiliated. God is the sovereign one.

3:20. 'And I will stretch out my hand and I will smite Egypt with all my wonders which I will do in her midst. And afterwards he will send you out.'

A word-play occurs in this verse. **'I will stretch out my hand'** is literally, 'I will send out my hand,' using the same verb as the later statement: **'He will send you out.'** The idea is that God will stretch out his hand so that Pharaoh will stretch out his hand. The first action is the cause of the second.

The word **'wonders'** is derived from a Niphal participle with the first person pronominal suffix, which means 'my'. This particular form of the word is used almost exclusively to refer to acts of God dealing with deliverance. So, for example, the Lord's dividing of the Red Sea (Ps. 78:12-13), his leading Israel through the wilderness (Ps. 78:14-16) and his separating the waters of the Jordan (Josh. 3:5) are all considered 'wonders' of the Almighty.

3:21. 'And I will give this people favour in the eyes of the Egyptians. And it will be when you go that you will not go empty-handed.'

Even though God will strike Egypt with great wonders (i.e., plagues), he will not allow his people to be the subject of great animosity on the part of the Egyptians. Rather, God will cause the Egyptians to be favourably disposed towards the Hebrews. The Hebrew word used here is generally descriptive of acts of kindness and generosity that one person bestows on another. These beneficent actions are almost always freely given and are indicative of an ongoing relationship.

One of the signs of the Egyptians' graciousness towards them will be that the Hebrews will not leave Egypt in poverty. God had promised in the original covenant with Abraham that the Hebrews would depart from Egypt with great property: 'And also the nation which they serve I will judge, and afterwards they shall come out with great property' (Gen. 15:14). This prophecy was realized in the exodus event (see Exod. 11:3; 12:35-36).[27]

This act of charitableness to slaves serves as a model for later slave laws given to Israel. Deuteronomy 15:13 says, 'And when you send him out free, you shall not send him out empty-handed.' The word 'empty-handed' in that verse is the same one used here in Exodus 3:21. In addition, the author of Deuteronomy provides a context for the law of showing grace to slaves: 'You shall remember that you were a slave in the land of Egypt' (Deut. 15:15).

Finally, it needs to be seen that when one person shows favour to another in the Old Testament it is because God is the source of it (see Gen. 39:21). Grace does not come to the Hebrews because of the Egyptians' soft and loving hearts; it comes because God has so willed it.

3:22. 'But a woman shall ask her neighbour and a woman living in her house for articles of silver and articles of gold and clothing; and you will put them upon your sons and upon your daughters; and you will plunder the Egyptians.'

The Hebrews had served the Egyptians for at least four centuries, and they were living in abject poverty. God now decrees that the people will be remunerated for their work. By a mere request the Egyptians will hand over gold, silver and clothing. In this non-hostile situation, the Israelites **'plunder'** the Egyptians. The verbal stem of that word literally means 'to strip off', and it is used in a physical sense in 2 Chronicles 20:25. So, in a sense, the people of God will take the clothing right off the backs of the Egyptians! This prophecy of God comes to pass in Exodus 11:2-3 and 12:35-36.

This plundered property is later used in the Exodus account for both good and evil. Some of it becomes part of the materials used to construct the tabernacle: 'And this is the contribution which you are to raise from them: gold, silver, and bronze, blue, purple and scarlet material, fine linen … and let them construct a sanctuary for me' (Exodus 25:3-8). But some of it was also employed to make the golden calf in Exodus 32:2-3.

Application

In the middle of the eighteenth century in America, a certain young man was attending Yale University as a full-time divinity student. His desire was to be trained for the pastoral ministry. He was an excellent student and after a few years of hard study he was close to completing his work. However, one day an unfortunate incident occurred. The student was talking to some friends and made the unguarded remark about one of his professors: 'That man is about as spiritual as this chair I'm sitting in!' The student was expelled from Yale, never to be readmitted. No doubt it was a sinful remark, and the student later repented and asked for forgiveness from the professor. Thus began perhaps the lowest, most depressing and most discouraging period in the life of David Brainerd.

But the Scriptures call us to understand that God uses even our most despicable acts to bring about his good purposes. For example, in the story of Joseph, when the patriarch confronts his brothers about the wickedness they had done to him, he says, 'And as for you, you meant evil against me, but God meant it for good in order to bring about this present result, to preserve many people alive' (Gen. 50:20).

And so, in the same way, God worked his good pleasure in the life of David Brainerd. After his expulsion from Yale, Brainerd agonized over his calling. But God opened up a service for him on the mission-field to the Indians. That had not been the field of service Brainerd had chosen, but God gave him the desire for that work. And God blessed his ministry with great revivals among the Indians.

The life of Moses provides a good illustration of this biblical principle: God uses even the misdeeds of man to bring about his purposes for creation. So, even though Moses' sin caused him to flee Egypt, God made use of it in his redemptive plans for his people.

The doubting Moses and miracles (Exodus 4:1-17)

As the story proceeds into Exodus 4, it should be observed that the chapter division is artificial. In reality, the scene at the burning bush continues, and it does not end until verse 17 of the chapter. This section, from verses 1-17, describes Moses' further objections to returning to Egypt and the various obstacles he sets up in order not to go back. It also relates how God equips Moses to confront Pharaoh and it gives details of the many provisions, often miraculous, that God makes for the prophet.

4:1. Then Moses answered and said, 'Behold, they will not believe me and they will not listen to my voice because they will say, "Yahweh has not appeared to you."'

Moses now raises a third objection. In chapter 3 he had questioned his own worthiness for the task of deliverance. Here he questions how the Israelites will react to him and his message. In other words, what if the people say he is deluded? Moses is demonstrating a lack of confidence in God's word. God had earlier promised that 'They will listen to your voice' (3:18), and now Moses declares that **'They will not listen to my voice.'** Thus Moses is sceptical and mistrusts God's pledge to him. That is ironic because failing to believe or trust his word is the very thing of which he is accusing the Hebrews!

There is no scriptural evidence that a theophany (an appearance of God) had occurred during Israel's sojourn in Egypt. The last recorded theophany was God's appearance

to Jacob at Bethel (Gen. 35:9-15). So, at least on a human
level, Moses had some justification for raising this concern.

*4:2. And Yahweh said to him, 'What is that in your hand?'
And he said, 'A rod.'*

In the original Hebrew there is an obvious word-play: God
asks Moses, **'What is this?'** *(māzzĕh)* and Moses responds, **'a rod'** *(māttĕh)*.

This is the first time we read of the staff by which Moses
and his brother later perform many signal wonders in
Egypt. With it they bring numerous plagues on the land
and destroy the Egyptian army in the Red Sea (14:16). The
use of a **'rod'** is a deliberate attack on Egyptian culture
and belief. The Egyptians held that a staff was a symbol of
authority, leadership and power.[28] The irony is that the two
Hebrew leaders possessed a rod, an emblem highly es-
teemed by the Egyptians, in order to humiliate and defeat
the Egyptians. That is to say, the physical symbol that was
considered to render glory, authority and power to Egypt
was the very object that was employed to vanquish Egypt.

In support of this use of the word is the fact that *māttĕh*
is of Egyptian origin, deriving from the hieroglyphic *mdw* (=
staff).[29]

*4:3. And he said, 'Cast it to the ground.' And he cast it to the
ground. And it became a serpent. And Moses fled from
before it.*

The turning of Moses' staff into a serpent is the first physical sign that God gives to the prophet as evidence of his
calling and task. It is a precursor of the serpent confrontation in Exodus 7:8-13, in which the Egyptian magicians
appear to perform the same feat. Moses' rod, of course,
swallows their staffs, thereby demonstrating God's sovereignty over Egypt.

This sign is a polemic against Egypt because its magicians prided themselves on being able to change inanimate objects into animate beings by means of a magical rod. For example, when attacked by enemies, the magician-king Nectanebo II (360-343 B.C.) uses his rod of enchantment to turn wax figures of soldiers and ships into a live fighting force. Numerous Egyptian scarabs attest to that practice by depicting scenes of magicians holding rods in their hands that could instantly be turned into snakes.[30]

The reality of the transformation of a rod to a snake is attested by the fact that Moses **'fled from before it'**. This was no mere sleight of hand; God miraculously altered the physical state of the object.

4:4. **And Yahweh said to Moses, 'Stretch out your hand and grasp its tail.' And he stretched out his hand, and he grasped it. And it became a rod in his palm.**

Another word-play appears in this verse. God's command to Moses is, **'Stretch out your hand.'** Back in chapter 3:20, that is exactly what God was going to do against Egypt ('I will stretch out my hand'), and what Pharaoh would do by releasing Israel ('He will stretch out [his hand]'). Now we learn that Moses, as the third participant in the drama, will also stretch out his arm.

An Egyptian document, the *Westcar Papyrus*, is a cycle of stories detailing the wonders performed by lector priests in the days of Pharaoh Cheops.[31] One of the tales concerns the priest Webaoner who fashioned a wax crocodile that came to life when he threw it in a lake. Later he bent down, picked it up, and it became wax again. In Exodus 4 (and in chapter 7) the author narrates a historical event in which a priest (Moses) actually transforms an inanimate object into an animal, and thereby he goes far beyond the Egyptian story and shows the superior power of the God he represents. Moses does what Egyptian mythology merely imagined.

4:5. 'In order that they might believe that Yahweh, the God of their fathers, the God of Abraham, the God of Isaac, and the God of Jacob, appeared to you.'

This statement begins with the Hebrew particle meaning **'in order that'**. It is used to state a purpose for a situation that has already been expressed. The point is that God has given Moses a sign in order that the Hebrews might believe that Yahweh had indeed appeared to him. This divine word is in direct response to Moses' objection in verse 1.

4:6. And Yahweh spoke to him again: 'Now bring your hand into your bosom.' And he brought his hand into his bosom. And he brought it out, and behold his hand was leprous like snow.

A second sign is now given to the prophet. God tells him to put his hand **into [his] bosom** and when he pulls it out it is struck with some kind of skin disease. That this disease is leprosy, as we know it, is dubious on the basis of the various uses of the word in the Old Testament.[32] Such skin ailments, of course, were common in the ancient Near East and certainly in ancient Egypt. And in Egypt, such a disease would be seen as a judgement and curse, the punishment of the gods on the person smitten with it.

As the first sign finds a later repetition in the serpent confrontation of Exodus 7, so there may also have been a recurrence of this sign in the plague of boils breaking out on mankind in Exodus 9:8-11.

4:7. And he said, 'Return your hand into your bosom.' And he returned his hand into his bosom. And he brought it forth from his bosom and, behold, it returned like his flesh.

It is likely that the skin disease that Moses was afflicted with was incurable. The fact that his hand was instantly restored by the mere act of placing it in his bosom signifies the miraculous, divine nature of the incident. The performance of this miracle certainly would be a grand testimony to the truth that God had appeared to Moses and that he had sent the prophet to deliver his people from Egypt. The sign was a physical witness that God was about to act through the man Moses.

4:8. 'And it shall be if they do not believe you and they do not listen to the voice of the former sign, then they will believe the voice of the latter sign.'

This verse defines the purpose of a second sign being given to Moses. It was simply a back-up sign in case the Hebrews disbelieved the performance of the staff turning into a serpent and then back to a rod. The idea that these signs were to serve as witnesses to the call of Moses by the deity is reflected in the use of the expression 'listen to the voice': **'If they do not listen to the voice of the former sign, then they will believe the voice of the latter sign.'** These signs, in effect, speak; they have voices and they declare the commissioning of Moses to deliver the Hebrews from bondage. Back in Exodus 3:18 God had declared to Moses that the sons of Israel 'will listen to your voice'. But Moses has made so many objections to his call that God now provides further 'voices' to call forth redemption in the land of Egypt for the people of God. Moses, then, is not the only herald in Egypt.

God equips Moses with more than one miraculous sign because the people are living by sight, and not by faith. The Hebrews are in need of physical confirmation, and God provides it. Living by sight, and not by faith, becomes a central theme of the exodus event from now until it is over.

4:9. 'And it shall be if they do not believe these two signs either and they do not listen to your voice, then you shall take from the water of the Nile and you shall pour it on the ground.

And the water you take from the Nile will become blood on the ground.'

Here is a third physical sign that God provides for Moses. This one, however, could not be performed at the burning bush, but only within the confines of Egypt. This sign (like the first two signs) is also a precursor of a coming event, because it later becomes the first plague that God inflicts upon Egypt (Exod. 7:15-25). But this instance of it is limited in its consequences, whereas the first plague strikes all Egypt.

As a miracle this would be particularly damaging to Egypt because the Nile was considered to be the life-blood of Egypt. From the Nile creation was believed to have sprouted, and it was the Nile that maintained and sustained life in Egypt. Herodotus even called Egypt 'the gift of the Nile'. The fact that God could transform Nile water into blood reflects his sovereignty and power over the life-giver of Egypt. More will be said regarding this matter when the first plague is discussed.

As an aside, the term **'water'** in the phrase **'water from the Nile'** is a plural construction meaning 'waters of'. It may be that the author's use of a plural mirrors the Egyptian concept of water being a plural entity: the hieroglyphic sign for water is: 〰〰〰.

In any event, Moses is now without excuse. God has provided him with three miraculous signs as proof of his call. He is fully equipped. The only question now is, will he obey?

4:10. And Moses said to Yahweh, 'Please, my Lord, I am not a man of words, not previously, nor since you have spoken to your servant. Because I have a heavy mouth and a heavy tongue.'

Moses now makes a further objection, and he sets up another obstacle against the divine call. He begins his resistance with a Hebrew particle of exclamation. In dialogue that word is always followed by the word **'Lord'** (Adōnāy). It is a plea that any guilt for what is about to be said would fall upon the speaker.[33] Moses has resorted to pleading his case with God.

Moses claims that he is not a man of words. And this has been the case, literally, **'from yesterday or from three [days ago]'**. This is a Hebrew figure of speech that simply means 'previously': he has never been eloquent. And he adds, **'nor since you have spoken to your servant'**. Moses' point is that nothing that has happened at the burning bush has changed the fact that he is not a polished orator. Nothing miraculous has occurred to change his speaking abilities!

The prophet argues that his lack of articulation is due to **'a heavy mouth and a heavy tongue'**. Exactly what the problem was is hard to know.[34] Some have supposed that Moses had a speech impediment, that he may have been a stammerer. Others think that it simply means he had lost his ability to converse in the Egyptian language. Whatever the problem, the point is that Moses felt incapable of speaking in the court of Pharaoh.

The fact that Moses had problems with his speech is a sardonic comment on Egyptian culture. Egyptian magicians, some of whom Moses was shortly to face, were thought to be eloquent speakers and they revelled in their splendid powers of speech.[35] Moses, however, was wholly dependent upon the God who was speaking through him.

4:11. And Yahweh said to him, 'Who gave man a mouth? Or who gave dumbness, or silence, or sight, or blindness? Is it not I, Yahweh?'

This part of the dialogue by Yahweh is tied together by the author's use of the co-ordinating conjunction **'or'** four times: **'Who gave man a mouth? Or who gave dumbness, or silence, or sight, or blindness?'** The particle 'or' is principally used to separate alternatives in main clauses. In this context it serves to identify merisms, pairs of opposites that are all-inclusive (i.e., the totality of polarity). The point is that God is sovereign over mankind, whether a person sees or not, hears or not, speaks or not. That fact that God is sending Moses is enough; it is by the Lord's power, and not by Moses' speaking abilities, that the mission will be accomplished.

What is spelled out in this verse is precisely part of the work and ministry of Jesus in the New Testament. In Matthew 11:4-5, Jesus responds to the question of whether he is the Messiah by saying, 'Go and report to John what you hear and see: the blind receive sight and the lame walk, the lepers are cleansed and the deaf hear, and the dead are raised up, and the poor have the gospel preached to them.' Such activity underscores the deity of Christ.

4:12. 'And now, go! And I will be with your mouth, and I will teach you what you will say.'

God follows the great teaching of his sovereignty with an imperative command: **'Now go!'** The time for talking is over; it is now time for action. This decree is then followed by the double first person singular (personal pronoun followed by verb): **'I, even I will be with your mouth.'** The emphatic nature of this verse indicates God's growing impatience with Moses. There have been enough objections; Moses must now do what God has commanded.

The 'I will be' used here is the same form that God employed back in 3:14 when he revealed his name as 'I will be who I will be' (or I AM THAT I AM). This signifies that the eternal, immutable, omnipresent, omniscient God Yahweh is in control of Moses' mouth and of the very things he will say to the Hebrews, to the Egyptians and to Pharaoh. In reality, God **'will teach'** Moses what to say. This verb 'to teach' is related to the word *torah*, which means 'teaching'. Torah later becomes the name for the five books written by Moses.

What great promises Moses receives from God! The prophet will go in God's strength, teaching and words. Moses' objection of verse 10 has been adequately answered.

4:13. And he said, 'Please, my Lord, send now by the hand of whom you will send.'

Moses makes one final plea of desperation: **'O Lord, send now by the hand of whom you will send.'** This is a grammatical construction called *idem per idem*.[36] It is a formula that leaves the action unspecified, and it gives freedom to the subject to act in any manner. At first glance the statement appears to be one of assent to God's providence — in other words, Moses is saying that God's will ought to be done. And if he is the one chosen, then he will obey and go. The problem is that he has already been selected to return to Egypt and to lead the people out. Moses should have responded with a resounding, 'Here I am. Send me!' But he does not react in that way, but tells God to send whomever. There is simply no enthusiasm on the part of the prophet to do what God has directed. Moses does not want to go back.

4:14. And Yahweh was angry with Moses. And he said, 'Is not Aaron, the Levite, your brother? I know that he speaks well. And, behold, he is coming to meet you. When he sees you, he will be joyful in his heart.'

The Hebrew is quite graphic: it says that **'The nose/nostrils of Yahweh burned/heated up.'** The anger of God is expressed in the metaphorical appearance of flaming nostrils, much like a raging bull ready to charge. The many objections raised by Moses have brought on God's disfavour.

As a consequence, God has sent Aaron to help Moses. This is the first time Aaron is mentioned in Scripture. He is called **'the Levite'**. It is an unnecessary designation because Aaron is Moses' brother and Moses, we know, is a descendant of Levi (Exod. 2:1). It may be anticipatory of the fact that Aaron will later become head of the Levitical priesthood. In any event, God makes another concession to Moses: he sends Aaron to be Moses' spokesman. Moses is not relieved of responsibility, but he is provided with an agent of communication.

We see providence at work again. God has anticipated Moses' response, and thus he has already set Aaron's departure in motion. God is controlling the entire situation.

4:15. 'And you will speak to him, and you will put the words in his mouth. And I will be with your mouth and with his mouth. And I will teach you what you will do.'

This verse is a repetition of the promise given in verse 12. God had said there that he would be with Moses' mouth and teach him what to say. Now the Deity proclaims that he will be with both Moses' and Aaron's mouths and he will teach them (**'you'**, second person plural) what to do and say. It simply means that God's promises are enlarged and now include two spokesmen.

Note that God says, **'I will be with your mouth and with his mouth.'** The **'I will be'** is the same Hebrew expression that is used in 3:14 of the revelation of God's name, and again in 4:12.

4:16. 'And he will speak to the people for you. And it shall be that he will become like a mouth for you, and you shall be like a god to him.'

Because of Moses' speech difficulty, God has provided him with another **'mouth'**, in the person of his brother Aaron. Aaron is the mouthpiece for Moses. Moses then will be like a god (or gods) to Aaron. What does that mean? It is in the sense of ancient Near-Eastern prophecy that is defined by a prophet's speaking the exact words that a god tells him. Aaron is not an interpreter but a mere channel for the words of Moses. That this is the case is confirmed by Exodus 7:1, in which God says to Moses, 'See, I make you like a god to Pharaoh, and your brother Aaron shall be your prophet.'

In ancient Egypt, there was a high official called 'the mouth of the king'. His duty was to act as an intermediary between Pharaoh and the Egyptian people. His principal activity was to speak Pharaoh's commands to the people, in the precise form in which they were uttered. Of course, Pharaoh was considered a deity in Egypt and his words were therefore not to be altered in any way.[37]

4:17. 'And this rod you will take in your hand with which you will do the signs.'

Moses is now ready for action. He is fully equipped and prepared to confront Pharaoh in Egypt. He knows the wilderness (i.e., escape routes, environment, etc.); he knows where Mount Sinai is located; he has the rod to perform miracles; his brother is to be with him as a mouthpiece; and he has been directly commissioned by God. There are no more excuses. Moses must simply obey.

So ends the burning-bush sequence. The reader now waits with great anticipation to see how the work of Moses will unfold in Egypt.

Application

It is easy to be critical of Moses' reluctance to return to Egypt. We ask, why did he not immediately obey and do what God commanded him? We need to be careful here. Moses was a man of flesh and blood and he had all the human emotions, including fear. The Scriptures are truthful in their portrayal of him as a man with faults and foibles. He had murdered an Egyptian and he had been forced to flee Egypt by the authorities. Now he was directed to go back there. Was there no room for fear?

In addition, if we look deep into our own hearts we shall soon realize that we would have acted no differently. How simple to look at Moses' life and to say he should have done this or that! Let us be honest: our hearts too would have faltered at such a daunting demand. So let us be compassionate to a frail man who was just like us.

Moses returns to Egypt
(Exodus 4:18-31)

This section covers the events between the theophany of the burning bush and the opening audience with Pharaoh in Egypt. It may be divided into three parts: first, Moses takes leave of his father-in-law in Midian; secondly, the journey to Egypt (including the event at the lodging-place); and, thirdly, the initial meeting with the Hebrew elders in Egypt.

4:18. And Moses went and he returned to Jethro, his father-in-law, and he said to him, 'Let me go, please, that I might return to my brothers who are in Egypt and I will see if they are still alive.' And Jethro said to Moses, 'Go in peace!'

Moses leaves the burning bush, and he returns to Midian to see his father-in-law Jethro. There he seeks permission from Jethro (a Hebrew particle is used by Moses that normally expresses a wish or request; it is often translated 'please') to go back to Egypt. Moses is recognizing the patriarchal authority of his father-in-law. Moses has been living with him and working for him (3:1), and he therefore needs to obtain his release from Jethro.

Moses tells Jethro the reason he wants to go to Egypt is to **'see if'** any of his own people **'are still alive'**. This is a Hebrew idiom that refers to their general welfare in a broad sense: Moses wants to see how they have been faring in Egypt since he left some forty years previously.[38]

Jethro responds by saying, **'Go in peace!'** The statement is an imperative followed by the word *šālôm*. That word designates prosperity, completeness and fulfilment. We do not want to make too much of the word, however, because it is often used as a formula, to greet someone, or to wish someone well. In any event, Jethro gives Moses leave to return to Egypt.

4:19. Now Yahweh said to Moses in Midian: 'Go! Return to Egypt! For all the men are dead who were seeking your life.'

Now that Moses is back in Midian, the Lord apparently must prod him again to go back to Egypt. The prophet is lingering. He appears to be afraid that there may still be men in Egypt who seek his life. God assures Moses by telling him that all those men are dead.

The passage also indicates that a significant period of time has elapsed since Moses had left Egypt. The book of Acts relates that forty years had passed since he had fled (7:30). As we saw earlier, the life of Moses may be divided into three periods of forty years: the first phase is his life in Egypt (Acts 7:23), the second phase his life in Midian, and the final phase his leading of the Hebrews through the wilderness (Deut. 29:5; 31:2; 34:7).

In the early life of Jesus, there is a typological event that is built on Exodus 4:19. In Matthew 2, Joseph takes his wife and son and flees to Egypt because Herod wanted the child killed. And then the Gospel writer explains: 'But when Herod was dead, behold, an angel of the Lord appeared in a dream to Joseph in Egypt, saying, "Arise and take the child and his mother, and go into the land of Israel; for those who sought the child's life are dead"' (vv. 19-20). That event is indeed reminiscent of Moses' situation: both deliverers are forced to flee from tyrannical rulers and they return only after those despots (and others) are dead. And it is ironic that Jesus flees to Egypt!

4:20. And Moses took his wife and his sons and he mounted them upon the donkey. And he returned to the land of Egypt. And Moses took the rod of God in his hand.

Moses thus obeys God's directive. Curiously, he takes his family with him. He must have finally been convinced that he would be safe in Egypt because of the protecting hand of the Almighty. It is interesting to note that Moses' family did not stay the entire course in Egypt: later, in Exodus 18:2-6, we are told that Jethro brings Zipporah and her sons to meet Moses in the wilderness after the prophet had led the people out of Egypt. Apparently the rigours of the journey to Egypt (see the incident in 4:24-26) or the difficulties in Egypt (the plagues, etc.) served as a catalyst for Moses' family to return to Midian.

Moses does not forget to take the rod that God had empowered to perform miraculous signs. Observe that it is called **'the staff of God'** because the miraculous power in it comes from, and belongs to, the Creator.

4:21. And Yahweh spoke to Moses when he went to return to Egypt: 'See all the wonders I have put in your hand, and you shall do them before Pharaoh. And I will harden his heart, and he will not send out the people.'

The concept of the hardening of Pharaoh's heart is a leading motif in the entire conflict between God and Pharaoh in Exodus 4-14. This first instance of it specifies that God is the one who hardens Pharaoh's heart. The word for **'harden'** bears the idea of Pharaoh's maintaining a strong, determined will not to accede to the Hebrews' demands. God is the cause of that hardening.

Ancient Egyptian texts teach that the heart is the essence of the person, the inner spiritual centre of the self. Pharaoh's heart was particularly important because the Egyptians believed it was the all-controlling factor in both history and society.[39] It was further held that the hearts of the gods Ra and Horus were sovereign over everything.[40] Because Pharaoh was the incarnation of those two gods, his heart was thought to be sovereign over creation.

Yahweh hardens Pharaoh's heart to demonstrate that only the God of the Hebrews is the Sovereign of the universe. That Yahweh controls the heart of Pharaoh is the basic point of the account. In addition, the fact that this passage is prophetic reflects divine dominion over the unfolding of history.

4:22-23. 'And you shall say to Pharaoh, "Thus says Yahweh, 'Israel is my son, my first-born. And I said to you, "Send out my son, that he might serve me." Yet you refuse to send him out. Behold, I am killing your son, your first-born.'"'

What Moses is to say to Pharaoh is, **'Thus says Yahweh...'** In the Bible, when a prophet invokes that expression he is employing a common Near-Eastern formula to preface the commands of a deity. The Egyptians would have been well aware of that idiom because many of their own texts, such as the *Book of the Dead,* introduce the directives of the gods with the words: 'Thus says...' It is an introductory formula that signifies that the words following it derive directly from the deity, and they are not to be altered or changed in any manner. The role of the prophet is to communicate that word without modification.

Such phraseology helps to underscore the idea that the confrontation about to occur in Egypt is between the gods of Egypt (including Pharaoh) and the God of the Hebrews.

Yahweh calls Israel his **'first-born son'**. He uses the language of a family relationship. The status of the first-born in antiquity was one of great privilege. In the laws of Israel, the first-born had the right of headship of the family after the father died, and the right of receiving a double portion of inheritance (Deut. 21:17). It was a position of prominence and pre-eminence.[41]

As the Hebrews were in a filial relationship with Yahweh their God, so were the Egyptians with their deity Pharaoh.

Because Pharaoh had oppressed and murdered many of the Israelites, God, measure for measure, would destroy Pharaoh's **'first-born son'**. This constituted a direct assault on the royal succession in Egypt. In all likelihood the first-born male was directly in line to follow his father on the throne: the new Pharaoh would be a god, the incarnation of Ra, eternal, omniscient, omnipotent and worthy of worship. The point here is that Yahweh is the one who decides who will sit on the throne of Egypt. He is the sovereign King.

These verses, of course, look forward to the final plague against Egypt (Exod. 11-12). This is the plague that will force Pharaoh to drive out the Hebrews from Egypt.

4:24. And it came to pass in the lodging-place on the way, that Yahweh met him and he sought to kill him.

It is assumed by many translations that Yahweh was here seeking to kill Moses. However, in the original text the name Moses does not appear. It simply says that **'Yahweh met him and he sought to kill him.'** The question then arises who is the person referred to by the **'him'** (the third person masculine singular), referred to in this verse. There is every reason to believe, as will be demonstrated below, that the author is speaking of Gershom, the first-born son of Moses.

4:25. And Zipporah took a flint and she cut the foreskin of her son, and she touched it to his feet. And she said, 'For a covenant-relative of blood you are to me.'

Again, the name of Moses does not appear in the original Hebrew text of this verse. It simply says, **'And Zipporah took a flint and she cut the foreskin of her son and she touched it to his feet.'** It is likely that Moses is not the central figure of this episode, but rather his son (cf. Gen. 17:14).

But what does one do with the word 'bridegroom' that is used in so many translations? Why would she call her son by that term? The Hebrew word is used in the Old Testament not only to refer to a bridegroom, but to a son-in-law, a father-in-law and even a mother-in-law. It is used of Jethro in 3:1 and 4:18 to describe his family relationship to Moses. The basic idea of the word stresses that a person has been made part of a family, that he or she has become a blood relative through a covenant relationship. Thus, Moses' son has been circumcised as a symbol of his entrance into the covenant community/family.

Zipporah then takes the blood of the foreskin and places it on the child's feet. On occasion the term for **'feet'** can be used of genitalia (Judg. 3:24; 1 Sam. 24:3), and that is perhaps where Zipporah smeared the blood of the circumcision. This act may serve as a precursor or preview of the forthcoming exodus event, in which God passes over the houses of his people who have blood smeared on their doorposts. The blood, in both cases, serves as a protective sign against Yahweh's wrath.

4:26. And he let him alone. Then she said, 'a covenant-relative of blood', because of the circumcision.

In support of the idea that this little episode is a paradigm of the later Passover event is the fact that after the son is circumcised and the blood-sign is put on him, the Lord **'let him alone'**. In regard to the tenth plague, God promises: 'And the blood shall be a sign for you on the houses where you live; and when I see the blood I will pass over you, and no plague will befall you to destroy you when I strike the land of Egypt' (Exod. 12:13). The Lord simply passes by the Israelite homes that have the blood-sign on them: that is the same as Moses' son.

Zipporah then repeats her statement to her son (**'Then she said'**) from verse 25, **'a covenant-relation of blood'**. And the reason is stated directly why the son is now considered part of the blood-covenant: **'because of the**

circumcision'.[42] The symbol of the covenant is performed on the son, and so he is considered a member of the covenant. God thus passes over him.

The immediately preceding context of verses 22-23 supports this interpretation. There it is dealing with the distinction between the first-born of Yahweh and the first-born of Pharaoh. The physical symbol of those who are in covenant with Yahweh, and are his first-born, is circumcision. Moses' son now bears the sign of belonging to Yahweh.[43]

4:27. And Yahweh spoke to Aaron, 'Go to the desert to meet Moses.' And he went, and he met him on the mountain of God. And he kissed him.

Here is a word-play with verse 24. The same verb **'to meet'** is used in both accounts. The two meetings are, however, antithetical in character: the first is wrought with danger, the second with joy.

Aaron's coming to Moses in the wilderness (at Sinai) is in fulfilment of the Lord's words in verse 14. Aaron kisses Moses at the mountain: that was merely a common manner of greeting between relatives (Gen. 27:26; 33:4; etc.).

4:28. And Moses told Aaron all the words of Yahweh which he sent him and all the signs which he commanded him.

Moses now explains to Aaron the nature of their mission and the means by which wonders will be performed before Pharaoh and all Egypt. Moses tells Aaron **'all the words of Yahweh'**. It should be remembered that Aaron was to serve as the mouthpiece of Moses and to speak the exact words of God that Moses revealed to him (see 4:16).

Obviously the brothers travelled together to Egypt because the next verse shows them in Egypt gathering together all the elders of Israel.

4:29-31. And Moses and Aaron went and they gathered all the elders of the children of Israel. And Aaron spoke all the words which Yahweh had spoken to Moses, and he performed the signs before the eyes of the people. And the people believed and they listened because Yahweh had visited the children of Israel and he saw their affliction. So they bowed down and prostrated themselves.

The text records that Moses and Aaron did four things. First, verse 29 begins with, **'And Moses and Aaron went/left'**; that is, they set off for Egypt. They are the only ones mentioned as departing, so perhaps Moses' family did not accompany him any farther than the lodging-place in verse 24. In any event, we do not read about his family again until they come to meet Moses as he leads the Hebrews out of Egypt (Exod. 18:5).

Secondly, once the two prophets arrived in Egypt we are told that their opening activity was to **'gather all the elders of the sons of Israel'**. Moses and Aaron did this in fulfilment of God's command back in 3:16.

Aaron, thirdly, performed his duty as prophet and mouthpiece for Moses. He did not hold back anything, but he spoke **'all the words'** of the Lord.

And, finally, all three of the signs given by God to Moses were produced in the presence of the Hebrews. It may be argued that it was Aaron who performed the miracles before the Hebrews since he is the closest subject in the sentence. That is unlikely, however; the verb **'he performed'** probably refers back to the beginning of verse 29 in which Moses is mentioned first as the one who gathered the elders of Israel.

The fact that all three signs had to be performed **'before the eyes of the people'** indicates that one miracle was not sufficient for them to be convinced. The Lord had anticipated the people's unbelief back in verse 8 when he gave Moses the second sign. He said, 'If they do not believe you or pay attention to the first miraculous sign, they may believe the second.' Apparently not even two signs were enough for these people who were living by sight. That, of course, becomes a major theme of the exodus event: the people of Israel frequently lived by sight and not by faith.

The final verse literally reads, **'And the people believed and they listened because Yahweh had visited...'** The Hebrews believed the message of Moses because of the three signs performed in their presence; in other words, they believed because of the physical manifestations.

The Hebrew verb for 'to listen' does not merely mean 'to hear'; it also signifies obedience and action. It is the same in English; for example, when a parent tells a child, 'Listen to your mother!', more is meant than the mere physical act of hearing. Obedience is required.

Finally, the people worshipped: **'They bowed down and prostrated themselves.'** Thus, this section ends on a note of praise and thanksgiving.

Application

In this section we have been introduced to the true nature of the confrontation in Egypt. It is not merely a hostile engagement between the two earthly powers of Egypt and Israel. Nor is it a conflict only between Moses and Pharaoh, or between the Hebrew prophets and the magicians of the court of Pharaoh. There is much more at stake. We are witnessing in the exodus event a contest between the God of Israel and the god of Egypt — that is, Pharaoh. It is a good example of what Paul declares in Ephesians 6:12: 'For our struggle is not against flesh and blood, but against the rulers, against the powers, against the world forces of this darkness, against the spiritual forces of wickedness in the heavenly places.' Thus, in the book of Exodus we are viewing something much greater than a simple national struggle against oppression. We are witnessing a heavenly, divine combat.

3. The opening foray

(Exodus 5:1 - 7:7)

First audience with Pharaoh
(Exodus 5:1-21)

The first encounter between Pharaoh and the Hebrew prophets is confrontational. The episode serves to demonstrate Pharaoh's true colours. He is playing at being a deity. He therefore persecutes the Hebrews still more by imposing even greater burdens upon them. The Hebrew prophets are certainly surprised by such a turn of events: they are rather confident that the King of Egypt will let the people go because Yahweh commands it. They are disappointed.

But God is at work here. He is in the process of hardening Pharaoh's heart so that the king will not release the Israelites. The reason is crystal clear: it is so that God will then bring judgements upon Egypt and miraculously bring his people out of the land. And, in this manner, Yahweh will be supremely glorified.

5:1. And afterwards Moses and Aaron came and they spoke to Pharaoh: 'Thus says Yahweh, the God of Israel, "Send out my people that they might sacrifice to me in the wilderness."'

Here is the beginning of the first audience that Moses and Aaron have with the King of Egypt. The opening words of their conversation are the formula, **'Thus says Yahweh'**, which, as we have already seen, was always associated with deity (see comments on 4:22), and thus what follows is to be understood as the final authoritative word of a god. Pharaoh, of course, knows that because a similar formula implying divine authority was employed in Egyptian documents.

So that Pharaoh will realize precisely which God is represented by the two brothers, the qualifying phrase, **'the God of Israel'** is appended to the name Yahweh. It is a clause that identifies a god with a people and a people with a god. And since Israel and Egypt are in an adversarial position, so too are their gods.

A couple of problems arise out of this verse. First, the elders of Israel do not accompany Moses and Aaron into the Egyptian court. Their failure to do so is in direct disobedience to the command of Yahweh in 3:18.[1] In addition, the prophets' proclamation to Pharaoh is different from what God had commanded Moses to say back in 3:18. **'Thus says Yahweh'** demands that the prophet speak the exact and precise words of God with no interpretation. Perhaps Moses and Aaron failed in their task in this opening scene.

As stated previously (see comment on 3:18), the prophets make a humble request of Pharaoh. In his response, the Hebrews will be shown how hardened the Egyptian king is against Israel and her God.

Work-lists from Deir el-Medina in Thebes reveal that workers had days off for a variety of reasons, including 'offering to one's god'.[2] Thus, the request made by Moses and Aaron was not all that remarkable or unexpected.

5:2. But Pharaoh said, 'Who is Yahweh that I should listen to his voice to send Israel out? I do not know Yahweh, and furthermore I will not send Israel out.'

The pride and arrogance of Pharaoh are in evidence here. The structure of the sentence is similar to that of Exodus

3:11, in which Moses asks, 'Who am I that I should go to Pharaoh?' If Moses is demonstrating humility with that question, it provides a striking contrast with Pharaoh, who asks, **'Who is Yahweh that I should obey him?'** Pharaoh's question is rhetorical; no answer is expected. The point is obvious without an answer: Pharaoh simply regards himself as the true deity of Egypt and far superior in power to the God of the Hebrews.

Pharaoh claims that he **'[does] not know Yahweh'**. This does not mean that he had never heard of the Israelite God. As we have already seen, the Hebrew verb 'to know' frequently bears the idea of having intimacy with something or someone (see Gen. 4:1; 25:27, where Esau is described as, literally, 'a man knowing hunting, a man of the field'). Pharaoh is refusing to acknowledge the power and authority of the Hebrew deity.

Pharaoh's stand is firm, his heart is stubborn and he will not yield at all. He announces, **'I will not send Israel out.'** The construction of this clause in the original is an apodictic, or definitive, 'No', followed by an imperfect. This is the strongest possible negative in Hebrew. And so the gauntlet has been thrown down. Who is sovereign? Who is in control of Egypt and the enslaved Hebrews — Pharaoh or Yahweh?

The biblical writer, with considerable relish, begins to describe how Pharaoh comes to know Yahweh and how he lets the people leave Egypt.

5:3. And they responded, 'The God of the Hebrews has met with us. Please let us go three days journey into the wilderness. And we will sacrifice to Yahweh our God, lest he fall on us with the plague or with the sword.'

In verse 1, Moses and Aaron had demanded that Pharaoh send the Hebrews out of Egypt (the imperative form was used there). After Pharaoh's harsh reply, the Hebrew prophets back off from this direct approach. In this verse, they appear to be almost pleading their case to Pharaoh. In

the original the word *nā'* is used, and it is generally understood to be a precative particle, meaning 'please'. It is
almost as if the two Hebrews are throwing themselves on
the mercy of the Egyptian king. In other words, Moses and
Aaron go to Pharaoh saying, 'Thus says Yahweh...', fully
expecting Pharaoh to relent. When the king so harshly
refuses them, they retreat from their imperious demands.

The terms for **'plagues'** and **'sword'** are common
symbols of judgement. They may, however, be used here
in anticipation of what is later to come upon the Egyptians
— not upon the Hebrews (see Exod. 9:3,15; 15:9; etc.).

5:4. And the King of Egypt said to them, 'Moses and Aaron,
why do you loose the people from their labours? Go to your
work!'

Pharaoh makes no concessions whatsoever. He becomes
the accuser, charging the two prophets with distracting
the Hebrews from their work. The Egyptian king then goes
on the offensive by ordering Moses and Aaron to return to
their work (literally, their **'burdens'**) along with the other
Israelites. It is a royal decree because the verb **'Go!'** is in
the imperative form. Apparently, Pharaoh is in no way
recognizing any authority that the two Hebrews might
have.

There is a play on words in this verse. The verb **'loose'**
(literally, 'cause to refrain', Hiphil stem) derives from the
root *pr'*. These consonants form the opening letters of the
title 'Pharaoh'.

5:5. And Pharaoh said, 'Behold, the people of the land are
now many. And you cause them to cease from their
burdens.'

This declaration by Pharaoh has been interpreted in
various ways. First, it may show a nervousness on his part
because the Hebrews were so numerous that they posed a

military threat. A cessation of work would give the Hebrews opportunity to plot sedition. Exodus 1:9 indicates that the Hebrew numbers constituted a grave danger to Egypt. On the other hand, this interpretation does not fit the immediate context very well: Pharaoh showed no fear and was, humanly speaking, in total control of the situation.

A second interpretation says that Pharaoh was upset over the economic loss that was occurring because of the work stoppage. It was costing him a great deal of money to feed, house and care for his slaves, and now he was not receiving anything in return.

A hint of pride may also be seen here. Cassuto remarks that **'Behold, the people of the land are now many,'** is the king's arrogant statement meaning: 'Now I am glad to see that I have many slaves, who are engaged in my service and bring me much benefit.'[3] In other words, 'See how great I am! Now, who are you, prophets, to take my people away from my work?'

The verb 'to cease' is *šābat*. Pharaoh does not give the Hebrews leave to rest, stop, or desist. The word 'Sabbath' *(šabbāt)* derives from that verb. Significantly, the God of the Hebrews later provides a Sabbath rest for the people of Israel (Exod. 20). Yahweh is the antithesis to Pharaoh.

5:6-7. On that day Pharaoh commanded the taskmasters over the people and their foremen, saying, 'You shall not gather in order to give straw to the people to make bricks like before. They shall go and they shall gather straw for themselves.'

As an immediate result of the first audience, Pharaoh gives a command to the **'taskmasters'** and to the **'foremen'**. These are two distinct offices. The 'taskmasters' were Egyptian wardens. The 'foremen' were Israelites who were appointed to direct the labours of their own people. The foremen answered directly to the taskmasters.

Brick-accounts from the time of Rameses II record that a group of forty Egyptian 'stable-masters' were assigned a quota of 2000 bricks.[4] Subsequent lists describe the progress of reaching that quota. The role of these men was the same as that of the Egyptian taskmasters in Exodus 5.

The directive of Pharaoh was not for the Hebrews to make bricks without straw, but rather to go out and collect it themselves in addition to their other work. Straw is essential to making bricks: it has holding power and helps to bind the bricks. The ancients made bricks by combining Nile Valley mud with straw and chaff, placing the mixture in rectangular moulds, and then letting them bake in the sun.

A famous brick-making scene is pictured on the walls of the Rekhmire Chapel in Thebes dating to the middle of the fifteenth century B.C. It illustrates the process of brick-making in ancient Egypt, and what is demonstrated there fits well with the biblical description of Exodus 5.

The opening verb of Pharaoh's command is 'to gather'. He tells the men, **'You shall not gather in order to give straw...'** Apparently one of the duties of the taskmasters had been to collect straw for the slaves' use in making bricks. It had not been part of the slaves' task. Now it would be, and thus their work would become much more arduous.

5:8. 'But the quota of bricks which they were making previously you shall set upon them. You shall not diminish it, because they are lazy. Therefore they cry out, saying, "Let us go that we might sacrifice to our God."'

The oppressive pharaoh charges the Hebrews with idleness as the reason for their desire to go to the desert to hold a festival. He does not acknowledge any religious or spiritual dimension to the request: the Hebrews simply want to stop working. In fact, Pharaoh does not even recognize Yahweh as God of the Hebrews. He does not call him by the divine name, but by the generic *'el.* To

Pharaoh, Yahweh has no authority as a god, just as Moses
and Aaron have no authority as his prophets. Pharaoh is
thus dismissing the possibility that there is any truth or
reality in the God of the Hebrews. Pharaoh is god and he
will countenance no other god for the Hebrews.

In order to deal with the people's apparent laziness, the
King of Egypt refuses to reduce or **'diminish'** the measure,
or quota, of bricks the slaves are required to supply.

5:9. 'You shall make the work heavy upon the men. And they
shall do it, so they shall pay no attention to deceitful words.'

The verb used here for 'to make heavy' is *kābēd*. That
same verb is later used when God makes Pharaoh's heart
'heavy' or 'hard' (see Exod. 10:1). Because of Pharaoh's
oppression of the Hebrews, God oppresses him.

The King of Egypt appears to believe the adage, 'Idle
bodies make for active minds.' He thus increases the
workload of the Hebrews so that they do not listen to
words of sedition. The lies, or, literally, **'words of deceit'**,
of which he speaks apparently refer to the words of deliverance and redemption that Moses and Aaron spoke to the
people in Exodus 4:29-31. In the final analysis, Pharaoh
proclaims that Moses and Aaron are false prophets,
promising a salvation that cannot be delivered.

The Hebrew verb for 'to pay attention' means to gaze at
something with great interest, with trust and devotion.
Pharaoh seems to have understood that the Hebrews were
believing the message of the prophets, and they were
holding great hope in it. He wanted to dispel any such
notion.

5:10. So the taskmasters over the people and their foremen
went out and they spoke to the people, saying, 'Thus says
Pharaoh, "I am not giving straw to you."'

Moses and Aaron are shunned as mediators between Pharaoh and the Israelites. The King of Egypt's own cronies serve as his mouthpieces (or prophets) to his slaves. Note that Pharaoh's commands are related to the Hebrews with the divine formula that was encountered in verse 1 of this chapter: **'Thus says...'** The directive of Pharaoh, in other words, is arrogantly announced in the same language in which Moses and Aaron earlier proclaimed the words of Yahweh.

Pharaoh thus lays down a challenge to Yahweh. The die has been cast. Let the contest begin. Who is God — Pharaoh or Yahweh? Whose 'Thus says...' will come to pass?

5:11. 'You go and take for yourselves straw from wherever you can find it because there will be no reduction from your work.'

This command begins with the personal pronoun **'you'** (plural) followed by the imperative, **'Go!'** Immediately succeeding it is another imperative, **'take',** with another pronoun, **'for yourselves'**. This is a chiastic structure. The pronouns are not needed grammatically in the directive, but they provide additional force and emphasis to Pharaoh's order.

The thrust of the command is the same as in verse 8. The responsibility to procure straw, or chaff, for making bricks has now been given to the Hebrew slaves. And this rigorous task is over and above their normal labours.

5:12. So the people scattered in all the land of Egypt to gather stubble for straw.

The pathetic Hebrew slaves are forced to scour the land of Egypt for straw. All that they find is **'stubble'** or 'chaff' — that is, the mere remnants of straw. It is all that is made available to them, and they must use it to build bricks. The condition of the Hebrews is quite pitiful.

The final clause literally reads, **'to gather stubble, stubble for straw'**. This is an example of paranomasia, or a play on words, in which the noun 'stubble' *(qāš)* derives from the verb stem 'to gather stubble' *(qāšāš)*. It is a grammatical construction employed in Hebrew for the purpose of emphasis. Chaff is simply the only thing they could find to gather for making bricks.

5:13. And the taskmasters pressed them, saying, 'Finish your work, the matter of the day in its day, as when there was straw.'

The Egyptian taskmasters then put pressure on the Hebrews to finish making the requisite number of bricks. The object of the pressure, **'them'**, appears to be ambiguous: some scholars think it refers to the Israelite foremen rather than all the people. However, verse 12 has as its subject 'the people', and that probably carries over into verse 13.

The verb 'to press' often means to hasten or hurry. The Septuagint, the Greek translation of the Old Testament from the third to second centuries B.C., renders it 'to quicken' with a prefix probably meant for intensification. This sense of crushing and pushing the Hebrews reflects the frantic and desperate situation in which the people were now working.

5:14. And the foremen of the children of Israel, whom the taskmasters of Pharaoh had placed over them, were beaten, saying, 'Why have you not finished your quota number of bricks today as previously?'

Apparently some time has passed since the directive was given in verse 13. The Hebrews have not been able to meet the demands put upon them, literally, **'yesterday and today'**. That phrase is figurative, signifying the recent past. That work of the recent past is then compared to their work of, literally, **'yesterday and the third day'**, a figure of speech meaning the distant past. So the point is simply that the Hebrews have not completed their work-load since Pharaoh added the burden of collecting straw.

Because of this failure, the foremen are thrashed. They are responsible for the amount of work done, and they will press their own people to work harder. The sorry condition of the Hebrews is affirmed again. Out of sheer spite, they are required to do what is impossible and then severely punished when they are unable to complete the tasks given to them. Here is a complete degradation of the mass of Hebrew workers. Moses and Aaron have provided Pharaoh with a reason to destroy the people of God, and he takes every advantage.

The word for **'quota'** is different from the term used in verse 8. This word, *hq,* bears the idea of what is due, that which is an obligation. In the eyes of the Egyptians, what the Hebrews are required to do is not oppressive but obligatory.

5:15. And the foremen of the children of Israel came and they appealed to Pharaoh, saying, 'Why do you deal thus with your servants?'

The Hebrew verb for 'to appeal' commonly means 'to cry out', and to do so in a distressful, trying situation. The Israelite foremen are showing their true colours as they cry out to Pharaoh for help. The Egyptian monarch is the recipient of their plea. The foremen do not appeal to Yahweh. They do not recognize his power, authority and sovereignty.

Later, at the Red Sea, when the Israelites are in a desperate situation, they 'cry out to Yahweh' (14:10). There the Lord demonstrates his might by dividing the sea that the people might pass through it.

Confirmation of the Hebrew foremen's allegiance to Pharaoh is to be found in their calling themselves Pharaoh's **'servants'**. In this verse and the next one that designation appears three times, as if the foremen are emphasizing their devotion and loyalty to the service of Pharaoh. These foremen are ones who sold out to Pharaoh.

5:16. 'No straw is given to your servants to make bricks, yet they keep saying to us, "Make!" And, behold, your servants are being beaten. But the fault is with your people.'

The plea that the Israelite foremen make to Pharaoh is that it is not their fault that brick-quotas are not being met. The problem is with Pharaoh's own people. That is probably a reference to the Egyptian taskmasters who were no longer supplying straw for bricks, but were requiring the same amount of bricks to be made.

Cassuto argues that the foremen intended to say that Pharaoh is the one really to blame.[5] But out of deference to, or fear of, the king, they change their wording at the last moment and instead blame Pharaoh's servants. The Septuagint also puts the blame on Pharaoh: it translates the passage, 'but you sin against your own people' (i.e., your Hebrew servants). The Hebrew Masoretic Text does not support this interpretation.

5:17. But he said, 'You are idle, idle. Therefore you are saying, "Let us go, that we might sacrifice to Yahweh."'

Pharaoh responds to the foremen with the same rationale as in verse 8. The Hebrews, be they foremen or the masses, are simply lazy. They ask to perform a religious rite in order to get out of work. Pharaoh's catch-phrase is emphasized here with the participial form (Niphal) of the verb (in a substantival use, in which it acts as a noun): **'Idle, you are idle.'** The point is that Pharaoh again refuses to yield an inch. He is truly and utterly hardened in his heart and ways.

5:18. 'And now go and work! And no straw will be given to you, yet you must fulfil your quota of bricks.'

Back in verse 3 Moses and Aaron asked that Pharaoh 'let us go'. The monarch now commands that the Hebrews **'Go!'**, but to the work he has given them to do. It is another imperative, and it underscores the weight of Pharaoh's directive.

A second imperative appears at the beginning of the verse and it is from the verb 'to serve'. And so the command begins, literally, **'And now, go, serve!'** This directive highlights the main issue of the exodus account: who is it that the Hebrews are to serve — Pharaoh or Yahweh? (cf. Exod. 4:23 and 8:1 in which 'to serve' is used for the service of the Lord).

5:19. And the foremen of the children of Israel saw themselves in trouble, saying, 'You must not reduce your number of bricks, a matter of a day in its day.'

The beginning of the verse literally says, **'The Israelite foremen saw that they were in evil'** — that is, in a grievous and serious plight. The Hebrew preposition **'in'**, however, can have the spatial sense of 'among/before/in the midst of'.[6] Perhaps the Hebrew foremen realized the true nature of Pharaoh at this point: he represents the evil one.

The word for **'trouble/evil'** is *rā'*. This may be a play on words, an allusion to one of the chief Egyptian deities — the sun-god Ra. Thus the foremen see themselves in dire straits because they are in the midst of the worshippers of Ra. Perhaps the reference is to Pharaoh himself, who is regarded as the incarnation of the god Ra in human form.[7]

5:20-21. And they met Moses and Aaron standing to greet them when they came out from Pharaoh. And they said to them, 'May Yahweh look upon you and judge that you have

caused us to stink in the eyes of Pharaoh and in the eyes of
his servants, to give a sword in their hand to kill us!'

The verse opens by saying, literally, **'They met Moses
and Aaron standing to greet them...'** The verb translated **'met'** frequently means 'to confront, assail, or attack'.
That verb is used to demonstrate the bitterness of the
foremen as they come out from their audience before
Pharaoh. It is clear to them that Moses and Aaron are the
source of their problems and they are resentful. That this
is an adversarial meeting is confirmed by the words of the
foremen.

The anger results in a verbal attack on the prophets.
The foremen are claiming that the fault of their ills lies with
Moses and Aaron. The prophets had announced that
Yahweh had seen the Hebrews' affliction and he was going
to act. It is a lie: see what has happened because of their
words! There is something that rings true about this
incident. The foremen are passing the blame for the
problem away from its true source. Was it really Moses
and Aaron who caused Israel to stink before Pharaoh? Or
was Pharaoh not the guilty one?

The foremen literally say that **'You have caused** [Hi-
phil] **our smell to stink in the eyes of Pharaoh.'** The
term 'smell' is a figure of speech, of course, representing
the reputation and standing of the foremen in the court of
Pharaoh. The Hebrew leaders were concerned with their
position and rank before the King of Egypt. It is ironic that
later Moses causes the Nile to stink (same verb as in the
present verse) before Yahweh.

The statement of the foremen is also reminiscent of
Exodus 5:3. There Moses and Aaron had asked Pharaoh
to release them so that Yahweh's 'sword' would not fall on
the Hebrews — but, in reality, it appears that their work
has caused Pharaoh's **'sword'** to be drawn against them.
What the prophets have been sent to do is seemingly not
coming to pass, but it is bringing about the opposite effect.

Application

At no time did God promise that Moses' and Aaron's task would be easy. In this section, we see that their work was fraught with danger and difficulties. Pharaoh responded to their demands by making life even more miserable for the Hebrews by forcing them to gather straw for making bricks. The Hebrew foremen were no consolation: they attacked the Hebrew leaders as the source of their misery. Moses and Aaron appeared to stand alone.

Often God's calls to his people are not simple or easily fulfilled. One need only think of a missionary like J. Hudson Taylor, whom God called to evangelize China in the mid-nineteenth century. He suffered great deprivations in his life and ministry, loss of loved ones in the field and illness. Yet God did wondrous things through that man, as many Chinese became believers. During one serious illness, Taylor admitted to a friend, 'I believe that God has enabled me to do more for China during this long illness than I might have done had I been well.' He knew his mission was wholly dependent upon the power of God. Even today, a century and a half later, Taylor's work lives on and is reaping great rewards in China. In our lives and ministries we are also to rely and depend upon God's power and the strength given by the Holy Spirit. Like Moses, we are called to live by faith, and not by sight.

Promise of redemption from Egypt
(Exodus 5:22 - 6:13)

In this section of the story Moses confronts the Lord over the reason why Israel has not yet been delivered from Egypt. Moses complains directly to Yahweh: 'Why did you send me? Why did you not rescue your people as you said?' The prophet is being quite forthright and bold in addressing God in this manner.

God does not rebuke Moses. Instead he patiently explains, in great detail, what is going to take place in Egypt and why it is going to happen. The Lord's forbearance with Moses is a concession to the prophet's weakness and impatience. He is being taught to wait upon the Lord who does things according to his own timing.

5:22. Then Moses turned to Yahweh, and he said, 'My Lord, why have you brought evil on this people? Why did you send me?'

Moses responds to the hostile circumstances by retreating into seclusion in the presence of God. The prophet immediately expresses his disillusionment, and he calls into question the very justice of God. How could God make matters worse for his oppressed people? How could he bring **'evil'** (Hebrew *rā*) on the Israelites? Moses is again doubting the call of Yahweh that he received at the burning bush, the call that proclaimed deliverance for the Hebrews.

5:23. 'And from the time I came to Pharaoh to speak in your name, he has done evil against this people. And you certainly have not delivered your people!'

The despair of Moses does not only stem from Pharaoh's refusal to grant the Hebrews' request, but also from the fact that the condition of the people has gone from bad to worse. Not only has Pharaoh not let the people go, but **'he has done evil'** against them.

The accusation that Pharaoh has brought evil upon the people is the same one that Moses levelled against Yahweh in verse 22, where he asked, 'Why have you brought evil on this people?' By employing the same phraseology Moses seems almost to be charging God and Pharaoh with being in league and having banded together to persecute the Israelites. His manner of addressing God is accusatory.

He also challenges God on the grounds that the Lord has not delivered the people out of Egypt as he promised: **'You certainly have not delivered your people.'** The construction of the Hebrew is an infinitive absolute followed by a finite verb for the purpose of affirmation and emphasis. The prophet's words are pointed and sharp: Yahweh has not done what he said he would do.

6:1. Then Yahweh said to Moses, 'Now you will see what I will do to Pharaoh. Because by a strong hand he will send them out, and by a mighty hand he will drive them from his land.'

This is a strong statement of sovereignty, a proclamation of who it is that is truly in control of the operation of the universe. Yahweh is claiming that he will cause Pharaoh to drive the Hebrews from the land. Pharaoh is in the hand of the Lord.

Back in Exodus 3:19, it was suggested that the 'mighty hand' there referred to the power of Pharaoh. Now here in chapter 6 the same terminology is being used for the all-encompassing strength of Yahweh. And it is Pharaoh who is being wielded by the omnipotent God. The point is that the hand of Pharaoh is weak before the **'mighty hand'** of Yahweh!

The verb meaning 'to drive out' is the same word employed in Exodus 2:17 when the shepherds drove Jethro's daughters away from the well. The name of Moses' son Gershom is also a derivative of this verb (see the commentary on 2:22).

Yahweh's declaration is an encouraging answer to Moses' complaint. God repeats his promise from the burning bush. He has not abandoned or forsaken his people, but he will fulfil his word — in his own way and timing!

6:2. And God spoke to Moses, and he said to him, 'I am Yahweh.'

God's declaration of what he is about to perform comprises verses 2-8. It commences with a statement of self-identification: **'I am Yahweh.'** This is a royal formula that was commonly used by kings in the ancient Near East to begin a royal edict. For example, the inscription of the *Legend of Sargon* from Assyria starts: 'I am Sargon, the mighty king, King of Agade.' One Phoenician text opens with: 'I am Azitawadda ... King of the Danunites.'[8] The 'I am' is also a formula applied to gods to whom royalty is attributed. In the Egyptian account of the creation of the universe, the god Atum says, 'I am Atum when I was alone in Nun; I am Re in his [first] appearances, when he began to rule that which he made.'[9] In our passage, the great King of creation announces his plans for his people in Egypt.

The importance of the 'I am Yahweh' formula is underscored by its appearance at the end of the speech in verse 8. Its use both to introduce and to conclude the passage places great stress, or emphasis, on the serious and secure nature of the promises in the decree.

6:3. 'And I appeared to Abraham, to Isaac and to Jacob as El Shaddai. But my name Yahweh was not made known to them.'

God now recounts his past history and relationship with the forefathers of the Hebrew people: Abraham, Isaac and Jacob. When God says that he **'appeared'** to the patriarchs that is precisely what happened (see Gen. 18:1; 26:2; 35:1,9). God appeared physically to the patriarchs in a theophany, but not in all his fulness and glory.

God did not reveal himself to the forefathers by the name Yahweh, but rather by the name **'El Shaddai'** (Gen. 17:1; 35:11). It is a biblical principle that the name of a person often reflects the character or actions of that person. El Shaddai possibly means 'God of blessing', and when it is used it is in the context of great blessing coming upon his people, in particular, the patriarchs (Gen. 17:1-2; 28:3; 35:11). They experienced the fulfilment of God's name coming to pass in their lives.

The patriarchs did not fully experience the essential nature and power of the name Yahweh. As we have seen, that name reflected a God who fulfils his promises. The promise of a coming exodus and redemption from slavery was not fulfilled during the time of the patriarchs but belonged to the distant future. The fact that the name Yahweh was made known to the Hebrews in the time of Moses meant that fulfilment was now imminent.[10]

'Abraham, Isaac and Jacob' is a formula used in the Pentateuch seventeen times (it appears only once outside of it in the Old Testament, in 2 Kings 13:23). It is first employed in Genesis 50:24, where we read, 'Then Joseph said to his brothers, "I am about to die. But God will surely come to your aid and take you up out of this land to the land he promised on oath to Abraham, Isaac and Jacob"' (NIV). That verse is a promise of the coming exodus. Our passage in Exodus 6 demonstrates the fulfilment of that promise to the patriarchs.

6:4. 'And also I established my covenant with them, to give them the land of Canaan, the land of their sojournings in which they sojourned.'

This statement begins with **'and also'**. The Hebrew word is a particle frequently used at the beginning of a sentence to serve an emphatic role. It thus affirms the fact and truth of the proclamation that follows.

God solemnly declares that he remembers the covenant of promise that he had made with the patriarchs so many centuries before. The forefathers, however, never witnessed the realization of that promise because they were **'sojourners'** or 'aliens', in a foreign land (that is, Canaan). An alien in the ancient Near East was one who possessed few of the rights and privileges of a native of the land (such as property rights).

A parallel exists between the circumstances of the patriarchs and Moses. Moses earlier claimed that he was 'an alien in a foreign land', with little hope of possessing an abiding home. The irony is that Moses should be so impatient with God in so short a time. God, in his own timing, did not fulfil his promise to the patriarchs until centuries had passed!

6:5. 'And also I have heard the groaning of the children of Israel, whom the Egyptians are enslaving. And I have remembered my covenant.'

This verse begins with the same particle as verse 4, **'and also'**. It is used to itemize a list, but it also serves to stress a point: thus it may be translated 'even' or 'indeed'; some of the older grammars render it 'yea'.

God here puts into words what had been put into action back in 2:24 (almost the exact same wording is used in the two verses — see the commentary on 2:24).

The term for **'groaning'** is found elsewhere in the Hebrew Bible to describe Israel's response to periods of oppression. The theme statement for the book of Judges, for instance, says, 'Whenever the Lord raised up a judge for them, he was with the judge and saved them out of the hands of their enemies as long as the judge lived; for the Lord had compassion on them as they groaned under those who oppressed and afflicted them' (Judg. 2:18). Much of the language of the latter passage is first found in the exodus incident. The exodus is a model, or paradigm, for later oppression and redemptive actions in the history of Israel.

The final phrase, **'I have remembered my covenant'**, means that God is ready to put the covenant and its promises into effect. In other words, he is prepared to act, and to do so soon.

6:6. 'Therefore, say to the children of Israel, "I am Yahweh. And I will bring you out from beneath the burdens of Egypt. And I will deliver you from their servitude. And I will redeem you with an outstretched arm and with great judgements."'

The opening word, **'therefore'**, frequently serves to introduce a divine command or directive after a statement on which the command is based.[11] And, indeed, here it is followed by a declaration in the form of an imperative: **'Say to the children of Israel...'**

God begins his oath with the royal formula of self-identification, **'I am Yahweh'** (see the commentary on 6:2). This is followed in verses 6-8 with seven verbs in the first person singular, all connected with *waw* conjunctions (meaning 'and'). The three verbs in verse 6 refer to the theme of freedom from Egypt.

The first verb proclaims, **'I will bring you out.'** It is a Hiphil or causative stem, probably being used to indicate God's part in Israel's escape from Egypt. It could properly be translated, 'I will cause you to be brought out.' In Exodus 3:10-12, God had said that Moses would be the agent of Israel's release (to bring the Israelites out). In this verse, Yahweh is identified as the source of their deliverance.

The second verb, **'I will free you'**, is also a Hiphil, and is the basic Hebrew word meaning 'to deliver/save/rescue'.

The third verb, **'I will redeem you'**, is a word of great significance in Hebrew. It is principally used to indicate the obligations of a near relative, or kinsman, in a family. The kinsman-redeemer had the duty to redeem, or deliver, his kin from difficulty or danger (such as having been sold into slavery; see Lev. 25:25,48-49). The Lord is here claiming that type of family relationship with Israel!

God's redeeming work will be accomplished by his **'outstretched arm'** in judgement against Egypt. When the plagues come upon Egypt, beginning in chapter 7, they arrive from the 'outstretched hand' and 'arm' of Yahweh (Exod. 7:5; 15:16).

6:7. 'And I will take you to me as a people, and I will be to you as God. And you will know that I am Yahweh your God who brings you from beneath the burdens of Egypt.'

The two first person singular verbs of this verse define the relationship between God and Israel: **'I will take you to me as a people and I will be to you as God.'** This phrase, or its equivalent, is employed throughout the Bible as the heart of the covenant relationship between Yahweh and the Hebrews. It is called the Immanuel principle.[12] The term 'Immanuel' means 'God with us'. The establishment of the covenant between God and Abraham in Genesis 17:7 is the first reference to it in Scripture. The formula is also central to the covenant at Sinai (Exod. 19:4-5). The intent of the phrase is to demonstrate God's purpose to make a people for himself.

The proof of the relationship is the deliverance from Egypt. The Hebrews **'will know'** that Yahweh is truly their God when that event takes place. The Hebrew 'to know', as has been mentioned previously (e.g. comments on 1:8; 2:25), bears the sense of intimacy in a relationship. Israel, as the covenant people, will have a close and loving bond with the Creator. Such an intimacy should be seen in contrast to the position of Pharaoh, who had earlier proclaimed, 'I do not know Yahweh' (5:2).

6:8. 'And I will bring you to the land which I swore that I would give to Abraham, to Isaac and to Jacob. Now I give it to you as a possession. I am Yahweh.'

The final first person singular verbs pertain to the divine gift of a land for the Hebrews' possession. The bestowing of a land was a central promise of the covenant from the beginning. In Genesis 12:7 God announced to Abraham, **'To your seed I will give this land.'** That covenant promise was often repeated to the forefathers (see Gen. 13:15,17; 15:18; 17:8). Now with the exodus event God's pledge was about to come to pass.

It is a pledge. The Hebrew literally says, **'I lifted my hand'**, which refers to a symbolic gesture that signals one's word of honour. The act denotes a divine guarantee.

The mention of Abraham, Isaac and Jacob connects the end of the divine speech with the beginning of it in verse 2. In addition, the divine formula of self-identification, **'I am Yahweh'**, concludes the speech as it begins it (6:2). These form a nexus between the beginning and conclusion of the divine communication.

6:9. And Moses spoke thus to the children of Israel. But they did not listen to Moses on account of a vexed spirit and on account of hard labour.

Moses again approaches the Hebrew people with the good news of salvation. When he did this the first time (with Aaron) the Israelites responded by believing the message and by worshipping (4:29-31). Now they react by paying no heed to his words.

The reasons for the Hebrews' refusal to acknowledge Moses' announcement are then given. The preposition translated **'on account of'**, or 'because of', is a *min* which is used to define the means or cause of a situation. The first reason is because the Hebrews have **'a vexed spirit'**: a literal translation says, 'on account of shortness of spirit/breath'. That description may signify that the Israelites were disheartened because of the severe oppression, or that they were physically beaten down and, therefore, losing heart. Either way, they did not listen to Moses because their bondage was now even harder and more cruel than it had been before his arrival.

The Hebrew for **'hard'** first appears in Exodus 1:14 (see the commentary on that verse).

6:10-11. And Yahweh spoke to Moses, saying, 'Go, speak to Pharaoh, the King of Egypt, that he might send the children of Israel from his land.'

Although the Israelites refused to give attention to Moses' announcement, that was no reason for Moses not to proceed with his calling. God makes this abundantly clear as he directly commands Moses in this passage with back-to-back imperatives: **'Go, speak...'** God appears to be anticipating an objection on the part of Moses — in fact, an objection that he has previously made: 'What if they do not believe me or listen to my voice?' (4:1). Moses might have used the Israelites' disregard of him as an excuse for not proceeding with the task to which he had been called. But God does not allow the prophet to go down that road.

6:12. And Moses spoke before Yahweh, saying, 'Behold, the children of Israel do not listen to me. How then will Pharaoh listen to me? And I have failing lips.'

Moses complains anyway. He argues that there are two problems with his continuing with the assigned task. First, if the enslaved Hebrews do not pay attention to him, why should Pharaoh, who reigns over the land? Secondly, Moses claims that the situation will only be exacerbated because, as he puts it literally, **'I am uncircumcised of lips.'** Many commentators link this statement with Moses' earlier admission of having 'a heavy mouth and a heavy tongue' (4:10). They see him as again bewailing his speech handicap, and that is how many translations understand it.

On the other hand, the word 'uncircumcised' is metaphorically used in the Scriptures of things that are profane and unholy. In this regard, Moses may perhaps be expressing his sinfulness and unworthiness to go to Pharaoh on behalf of Yahweh. It may be a response similar to that of Isaiah when he proclaimed himself 'a man of unclean lips' (Isa. 6:5).

6:13. **And Yahweh spoke to Moses and to Aaron. And he commanded them [to go] to the children of Israel and to Pharaoh, the King of Egypt, to bring out the children of Israel from the land of Egypt.**

God will have none of it. He orders the two prophets **'to bring out'** (Hiphil causative stem) God's people from Egypt. Their mission is to continue despite the objections of Moses, the apathy of the Hebrews and the hatred of the Egyptians. So God does not enter into dialogue with the prophets, but he responds with a charge, a command, that requires Moses and Aaron to stand as men in the gap.

Application

The promises that God gives to Israel in Egypt are the same ones he makes to his church throughout the ages. He is our Kinsman-Redeemer, the one who delivers and protects his people. Believers have been rescued from their slavery — that is, slavery to sin. As

Peter remarks, 'knowing that you were not redeemed with perishable things like silver and gold from your futile way of life inherited from your forefathers, but with precious blood, as of a lamb unblemished and spotless, the blood of Christ' (1 Peter 1:18-19).

The Immanuel principle certainly applies for ever. The New Testament makes explicit reference to this concept in regard to the church after the death and resurrection of Christ. In Paul's argument against Christians becoming involved in idolatrous practices he says that the believer belongs to God only, for God said, 'I will be their God, and they shall be my people' (2 Cor. 6:16).

It is also certain that the promise of a land continues throughout church history. Peter explains, 'Blessed be the God and Father of our Lord Jesus Christ, who according to his great mercy has caused us to be born again to a living hope through the resurrection of Jesus Christ from the dead, to obtain an inheritance which is imperishable and undefiled and will not fade away, reserved in heaven for you...' (1 Peter 1:3-4).

And, so, when we view Israel in bondage in Egypt and her miraculous deliverance from that land, we are to be reminded of our own redemption. We are to remember the work of Christ that has delivered us from bondage and has brought us to the glorious freedom of being children of God.

Genealogy of Moses and Aaron (Exodus 6:14-27)

The placement of a genealogy at this point strikes modern readers as somewhat odd. It does not fit the overall stream of the narrative. Actually, this is not an uncommon literary digression in ancient Near-Eastern literature. There has been great dramatic tension in the exodus story thus far, leading up to the installation of Moses and Aaron as the intercessors on behalf of Israel. A natural question for the reader is, what was their genealogical status? What place did they occupy among the sons of Israel?

Genealogies in the Bible serve a variety of purposes. The primary reason for them is to record the lineage and descent of the promised seed from Genesis 3:15. (Genealogies also catalogue the line of the seed of the serpent — see Gen. 4:16-24.) They also have a more mundane intent — to demonstrate physical, tribal descent from the various sons of Jacob. The latter purpose appears to be at the forefront in the introduction of the present genealogy.

6:14. These are the heads of their fathers' houses: the sons of Reuben, the first-born of Israel: Hanoch and Pallu, Hezron and Carmi; these are the families of Reuben.

The biblical author recounts the genealogy on the basis of 'the house of the father'. This was the central family unit in Israelite society, and it would be somewhat equivalent to the extended family today. Numbers of extended families united by ties of blood comprise a 'clan'.

The writer does not begin his genealogy with the clan of Levi, to which Moses and Aaron belonged, but with the clans of Reuben and Simeon. First, this list reflects the same genealogical order of the sons of Jacob as that in Genesis 46:8-10. Perhaps this indicates that the author of Exodus had the book of Genesis in front of him. He seems to have been copying a genealogical text. Secondly, it may demonstrate the importance of recognizing the first-born in Israel and the proper order of posterity. The place of the Levitical tribe as descending from the third son of Jacob is thus illustrated.

6:15. And the sons of Simeon: Yemuel and Yamin and Ohad and Yacin and Zohar and Shaul, the son of the Canaanite woman; these are the families of Simeon.

One exceptional note is added to the genealogy of the posterity of Simeon: we are told that Shaul was **'the son of a Canaanite woman'**. Intermarriage with the pagan peoples of the land was greatly frowned upon, even in the early stories of Genesis (see, for instance, Gen. 26:34-35). This statement perhaps serves as a subtle warning to the Hebrews coming out of Egypt not to do the same (cf. Exod. 34:15-16; Deut. 7:3).

6:16. And these are the names of the sons of Levi according to their generations: Gershon and Kohath and Merari. And the years of the life of Levi were 137 years.

The three sons mentioned here were the progenitors of the Levitical clans that were later to have the duty of service in the tabernacle. In Numbers 3:25-37 the specific tasks of each clan are described in the same order of the names as is given here: **'Gershon, Kohath and Merari'**.

No ages are given for anyone in the tribes of Reuben and Simeon. The years of Levi's life are recorded, and in verses 18-20 those of his descendants. The purpose of including these dates is to provide a chronology for the exodus period. Numerous scholars, however, have questioned the chronology of this genealogy on the basis of Exodus 12:40, which says, 'Now the time that the sons of Israel lived in Egypt was 430 years.' The issue is how to harmonize that number of years with a mere four generations living in Egypt. How could that equal 430 years? In reality, it does not seem so far-fetched when one considers the numbers:

Levi lived	137 years
Kohath lived	133 years
Amram lived	137 years
Aaron was	83 years old at this time (Exod. 7:7)
Total	490 years

Allowing for such factors as Levi's age when he came to Egypt and the ages of the fathers at the birth of their sons, there appears to be a strong possibility of harmonization.

On the other hand, in the Old Testament numbers may at times be used metaphorically.[13] Whether or not we are witnessing an example of this in the present instance is debatable.

6:17. The sons of Gershom: Libni and Shimei according to their families.

The genealogy recorded in this section of the book ought to be compared with the one reported in 1 Chronicles 6:16-30. The two registers are identical in the order of the names of the clans and the names of the sons.

The specific duties of the Gershonite clan of the Levites regarding the service of the tabernacle can be divided into three main categories. First, they were to care for and carry the curtains of the tabernacle. Secondly, the screens for the doorways of the court and the tent were under their guardianship. And, finally, the Gershonites were to keep watch and ward over the hangings of the court of the tabernacle (Num. 3:25-26).

6:18. And the sons of Kohath: Amram and Yizhar and Hebron and Uzziel. And the years of the life of Kohath were 133 years.

The clan of the Kohathites was later set apart in the tabernacle service to carry and guard the various furniture pieces used for worship. Included were the ark of the covenant (which they were to carry with poles), the table of showbread, the altars of sacrifice and incense, the menorah and the utensils (pans, etc.) of the sanctuary (Num. 3:27-32). It is to this clan that Moses and Aaron belonged.

6:19. And the sons of Merari: Machli and Mushi. These are the families of the Levites according to their generations.

The third clan mentioned is Merari. Their occupation in the tabernacle was to oversee the frames, bars, pillars and sockets of the structure (Num. 3:33-37).

The Hebrew term translated as 'generations' is a derivative of the verb meaning 'to bear, give birth'. It is most frequently used in the Hebrew Bible in the expression 'these are the generations of ...', and it appears ten times in Genesis and once in Numbers. The formula is often employed in genealogical contexts to provide a coherent framework for the unfolding history of the Pentateuch. In this passage, it serves to tie the exodus account to the history of Genesis and the general unfolding of redemptive history.

6:20. And Amram took Jochebed, his father's sister, to himself for a wife. And she bore him Aaron and Moses. And the years of the life of Amram were 137 years.

For a discussion of the fact that Aaron and Moses were grandsons of the patriarch Levi, see the commentary on 2:1.

Later Mosaic legislation promulgated at Sinai prohibits the marriage of a man to his aunt (see Lev. 18:12; 20:19). The Septuagint appears to have projected that later law upon the current situation. It translates the beginning of verse 20 as 'Amram married the daughter of the brother of his father', i.e., his cousin. Such a relationship would not have been forbidden by the Mosaic code.

The name of the woman is **'Jochebed'**, and it means 'Yahweh is heaviness' or 'glory'. The latter noun, kābēd, is an important one in the exodus account. It is later used of Pharaoh's heart being heavy, or hardened (8:15,32; 9:34; 10:1). Thus, in one sense, the prophecy contained in Jochebed's name comes to pass in the exodus incident itself.

6:21. And the sons of Yizhar: Korah and Nepheg and Zicri.

Although it is Amram's line that the author is most interested in, he also records the descent of Amram's brother. There are two likely reasons for this: first, the inquisitiveness of the Hebrew population regarding issues of ancestry; and secondly, in order to draw attention to the lineage of Korah, who was later to become a thorn in Moses' flesh. In Numbers 16, Korah leads a rebellion against the authority of Moses and Aaron. Korah and Moses were first cousins.

6:22. And the sons of Uzziel: Mishael and Elzaphan and Sithri.

Mishael and Elzaphan later appear in Leviticus 10. In that episode, Nadab and Abihu offer strange fire before Yahweh and are consumed by fire because of that activity. It is Mishael and Elzaphan who drag their bodies away from the tabernacle to outside the camp of Israel (Lev. 10:4). Part of the reason for the genealogy at this early stage of the exodus account is certainly to introduce some of the characters who make an entrance later during the escape and wanderings.

6:23. And Aaron took Elisheba, the daughter of Amminadab, the sister of Nahshon, to himself for a wife. And she bore him Nadab and Abihu, Eliezer and Ithamar.

The sons of Aaron are perhaps recorded because they played such a prominent and, in the case of the first two, infamous role in the priesthood of early Israel. Nadab and Abihu, of course, were the priests who disobeyed God by offering foreign fire in the tabernacle (see Lev. 10:1-5). They had been previously singled out with Moses and Aaron to ascend Mount Sinai (Exod. 24:1-9).

The fact that Elisheba, Aaron's bride, was the daughter of Amminadab and the sister of Nahshon is important because these two men were ancestors of King David (see Ruth 4:20). That reflects a tie between the royal and priestly leaders at the beginning of Israel's history.[14]

No lineage is provided for Moses. Perhaps it is because Gershom has already been mentioned (2:22). On the other hand, the silence may be to protect the reputation of Moses because his descendants apparently later became idolaters. In Judges 18:30, the original Hebrew text ascribes the erecting of the idol in Dan to 'Jonathan, son of Gershom, son of Moses'.[15]

6:24. And the sons of Korah: Assir and Elkanah and Abiasaph. These are the families of the Korahites.

The lineage of Korah is particularly registered because in the later rebellion of Korah (Num. 16) his posterity was not destroyed (Num. 26:9-11). In the Levitical service of the tabernacle it was the Korahites who acted as keepers, or guards, at the entrance to the structure (1 Chron. 9:19). They also played a part in the official singing in the tabernacle and, later, the temple, and even penned some of the psalms (e.g., Ps. 45; cf. 2 Chron. 20:19).

6:25. And Eliezar, the son of Aaron, took to himself a wife from the daughters of Putiel. And she bore him Phinehas. These are the heads of the houses of the Levites according to their families.

After registering the infamous progeny of Aaron in verse 23 (Nadab and Abihu), the biblical writer now refers to a famous descendant of Aaron, Phinehas. During the later wilderness wanderings Phinehas proved to be faithful in the midst of a severe crisis of idolatry and harlotry among the Hebrews (Num. 25:1-13). Because of this courageous act, he was rewarded and made a leader of the Israelite army (Num. 31:6). Phinehas went on to enter the promised land (Josh. 22:30-32) and served as high priest before the tabernacle (Judg. 20:28). The great Hebrew leader, Ezra, was a descendant of Phinehas (1 Chron. 9:20). Thus the genealogy ends on a high and positive note.

6:26-27. It was Aaron and Moses to whom Yahweh has spoken: 'Bring out the children of Israel from the land of Egypt by their hosts.' They were the ones speaking to Pharaoh, the King of Egypt, to send out the children of Israel from Egypt, that Moses and Aaron.

These two verses form an *inclusio*, a short section which begins and ends with the same concept. Verse 26 opens with, **'It was Aaron and Moses'** and verse 27 ends with **'It was Moses and Aaron'**. The only difference between the two phrases is the order of names, and that reversal reflects a chiastic structure, which, as we have seen, was a common literary device. The purpose of these two literary features is for emphasis. There is to be no mistake — the

Moses and Aaron we have met elsewhere in the account
are the same figures who appear in the genealogy that the
author just completed.

Verse 26 says that God ordered Moses and Aaron to
rescue the Hebrews 'by their hosts'. The Hebrew term for
'hosts' almost always has military overtones. Frequently,
during the wilderness journeys, the Israelites were organized or deployed in a military scheme (see, e.g., Num.
33:1-49).[16]

Application

Genealogies in the Bible are worthy of our study. They are not
merely registers of names and dates. Rather, genealogies have
great historical and theological import.

In a general sense, such catalogues reflect the fulfilment of
God's cultural mandate that man should 'be fruitful and multiply'
(Gen. 1:28). While that command refers to productivity in all areas
of life, it certainly includes the promulgation of the race. Genealogies also demonstrate the cessation of life. God's curse is in effect
as man is mortal and dies.

But, most importantly, genealogies trace the two different lines
of Genesis 3:15, the seed of the woman and the seed of the
serpent. The godly line, of course, reaches its climax and fulfilment
in the coming of Jesus Christ. He is the unnamed 'he' of Genesis
3:15. Even today, all people belong to one line or the other. John,
in the book of Revelation, comments that the seed of the woman
are those 'who keep the commandments of God and hold to the
testimony of Jesus' (Rev. 12:17). May our names be written in the
Book of Life!

Judgement on Egypt foretold
(Exodus 6:28 - 7:7)

Back in 6:12 Moses had asked the question of God: 'Will Pharaoh listen to me?' God did not answer him at that time. So Moses repeats the interrogative in the section before us. Is there any reason why the King of Egypt will listen to the Hebrew prophet? The Lord's answer is surprising: Pharaoh will not give heed and he will not acquiesce to Moses' demands. But Moses needs to understand that even Pharaoh's denial is part of God's unfolding plan. Even the Egyptian king's heart is under God's control. Yahweh is sovereign.

6:28-30. And it came to pass on the day Yahweh spoke to Moses in the land of Egypt, that Yahweh spoke to Moses, saying, 'I am Yahweh. Speak to Pharaoh, the King of Egypt, all that I am speaking to you.' And Moses answered Yahweh, 'Behold, I have failing lips. Why will Pharaoh listen to me?'

In these three verses the biblical author returns to the story after his digression into the genealogy. He succinctly summarizes what had happened before the lineage was given. The writer repeats the complaint Moses had made in verse 12: 'Why would Pharaoh listen to me, since I speak with faltering lips?' But note that verse 30 inverts the two clauses of the question: **'Since I speak with faltering lips, why would Pharaoh listen to me?** This is another chiastic structure used for the purpose of emphasis. The same question still remains unanswered. How will God respond?

7:1. And Yahweh said to Moses, 'See, I have made you a God to Pharaoh, and Aaron your brother will be your prophet.'

The beginning of God's response to Moses is emphatic: the word **'see'** is an imperative. Thus, Yahweh is urging Moses to consider seriously the words which follow.

The promise Yahweh gives to Moses is that he will be 'like God to Pharaoh'. However, the language of the original text is even more forceful. Instead of the simile, '*like* God', it employs the stronger imagery of a metaphor: **'I have made you a god to Pharaoh.'** Moses will operate with divine authority and, like the true God, will make his word known through a prophet. This declaration by Yahweh puts Moses on an equal footing, at the very least, with Pharaoh, who, as we have already noted, was considered a deity in ancient Egypt.

Aaron's role is to be the **'prophet'** of Moses. The task of the prophet in the ancient Near East was the organ of the message. He is not to alter the deity's words in any manner but to present them untainted and in their entirety (for further commentary see 4:16).

7:2. 'You will speak all that I have commanded you, and Aaron your brother shall speak to Pharaoh that he send out the children of Israel from his land.'

Although Moses will be 'a god to Pharaoh' he must remember that he is not really a god. He (and Aaron, for that matter) is merely an agent of Yahweh. It is Yahweh's will, intention and desire that are at work in this story.

7:3. 'But I will harden the heart of Pharaoh. And I will multiply my signs and my wonders in the land of Egypt.'

This is the second time the phrase is used that God **'will harden'** Pharaoh's heart. It first appeared in 4:21 (see the commentary on that verse). Here, however, a different verb is used for 'harden'. It means 'to be difficult, stubborn'. In this scene it is ironic because the noun derived from it was used earlier (1:14) to characterize Pharaoh's cruelty to, and oppression of, the Hebrews. Now God is cruel to Pharaoh by hardening him in his cruelty.

It is clear that God does not make Pharaoh evil. Pharaoh is evil in and of himself. What God simply does is harden Pharaoh in his nature by giving him completely over to his sin (Rom. 1:24-26). Is that unfair of God? Absolutely not. As Paul comments, God 'has mercy on whom he desires, and he hardens whom he desires' (Rom. 9:18). Moreover, Pharaoh is responsible for his condition. It is not as if God is hardening a good person. Frankly, Pharaoh has no claim upon God's mercy, for he has sinned wilfully and maliciously. He is no innocent by-stander, but a willing, desiring compatriot of sin and vileness.

And although Yahweh brings great miracles and wonders of judgement against Egypt, Pharaoh will remain unrepentant and wholly in his sin.

7:4. 'But Pharaoh will not listen to you. And I will set my hand against Egypt, and I will bring out my hosts, my people the children of Israel, from the land of Egypt with great judgements.'

Moses is not to have unreal expectations, however. Pharaoh will not listen to him and he will refuse to let the people go from his land. But the prophet is called to understand that even the rejection of Pharaoh is part of God's plan for the exodus. The Egyptian king's rebuff and refusal to grant Moses' demands are the very catalysts for the plagues which are soon to come. Again, the doctrine of the sovereignty of God shines forth in this episode.

7:5. 'And the Egyptians will know that I am Yahweh when I stretch out my hand upon Egypt and I bring out the children of Israel from their midst.'

Pharaoh, the king and leader of the Egyptians, had earlier responded to Moses' request for the Hebrews' release by announcing, 'I do not know Yahweh' (5:2). God now proclaims that one of his purposes in the coming plagues is to cause all Egyptians to **'know that I am Yahweh'**. In other words, through the coming divine judgements upon the land, the Egyptians will be convinced that there truly is a deity named Yahweh.

God's intention in bringing the plagues on Egypt is primarily judgemental. However, in another sense it is evangelistic. During the plagues, for example, some of the Egyptian people came to believe the words of God and subsequently acted upon them (Exod. 9:20). And perhaps some of the Egyptians participated in the Hebrew escape from Egypt.

7:6. And Moses and Aaron did as Yahweh commanded them, thus they did.

A literal reading of this verse contains a repetition: **'And Moses and Aaron did as Yahweh commanded them, thus they did.'** Iteration is a common Hebrew tool for the purpose of emphasis. The biblical writer is forcefully stating that the two prophets are now being completely faithful to their calling of proclaiming God's message. This is no small matter. For the last few chapters, Moses has continuously doubted God's word and he has been hesitant in carrying out his mission. No more, because from this point until the crossing of the Red Sea Moses expresses no uncertainties. He is the man in the gap.

7:7. And Moses was eighty years old and Aaron was eighty-three years old when they spoke to Pharaoh.

Moses was eighty years old when he began his ministry in Egypt. By scriptural standards, eighty years is considered a full life and one that is strong (see Ps. 90:10, written by Moses himself). Thus the prophet was commencing his ministry at an age when most are either no longer working or dead. As we have seen earlier, Moses' life may be divided into three periods of forty years (see the commentary on 2:23).

In Hebrew culture, the first-born son had many privileges. We see here, however, that Aaron, the eldest, is mentioned second to Moses. That reflects Aaron's subservient position to his younger sibling. That situation would have been somewhat shocking to a Hebrew reader. However, God is not bound by cultural mores; he had chosen Moses to lead the children of Israel.

Application

God uses his people to proclaim his Word. This is a two-edged sword. On the positive side, people come to faith through proclamation of God's Word — one need only consider the ministries of Jonah, Philip, Paul and, especially, Christ himself. On the other hand, sometimes believers are called to preach to those who will not repent. In the call of the prophet Isaiah, he is told by God that he is being sent to a people who

> Keep on listening, but do not perceive;
> Keep on looking, but do not understand
>
> (Isa. 6:9).

And his preaching task was to

> Render the hearts of this people insensitive,
> Their ears dull,
> And their eyes dim
>
> (Isa. 6:10).

The parables of Jesus also reflect the double aspects of grace and judgement (see Matt. 13:10-17).

Moses' work in Egypt had a similar double result. Unbelievers, such as Pharaoh, were hardened in their unbelief and judged accordingly. God's people, in contrast, were freed from their slavery and oppression.

Our ministries have a dual nature. When I was in Tunisia several years ago, I met a missionary who had yet to see a convert in fourteen years of labouring for Christ. He still proclaimed the gospel diligently. The missionary explained that he was called to preach God's Word with no guarantee of people coming to Christ. God will use his Word how and when he sees fit. Our job is to obey by preaching his Word.

4. God's judgement upon Egypt
(Exodus 7:8 - 10:29)

The serpent confrontation (Exodus 7:8-13)[1]

Exodus 7:8-13 is critical for our understanding of what follows because it is a paradigm of the plague narratives. The serpent confrontation foreshadows Yahweh's humiliation of Egypt through the plagues and at the Red Sea. [2] The incident involving the serpents and the crossing of the Red Sea are the two boundaries of the entire narrative, reinforcing its single theme. Supporting that contention is the word **'swallow'**, which appears in Exodus 7:12, where Aaron's rod 'swallowed' the magicians' rods, and in Exodus 15:12, where the Egyptian army was 'swallowed' in the Red Sea. In addition, the staff that swallows the sorcerers' snakes points to the staff that will cause the waters to engulf the Egyptian army (Exod. 14:16,26). Such parallels establish Exodus 7:8-13 as a microcosmic prototype of the imminent national catastrophe coming upon Egypt. Therefore the plague narrative must be considered in the light of the serpent confrontation.

Exodus 7:8-13 also defines for the reader the true issue at stake in the entire exodus struggle. The hostilities are not primarily between Moses and Pharaoh, or between Moses and the Egyptian magicians, or for that matter between Israel and Egypt. What the serpent contest portrays is a heavenly combat — a war between the God of the Hebrews and the deities of Egypt. For the biblical writer the episode was a matter of theology. It was a question of who was the one true God, who was sovereign over the operation of the universe, and whose will would come to pass in heaven and on earth. The serpent drama introduces us to that theological issue in grand form: Yahweh, God of the Hebrews, engages Pharaoh, a god of Egypt, in a contest of power and will.[3]

7:8-9. And Yahweh spoke to Moses and Aaron, saying, 'When Pharaoh speaks, saying, "Make a miracle for yourselves," then you will say to Aaron, "Take your rod and cast it before Pharaoh that it may become a serpent."'

Yahweh anticipates what Pharaoh will request of the prophets: he will ask for a miracle. It is the same request unbelievers have made throughout the ages (Matt. 12:38). Pharaoh is testing Moses and Aaron, as well as Yahweh, to determine how much power is in their magic. It is the beginning of a contest, because in the ancient Near East the god with the most magic was supreme.

For example, in the Mesopotamian creation text, *Enuma Elish*, creation occurs because of a battle between the gods of chaos and the gods of order. Marduk (order) is victorious over Tiamat (chaos) because he possesses greater sorcery. One sign of his powerful magic is the red paste he wears on his lips during battle. In addition, Marduk calls forth various spells and enchantments in the course of fighting.

Some scholars argue that the **'serpent'** of this episode is a crocodile rather than a snake. A crocodile is 'most appropriate to the Egyptian milieu'.[4] That is unlikely, however. The Hebrew term probably merely refers to a large snake, such as a cobra. The cobra truly was the symbol, or emblem, of ancient Egypt.[5]

7:10. And Moses and Aaron came to Pharaoh and they did just as Yahweh had commanded. And Aaron cast his rod

before Pharaoh and before his servants and it became a
serpent.

This begins the second audience that the Hebrew prophets
have with the Egyptian king. It is a direct confrontation. In
this activity of changing a staff into a serpent the Israelite
leaders attack Pharaoh and his people at the very heart of
their beliefs.

In the first place, depicted on the front of the king's
crown was an enraged female cobra, or serpent. This
uraeus was thought by the Egyptians to be energized with
divine sovereignty and potency. It was considered the
emblem of Pharaoh's power.[6] It symbolized his divinity and
majesty. When Aaron flings down the rod-snake before
Pharaoh, he is therefore directly assaulting that token of
Pharaoh's sovereignty; the scene is one of polemical
taunting.

Secondly, casting down the rod is a challenge to the
power of Egyptian magic as described in many of Egypt's
mythological texts. Examples abound of priests performing
extraordinary feats, including changing inanimate objects
into animals. One text tells of a priest who made a wax
crocodile that came to life when he threw it into a lake.
Later he bent down, picked it up, and it became wax
again. Exodus 7 may be a polemic against Egyptian
mythology: Moses and Aaron truly perform what Egyptian
mythology merely fantasized about doing.

7:11. And Pharaoh also called for the wise men and for the
sorcerers. And the Egyptian magicians also did in like
manner with their secret arts.

The opening phrase literally says, **'And also Pharaoh
called for...'** The Hebrew particle 'also' may be used for
emphasis, but here its usage is perhaps for comparison.
As Moses (the 'god') calls for Aaron (the 'prophet') to throw

down his rod, Pharaoh (the 'god'), in like manner, summons his court magicians to cast down their staffs.

The Hebrew word for **'magician'**, *hărtōm*, is an Egyptian loan-word. It is an Egyptian title referring to a lector
priest, someone who is not only a magician but a member
of the priestly caste and a teacher of wisdom.[7]

How the magicians of Egypt were able to transform
their rods into snakes is a debated point. Some scholars
maintain that it was mere illusion, a sleight of hand. It is
well known that a group in Egypt called the Psylli were
able to put a serpent into a state of catalepsy by pinching
its neck. Other interpreters maintain that the ancient
Egyptians could truly change rods into serpents because
they possessed some sort of evil supernatural power.[8]

*7:12. And each cast his rod, and they became serpents. But
the rod of Aaron swallowed their rods.*

Aaron's staff **'swallowed'** the rods of the Egyptian magicians. The act of swallowing was of great significance in
Egyptian magical praxis.[9] Swallowing an object had a
hostile function meaning 'to destroy', but it could also
signify the acquisition of various traits associated with the
object. Therefore, when Aaron's rod devoured the staffs of
the magicians it was destroying the authority and power
that those rods symbolized. The act, in addition, demonstrated that true sovereignty lay in the hands of Yahweh.

*7:13. But Pharaoh's heart was hard and he did not listen to
them, as Yahweh had said.*

Back in 4:21 God had said, 'I will harden his heart.' The
Hebrew verb he used was *hāzāq*, and it means 'to be
strong'. In that earlier passage the verb was in the imperfect tense, indicating uncompleted action; the hardening of
Pharaoh's heart had not yet occurred at that stage. But
now in this verse we are told, **'But Pharaoh's heart was**

hard'; the verb is an imperfect introduced by a *waw* conversive that makes it act like a perfect. The perfect tense signifies completed action. It is not that Pharaoh's heart was in the process of hardening, but it was already hardened by this point in time.

Application

Pharaoh is a typical example of an unbeliever. He asks for proof, a miracle that will attest to the truth and power of Yahweh. The Lord responds. However, even with the physical evidence before him, Pharaoh does not believe. He simply will not be persuaded, no matter how much evidence is placed before his eyes. And that is true of unbelievers throughout the ages. Even many of those who saw Jesus, heard him preach and witnessed his miracles did not believe in him, for 'While seeing they do not see, and while hearing they do not hear, nor do they understand' (Matt. 13:13).

The same is true today. People cannot be talked into the kingdom of God. There is no burden of proof in human logic or physical attestation. People need to have their hearts changed by the will and power of the Creator. There is no other way.

The first plague: the Nile changed to blood (Exodus 7:14-25)

The plague sequence commences with God striking the Nile river. Why did God bring judgements upon Egypt, beginning with the changing of the Nile to blood? The answer is suggested in the words of the Greek historian Herodotus: 'For even though a man has not before been told, he can at once see, if he have sense, that that Egypt to which Greeks sail is land acquired by the Egyptians, given them by the river.'[10] The idea that Egypt is the gift of the Nile was hardly a new one when Herodotus wrote those words so many centuries ago.[11] The ancient Egyptians themselves looked upon the Nile as the primary source of their existence.

In its inundation stage the Nile was considered to be 'the giver of life to the two lands', 'the lord of sustenance', the one 'who causes the whole land to live through his provisions', and the like. The celebrated 'Hymn to the Inundation' proclaims:

> Hail to your countenance, Hapi,
> Who goes up from the land, who comes to deliver
>   Kemet [Egypt]…
> Who brings food, who is abundant of provisions,
> Who creates every sort of his good things…
> Who is enduring of customs, who returns at his due
>   season,
> Who fills Upper and Lower Egypt…

> Everything that has come into being is [through] his
>   power;
> There is no district of living men without him.[12]

All the blessings of Egypt evaporate when the Nile cannot supply its goods. Thus Yahweh attacks Egypt at the very heart of her existence.

7:14. **Then Yahweh said to Moses, 'Pharaoh's heart is heavy; he is refusing to send out the people.'**

A third Hebrew term is now engaged to present the nature of Pharaoh's heart.[13] It is *kābēd*, which in its most basic sense means 'to be heavy'. The term is used in a literal quantitative sense: for example, Absalom's hair (2 Sam. 14:26) and Moses' hands (Exod. 17:12) were both heavy. But *kābēd* may also bear a qualitative sense — that is, that something is weighty, or full of a particular quality or trait.[14] Therefore, this verse is saying that Pharaoh's heart is weighted down with something. But what is it?

The idea that **'Pharaoh's heart is heavy'** is an intriguing expression in view of the Egyptian background of the New Kingdom period in which the exodus occurred.[15] At this time the Egyptians believed that when someone died the person went to judgement in the underworld. The individual's heart — which was thought to be the very essence of the person — was weighed on the scales of truth. On one pan sat the feather of truth and righteousness; on the other lay the heart of the deceased. If the heart was heavy or weighty with misdeeds, the person was unjust, condemned and thrown to the Devouress to be eaten. If the heart was pure, the deceased would go to the Egyptian afterlife.

In the exodus account the verdict that Pharaoh's heart was heavy reflects the concept of his heart being filled with iniquity and injustice. His dealings with Israel, and for that matter his own character in general, were unrighteous.

God was simply judging Pharaoh as one with a heavy, sinful heart!

7:15. 'Go to Pharaoh in the morning. Behold, he will be going to the water. And you will stand upon the bank of the Nile to meet him. And you shall take in your hand the rod which was turned into a serpent.'

God responds to Pharaoh's hardness by commanding Moses to confront the Egyptian king. The Lord employs the imperative **'Go!'** to direct Moses in his activity.

Moses is told to meet Pharaoh as the king advances to the Nile river at the beginning of the day. The text does not tell us why Pharaoh was going to the water in the morning, although that act seems to have been habitual (cf. 8:20). Perhaps he was merely going for a morning stroll, or maybe even using the Nile for a bath (cf. 2:5). However, it may have been a daily ceremonial or ritual act to pay homage to the god of the Nile. The commencement of the plagues with the act of striking of the Nile waters, and the god personified in them, adds further support to this theological interpretation of Pharaoh's activity.

The language of this verse is reminiscent of Exodus 2:3-4. In that episode, Moses' sister 'stood along the bank of the Nile' to see what would happen to the child that had been placed in the basket. The reason for the literary parallel is to point out that both scenes serve as the moment of 'incipient redemption'.[16] In the first episode Moses is soon to be delivered from death; in the second the entire nation of Israel is about to be redeemed out of Egypt, the land of death.

7:16. 'And you shall say to him, "Yahweh, the God of the Hebrews, has sent me to you, saying, 'Send out my people that they might serve me in the wilderness but, behold, you have not listened until now.'"'

A play on words appears in this verse. The verb describing the activity of God in sending Moses to Pharaoh is to 'send out'. This is the same verb that God employs in commanding Pharaoh to **'Send out my people'**. The latter form, however, is a Piel imperative. The Piel stem is properly understood to mean the putting of something into action.[17]

7:17. 'Thus says Yahweh: "In this you will know that I am Yahweh." Behold, I am striking the waters in the Nile with the rod which is in my hand, and they will change to blood.'

Here begins the announcement of the first plague on Egypt. It starts with the formula denoting divine authority, **'Thus says Yahweh...'** (see the commentary on 4:22 and 5:1).

God commands Moses to strike the Nile river with his staff and transform its waters to blood. What purpose is there in this activity? To the Egyptians, the Nile in its inundation was deified and personified as the god Hapi. In reliefs, Hapi is pictured as a bearded man with female breasts and a hanging stomach (signifying pregnancy?), all characteristics that reflect fertility. Egyptian texts speak of Hapi as the one who gave birth to Egypt and sustains it.[18] Yahweh confronts this god and defeats it. God is the one who truly gives life and maintains it.

Some scholars want to see this plague as a mere metaphor. In other words, they say the waters only took on the appearance of blood. The red colour was really due to a high inundation that made the river red with sediment.[19] However, there is simply no textual support for such an explanation. The biblical author is reporting a transformation of one substance to another. In support of this is the fact that the waters of pools and reservoirs were turned to blood — waters that would not have been affected by an inundation.

7:18. 'And the fish which are in the Nile will die and the Nile will stink. And the Egyptians will not be able to drink water from the Nile.'

A major consequence of the changing of the Nile to blood was the death of the fish, a staple of the Egyptian diet. The people would be unable to eat or drink from the river. Hapi, therefore, could not supply the people's needs. This plague, then, served as a demonstration that true sustenance comes only from the hand of Yahweh and not from a false pagan deity venerated by the Egyptians.

7:19. And Yahweh said to Moses, 'Say to Aaron, "Take your staff and stretch out your hand over the waters of Egypt, over their rivers, over their streams, and over their pools and over all the reservoirs of water, and they will become blood. And blood will be in all Egypt, on the wooden things and on the stone things."'

Three imperatives are used in this verse. The first is God's command to Moses, which literally says, **'Speak to Aaron!'** The final two directives are to proceed from Moses to Aaron: **'Take your staff!'** and **'Stretch out your hand!'** These expressions denoting volition require immediate and specific action on the part of the person to whom they are addressed. They bear a sense of urgency.

The final sentence of the verse reads literally, **'Blood will be on all the land of Egypt and on the wooden [things] and stone [things].'** The terms 'buckets', 'jars', and 'vessels' etc. supplied by many translations are not found in the Hebrew text. To what, then, do 'wooden [things] and stone [things]' refer? Usually when the terms 'wood' and 'stone' are employed together they make reference to the physical substance of idols (see, for example, Deut. 28:36,64; 29:17). Egyptian priests washed the images of their gods in water every early morning.[20] Thus, it may be that the water was turning to blood as they poured it on the idols. Perhaps this episode provides another example of mockery at the expense of Egyptian deities.[21]

7:20-21. And Moses and Aaron did just as Yahweh had commanded. And he lifted up the rod, and he smote the waters which were in the Nile before the eyes of Pharaoh and before the eyes of his servants. And all the waters which were in the Nile changed to blood. And the fish which were in the Nile died, and the Nile smelled. And the Egyptians were not able to drink water from the Nile. And there was blood in all the land of Egypt.

The fact that it happened exactly as God had said underscores the doctrine of the sovereignty of God. Matters simply unfold according to Yahweh's decree, will and plan.

7:22. But the Egyptian magicians did the same thing with their secret arts. So the heart of Pharaoh was hardened. And he did not listen to them, as Yahweh had said.

Apparently there must have remained a few areas over which Aaron did not stretch out his hand. The Egyptian magicians succeed in transforming those waters to blood: the text is clear as it literally says, **'And they did thus'**, or 'in like manner'. There is a sense of ironic justice about the success of the magicians. They merely succeeded in adding to the plague against their own people. The sorcerers were seemingly unable to reverse the plague brought by God, but could only intensify it.

The accomplishment of the Egyptian magicians provided Pharaoh with a reason for not turning from his **'strong heart'**. Because the king saw his servants succeeding with their secret arts/magic he no doubt concluded that the Hebrew prophets were using the same sorceries. The changing of the Nile to blood, therefore, did not prove to him the existence or power of Yahweh.

7:23. Then Pharaoh turned and went into his palace. And he
did not pay heed to this either.

A common Hebrew phrase is used at the close of this
verse: literally, **'he did not set his heart upon'**. This idiom
means that Pharaoh paid no heed and gave no attention to
the first plague. He saw no differences between the two
miraculous transformations of water to blood. This, therefore, signifies an instance of total dismissal. Pharaoh's
heart remained hard, stubborn and strong.

7:24. And all the Egyptians dug around the Nile for water to
drink because they were not able to drink from the water of
the Nile.

The audience with Pharaoh is completed. An editorial note
is added by the biblical author that relates what the
Egyptians attempted to do in order to find fresh water.
There is, however, no mention of success on the part of the
diggers. It appears to have been a scene of futility and
desperation.

7:25. And seven days passed after Yahweh struck the Nile.

Some commentators want to interpret this verse to mean
that the second plague arrived one week after the first
plague came to an end. But the Masoretic Text literally
says, **'And it was filled seven days after Yahweh struck
the Nile.'** That may perhaps indicate that the Nile was
filled with blood for seven days. Seven is the number that
often symbolizes completion in the Bible. That length of
time would signify the complete conquest and derision of
the river god Hapi by Yahweh.

Chapter 7 of the English Bible ends at this point. The
Masoretic Text, however, continues for four more verses.
Why the disparity? The division of the Bible into chapters
is far from original to the text, having been established in

the thirteenth century A.D. by Archbishop Stephen Langton. Chapter divisions first appear in the Paris manuscript of the Latin Bible known as the Vulgate. From the Vulgate, they were later transferred to various manuscripts and editions of the Hebrew Bible. However, the many editions of the Masoretic Text do not always agree with the Vulgate, or with one another, in regard to chapter divisions.[22] Here at the end of Exodus 7 we have an example of such a divergence. This commentary will follow the generally accepted divisions of the English Bible.

Application

The entire plague account is a mere foreshadowing of the plagues that will strike the followers of Satan at the end of time (see Rev. 16). It is a model, or paradigm, of judgement that will come upon all unbelievers. The first plague in Egypt is prominently repeated in the end-time. Revelation 16:3-4 describes the second and third bowls of wrath in that light: 'And the second angel poured out his bowl into the sea, and it became blood like that of a dead man; and every living thing in the sea died. And the third angel poured out his bowl into the rivers and the springs of waters; and they became blood.' The similarities between this description and the account in Exodus are obvious. The only difference is that the extent and intensity of the plagues in Revelation are so much greater. Thus the episode in the Old Testament is a mere foretaste of what will come upon unbelievers in the final days.

The second plague: frogs
(Exodus 8:1-15)

Here begins the second plague on Egypt. It appears to arrive immediately on the heels of the first plague. There is no relief, no respite, no let-down of the drama.

8:1. And Yahweh said to Moses, 'Come to Pharaoh and you shall say to him, "Thus says Yahweh, 'Send out my people that they may serve me.'"'

The message that Moses is to proclaim is the same as at the beginning of the first plague (see commentary on 7:16). In this instance, however, the divine formula, **'Thus says Yahweh...'**, opens the declaration.

The last clause says, **'so that they may serve me'**. That is a crucial translation because a major issue of the exodus event is being underscored: who is it that the Hebrews are to 'serve' — Pharaoh or Yahweh? At this point in time the Hebrews are serving the King of Egypt. Yahweh wants their service. Therefore, Moses' proclamation is a direct assault on the power of Pharaoh.

8:2. 'But if you refuse to send [them] out, behold I will plague all your territory with frogs.'

The Hebrew word translated **'plague'**, in both noun and verb forms, is rare in the account of the plagues, except in regard to the tenth and final one (see 12:13,23,27). 'Plague' is, however, an appropriate designation for all the disasters that come upon Egypt because the term appears in this verse.

The means of plaguing the Egyptians is with frogs (the preposition *beth*, signifying instrumentality, is used by the author). Why frogs? This plague, like the previous one, appears to be part of a contest to establish who was the true God. The Egyptians regarded the frog as a symbol of divine power and a representation of fertility. One of the major goddesses of Egypt was Hekhet, who is depicted as a human female with a frog's head. She was the spouse of the creator-god Khnum. He was thought to fashion human bodies on his potter's wheel, and Hekhet would then blow the breath of life into them. Hekhet also had the responsibility of controlling the multiplication of frogs in ancient Egypt by protecting the frog-eating crocodiles.[23] But Yahweh overwhelms Hekhet and causes her to be impotent in her task. She is powerless to repel or resist Yahweh's overpowering regeneration of frogs. It is the Hebrew God who really bestows fertility; he rapidly produces frogs so that they become a curse upon Egypt. God is sovereign over fertility, over Egypt and over the Egyptian gods.

8:3. 'The Nile will teem with frogs. And they will come up and they will come into your house and into your bedroom and upon your bed, and into the houses of your servants, and on your people, and into your ovens and into your kneading bowls.'

The immensity and intensity of the second plague is stressed in this verse in a variety of ways. First, God says that the Nile River will **'teem'** with frogs. That verb in Hebrew bears the basic meaning 'to swarm/to be innumerable'. It is used in this sense in Genesis 1:20, in which God commands the newly created animals to swarm over all the earth. In Genesis 9:7, mankind is directed to multiply abundantly on the earth by 'swarming' over it. This is, in fact, the same verb that the Exodus writer uses in 1:7 to

express the rapid population growth of the Hebrews in
Egypt.

Three levels of social status will be afflicted by the
invasion of frogs: the king, his people and his **'servants'**.
The last-mentioned word in Hebrew in its most basic
sense means 'slave, servant, subordinate'. In this episode it
may perhaps refer to those non-Egyptians employed by, or
in bondage to, Pharaoh. Although the Hebrews are not
specifically mentioned, they would probably not have been
excluded from this grouping. The point of the three levels
is to verify that all Egypt would be subject to the consequences of the plague.

8:4. 'And the frogs will go up on you and on your people and
on all your servants.'

The three classes, or castes, are mentioned again for the
purpose of emphasizing the all-inclusiveness of the disaster. Further intensity is revealed by the word order in the
Masoretic Text, which literally reads, **'And on you and on
your people and on all your servants will arise frogs.'**
Normal Hebrew word order is verb-subject-object. Here the
object comes first in the sentence in order to accentuate it.
Pharaoh is not immune to the plague, for the frogs will
even climb up onto his royal person!

8:5. And Yahweh said to Moses, 'Say to Aaron, "Stretch out
your hand with your rod over the rivers, over the watercourses and over the pools, and bring forth the frogs upon
the land of Egypt."'

Three spheres of natural water in Egypt will be affected by
the multiplication of frogs. The first is best translated as
'rivers', and this designation would certainly include the
Nile.[24] The second object is the **'watercourses'**, or
'streams'. This term is an Egyptian loan-word. In the
singular it signifies the Nile river. In the plural, as in this

verse, it means the various watercourses of the Nile. And the final word, translated **'pools'**, refers to marshes that contain reeds, which were so common in the Egyptian environment. All natural water sources, therefore, were struck by the second plague.

8:6. So Aaron stretched out his hand over the waters of Egypt, and the frogs came up and they covered the land of Egypt.

Aaron did as God commanded and brought forth frogs out of the waters of Egypt that had suffered the first plague. This was an astounding event because the Nile and other waters had become rancid and unable to support marine life (see 7:21). The frogs multiplied so greatly that **'they covered the land of Egypt'**. The verb 'to cover' is used throughout the exodus account to demonstrate an over-whelming superimposition of one object upon another. In Exodus 10:5 and 15 the plague of locusts on Egypt is described as 'covering the surface of the land, so that no one shall be able to see the land'. The Egyptian army is drowned in the Red Sea by being 'covered' by water (Exod. 14:28; 15:5,10). After the escape, God 'covers' the camp of Israel with quails for food (Exod. 16:13).

The amount of time it took for the frogs to cover the land is not mentioned in the text. According to the rabbini-cal account in the *Haggadah*, the swarming of the frogs occurred over a seven-day period like the first plague.[25]

8:7. But the magicians did the same with their secret arts, and they brought up frogs upon the land of Egypt.

The verse opens with the statement, literally, **'And they did thus'**, or 'in like manner'. The same introductory formula was used when the magicians replicated the first plague (7:22).

'Secret arts' seems to be a technical term for the practices of the Egyptian magicians (see 7:11,22; 8:18). The writer in no way dismisses these methods as mere sleight of hand or magical tricks. The magicians were part of an ancient religious guild that was steeped in secret learning and lore.[26]

8:8. And Pharaoh called for Moses and for Aaron, and he said, 'Pray to Yahweh that he might remove the frogs from me and from my people. And I will send out the people that they might sacrifice to Yahweh.'

Pharaoh receives no relief from his magicians. The power of the gods fails to help him. He is beginning to weaken, so he calls for Moses and Aaron. He asks that the two prophets serve as mediators between the Egyptians and the God of the Hebrews. And for the first time he acknowledges the name **'Yahweh'**. Back in 5:2, he had said, 'I do not know Yahweh'; now he apparently is coming to know Yahweh all too well!

Pharaoh's request is that the Hebrew prophets should **'pray'** to Yahweh to remove the plague.[27] The Hebrew verb means 'to make supplication/entreat', and in the Scriptures it is always addressed to God. Pharaoh is asking that Moses and Aaron serve as intercessors on his behalf with Yahweh. Pharaoh offers no prayer for himself because this is merely a ploy to get rid of the frogs.

The king then pronounces a lie by saying he will let the people go. He has no intention of doing any such thing.

8:9. And Moses said to Pharaoh, 'I give you the honour [of deciding] when I should pray for you and for your servants and for your people to cut off the frogs from upon you and from your houses; only in the Nile will they remain.'

Moses' response at first glance is curious. He says, literally, to Pharaoh, **'Glorify yourself over me as to when I**

should pray for you' (the opening verb is a Hithpael, reflexive). What Moses seems to be saying is, 'I trust in my God to the point that I will give you the advantage.' In other words, Pharaoh is given the choice as to the time when the frogs will be removed from the land.

8:10. And he said, 'Tomorrow.' And he said, 'As you have said, so that you will know that there is no one like Yahweh our God.'

Pharaoh, of course, makes an unreasonable request. He wants all the frogs which cover the land of Egypt to be removed by **'tomorrow'**. The word 'tomorrow' is preceded by the preposition *lamed* which is perhaps serving in an emphatic manner.[28] The king's demand would require a miraculous response. And Moses answers by saying it will happen in one day so that Pharaoh will **'know'** (cf. 5:2) and recognize the authority and power of Yahweh.

8:11. 'And the frogs will depart from you and from your houses and from your servants and from your people; only in the Nile will they remain.'

Moses promises that the frogs will depart from Egypt. However, he does not tell Pharaoh how they will leave, and the fulfilment of this oath occurs in a surprising manner in the next three verses. The frogs will remain in the Nile only. In other words, God will cause them to return to their natural habitat from which they originally sprang. He will once again cause nature to operate according to its normal laws.

8:12. And Moses and Aaron went out from the presence of Pharaoh. And Moses cried out to Yahweh concerning the matter of the frogs that he had set upon Pharaoh.

Moses is true to his word and he prays to God regarding the second plague. Of course, he does this, not to benefit Pharaoh, but to honour God. Observe that the prophet does not pray in the presence of the Egyptian king; he is not interceding on behalf of Pharaoh.

The verb 'to cry out' is used frequently in the story of the exodus from Egypt. It is always employed in situations of great peril. In 5:15, the Hebrew foremen 'cry out' to Pharaoh because of the oppression of the Egyptians. When the Egyptian army bears down on the Hebrews at the Red Sea, the people 'cry out' to Yahweh for salvation. Here, in this passage, Moses **'cried out'** to Yahweh because so much was at stake: to show Pharaoh the power of Yahweh and to legitimize Moses' mission, it was important that Yahweh should answer the prophet's prayer. Moses had put his word on the line, and it was necessary that the Lord should respond.

8:13. And Yahweh did as Moses said. And the frogs died in the houses, in the courtyards and in the fields.

God responds favourably to Moses' request. He causes the death of all the frogs, literally, **'from the houses, from the courtyards'** (perhaps cattle-yards)' **'and from the fields'**. The preposition is probably a *min* indicating location, which may be translated 'out of/in'. Apparently the only place left for the frogs to live was the Nile River and the other waterways (see 8:11).

8:14. And they piled them up in heaps. And the land smelled.

Even with the removal of the plague, consequences of it still remained. First, the Egyptians had to expend a great deal of effort to deal with the remains of all the frogs. The extent of that work is emphasized in a literal reading of the passage: **'And they heaped them up, heaps, heaps.'** The repetition of the noun 'heaps' is an example of a common

Hebrew literary device to express emphasis and distribution. Because of the great number of frogs and the all-encompassing nature of the plague, the clean-up required of the Egyptians was a massive effort.

A second consequence was that the entire land of Egypt stank, or reeked, of dead frogs. The result of the first plague was that the Nile River smelled (7:18,21 — the same verb as in the present verse); now a stench pervaded the entire country. This is a reversal of the situation in 5:21, in which the Hebrew foremen complained to Moses that he had caused them to 'stink' (same verb) before Pharaoh. God now causes Egypt to stink before him.

8:15. But Pharaoh saw that there was relief, and he hardened his heart. And he did not listen to them, as Yahweh had said.

Once the plague had passed, the true character of Pharaoh was once again revealed. The verse begins, literally, with the words: **'When Pharaoh saw there was room...'** The Hebrew term for 'room' means 'space', or 'an interval'. Pharaoh simply determined that there was room to manoeuvre, to back off from his promise and to return to business as usual.

In response to the withdrawal of the plague, Pharaoh hardened his heart. The verb used is *kābēd,* 'to make heavy' (see the commentary on 7:14).

Application

The second plague is repeated and intensified in the book of Revelation, where we read, 'And I saw coming out of the mouth of the dragon and out of the mouth of the beast and out of the mouth of the false prophet, three unclean spirits like frogs; for they are spirits of demons, performing signs, which go out to the kings of the whole world, to gather them together for the war of the great day of God, the Almighty' (Rev. 16:13-14). In a dramatic reversal of the exodus account, the frogs here are produced by the evil ones to do battle against God and his people. These frogs are not mere animals, however; they are symbols of evil, unclean spirits.

The third plague: gnats
(Exodus 8:16-19)

The third plague arrives without warning to the Egyptians. There is no audience before Pharaoh, as there was for the previous two plagues. There is no need for it. The Egyptian king is deserving of the disaster because he has just lied and hardened his heart.

8:16. Then Yahweh said to Moses, 'Speak to Aaron, "Stretch your rod and strike the dust of the land so that it becomes gnats in all the land of Egypt."'

Aaron is directed to strike **'the dust of the earth'**. Why the dust of the earth? This is a common Hebrew expression that reflects great enormity and intensity. For example, when God promises that Abraham will have an immense number of descendants he says they will be as 'the dust of the earth' (Gen. 13:16). That same promise is given to Jacob in Genesis 28:14. The point is that the gnats which will descend upon Egypt will be innumerable.

The meaning of the Hebrew term for **'gnats'** is unclear. Many scholars translate it as 'gnats', but other suggested translations include 'vermin', 'lice', 'maggots', or 'mosquitoes'.

8:17. And so they did. And Aaron stretched out his hand with his rod and he struck the dust of the land, and it became gnats on man and on beast. All the dust of the land was gnats in all the land of Egypt.

The verse begins with the formula, **'And they did thus,'** which has been used before in Exodus, principally to signify the repetition of the plagues by the magicians of Egypt (see 7:22; 8:7). Here Moses and Aaron do exactly as God commands them.

The Hebrew terms for **'man'** and **'beast'** are frequently connected in Hebrew to indicate all humanity and all the animal kingdom together (e.g. Num. 3:13; 8:17; 18:15). The scale of the third plague was so vast that no creature of the ground was left unscathed.

The final clause is hyperbolic. The statement that **'all the dust of Egypt'** turned to gnats is employed by the author to highlight the severity of the plague.

8:18. And the magicians did in like manner with their secret arts to bring forth gnats, but they were not able to. And gnats were on man and on beast.

This attempt by the magicians to replicate Aaron's action begins just as in the first two plagues: **'And they did thus...'** (see 7:22; 8:7). Yet, the biblical author adds a new phrase to the formula, **'but they were not able'**. The point is simply that the magicians tried to repeat the act of the Hebrew prophets but they failed.

The fact that the **'gnats'** are again mentioned as being on **'man and beast'** emphasizes the impotence of the magicians. Not only could they not imitate the plague, but they could not counteract it either. The magicians themselves would, of course, have been covered with insects.

8:19. And the magicians said to Pharaoh, 'It is the finger of God.' But the heart of Pharaoh was hardened and he did not listen to them, as Yahweh had said.

Because of their failure, the magicians are perplexed. Therefore, they admit to Pharaoh that there exists a power greater than their magic. Their powers have been exhausted, and they have been defeated. Although the magicians appear again in the story (9:11), they never try to reproduce another plague. For all intents and purposes, they leave the scene of battle.

It should be noted that the magicians do not ascribe the power to the finger of Yahweh but to **'the finger of Elohim'**. Elohim can be used as a very general name for Deity or deities (the word is a plural form). The magicians are not acknowledging Yahweh here but rather some generic greater spiritual force.

Although the magicians are now convinced that there is a spiritual battle which they are losing, Pharaoh responds in the same way as he did to the earlier plagues. His heart has not been softened.

Application

In pagan myth the gods do not represent the greatest power of the universe; there is something even stronger — magic. Through the use of magic an external and mystical force beyond the ordinary power of both gods and humans can be brought to bear on natural and human events. The present episode, however, testifies to the limited nature of the power of magic. Magic is not omnipotent, but it is severely confined. Only Yahweh is omnipotent. This point is confirmed by his defeat of the Egyptian magicians in our story.

The fourth plague: stinging flies
(Exodus 8:20-32)

Moses is ordered by God to meet Pharaoh early in the morning by the Nile river and proclaim to him, 'Thus says Yahweh…' This is the same scenario as the opening plague (see 7:15). The similarity may indicate that a second cycle of plagues is beginning here.

8:20. And Yahweh said to Moses, 'Get up in the morning and stand before Pharaoh as he is going to the water, and you shall speak to him: "Thus says Yahweh, 'Send out my people that they might serve me.'"'

God's directive is in the form of a Hithpael imperative: literally, **'Take your stand before Pharaoh.'** The verb bears the sense of holding one's ground and maintaining a position. This, then, is clearly a situation of direct confrontation.

The imperative is followed by the particle **'behold'** in the clause, **'Behold he is going to the water.'** It is employed for the purpose of vividness and clarity: Pharaoh is returning to the water in the morning. Earlier (in the comment on 7:15) the suggestion was made that he may have been there to worship the Nile god Hapi. If that is true, it reflects Pharaoh's hardened heart. Even after that god has been humiliated and defeated, the King of Egypt returns to it.

8:21. 'If you do not send out my people, behold, I will send out on you and on your servants and on your people and on

your houses swarms of insects. And the houses of Egypt will
be filled with swarms of insects and also the ground on which
they will be.'

The announcement of the fourth plague includes a play on
words: 'If you do not *send out* my people, behold, I will
send out swarms of insects on you...'

This plague arrives in the form of a stinging fly, possibly
a mosquito.[29] It may be directed against the Egyptian self-
generated god of resurrection, Kheprer, who is symbolized
by the flying beetle.[30]

The extent of the plague is accentuated by the fact that
not only will the Egyptian houses be filled with flies, but
the very ground upon which the Egyptians walk will be
covered with them. It is as if a cloud, or shroud, of flies will
descend upon Egypt and there will be no open space.

8:22. 'But on that day I will set apart the land of Goshen on
which my people are standing. No insect will be there, in
order that you might know that I am Yahweh in the midst of
the land.'

In the opening part of the verse God declares, **'I will set
apart the land of Goshen.'** The verb is a Hiphil (causative)
that means 'to make separate, distinct'. It is an example of
election, in which God, out of his own mercy, is gracious to
the Hebrews by shielding them from the fourth plague.
This is the first time that the text specifically mentions that
the land of Goshen did not suffer a plague.

The purpose of the division is stated plainly (again!). It is
so that the Egyptians might recognize the power and
authority of Yahweh. It is Yahweh who is sovereign. He
specifically directs a plague to fall on one people and not
on another.

The name Goshen is not Egyptian and it has not been
found in any Egyptian texts.[31] It is where the Hebrews
settled in the days of Joseph according to Genesis 45:10

and 46:28. Goshen appears to be a Semitic word and it may be the Hebrew name for a region in Egypt. The area of the Eastern Delta is commonly assumed to be Goshen. That region demonstrates extensive Semitic influence throughout the history of Egypt.[32]

8:23. 'I will make a distinction between my people and between your people. Tomorrow this sign will occur.'

The beginning of this verse literally says, **'I will set a redemption between my people and your people.'** The Hebrew word means 'ransom/redemption'.[33] The meaning seems to be that Yahweh will deliver his people from the plague and hand over Pharaoh's people to it.[34] Pharaoh, of course, can do no such thing. As a further demonstration of his sovereignty, God tells Pharaoh when the plague will occur. In the second plague, God had removed the affliction according to Pharaoh's timing; now he brings a plague at the time that he himself predicts.

8:24. And Yahweh did so. And great swarms of insects came into the palace of Pharaoh and the houses of his servants and in all the land of Egypt. The land was ruined on account of the swarms of insects.

The formula, **'And the Lord did thus'**, begins the verse (cf., 8:7,17). It shows that what had been proclaimed and promised in verses 20-23 came to pass exactly as had been said.

The scope of the plague is emphasized by the use of the Hebrew word *kābēd*, meaning 'heavy' or 'weighty'. The second clause of the verse literally reads, **'And the flies came heavily.'** This is a satirical description of the plague because *kābēd* is used throughout the exodus story to characterize the nature of Pharaoh's heart (see 7:14).

One of the results of the fourth plague is that the land was **'ruined'** because of the flies. The verb form is a Niphal imperfect. The imperfect tense here probably serves as a habitual non-perfective expressing continuous action. In other words, the land was in the process of being destroyed.

8:25. Then Pharaoh called for Moses and for Aaron and he said, 'Go, sacrifice to your god in the land!'

Pharaoh does not call for his magicians. He realizes they have been defeated and they are no use to him in the battle against Yahweh. So the King of Egypt resorts to his own cunning. At first glance, it appears that Pharaoh has acceded to the Hebrews' request. But consider how the seed of the serpent operates, as he adds the words, **'in the land'**. This is a great restriction on the people of God who had asked to go into the wilderness (5:1) and leave Pharaoh's land (6:11). Pharaoh still desires to be in control of the situation and to keep the Hebrews under his authority.

Note also that Pharaoh does not use the personal name for God, Yahweh, in his directive. He makes reference only to Elohim, which again can be a generic name for gods. There really is no acknowledgement of Yahweh by Pharaoh.

8:26. And Moses said, 'We are not able to do so, because [it will be] an abomination to the Egyptians when we sacrifice to Yahweh our God. If we sacrifice an abomination to the Egyptians before their eyes, will they not stone us?'

Moses sees the treachery and he responds with a forceful negative, literally, **'Not right'**. The prophet's response is an apodictic 'No', the most emphatic form of the negative in the Hebrew language.

The Hebrew leader, who was well versed in Egyptian culture, understood that the animals they would use in their sacrifices were regarded as sacred by the Egyptian people. Certain sacrificial animals were symbols of

Egyptian gods. The Egyptians would take great offence at such practices within the confines of their own land. The sacrifices would be **'an abomination'** to them.

The punishment for such heretical acts was apparently stoning. This may have been exactly what Pharaoh had in mind for God's people at this point. In other words, the king is saying, 'If they do not serve me, then they will die.'

8:27. 'We will go three days' journey in the wilderness, and we will sacrifice to Yahweh our God, as he said to us.'

Although Pharaoh is beginning to bend and grant some concessions to the Hebrews, the Lord, by contrast, refuses to yield an inch. The demands of the Hebrew God remain the same. For commentary on the content of the request, see Exodus 3:18.

8:28. But Pharaoh said, 'I will send you out and you may sacrifice to Yahweh your God in the wilderness, only you shall not go very far away. Pray for me!'

Pharaoh seemingly makes a further concession. But the manner of his consent belies his self-obsessed and untrustworthy character. At the onset of his speech he employs an added personal pronoun, so that it literally reads **'I, I will let you go.'** This use of pleonastic language emphasizes his view of his own majesty. Pharaoh is still playing at being sovereign.

The totalitarian nature of Egypt's king is further confirmed by his setting conditions for the release of the Hebrews. His main restriction begins with a word normally translated 'only', but it is used primarily to indicate restrictive force. The prohibition is stated quite harshly: literally, **'only the distance you shall not go far to go'**. Here we have the apodictic, or strongest form of, negative in Hebrew. Pharaoh once again attempts to impose his will upon the situation.

As the icing on the cake, the king then makes the request (for a second time — see 8:8) that the Hebrew leaders pray for him.

8:29. And Moses said, 'Behold I am going out from you and I will pray to Yahweh that he might remove the swarms of insects from Pharaoh, from his servants and from his people tomorrow. Only let not Pharaoh again deal deceitfully by not sending out the people to sacrifice to Yahweh.'

Moses agrees to act on the request of Pharaoh. However, as Pharaoh places a restriction on his plea with 'only' (8:28), Moses puts an 'only' limitation on his fulfilment of it. The caveat is that Pharaoh should **'not deceive again'**. The verb 'to mock/deceive' in this case signifies the pretence of doing something, but wilfully failing to execute it. Pharaoh has been acting the part of the conniver, the schemer, the liar: Moses sees right through the false swearing and misrepresentations and he does not countenance such activity.

8:30-31. And Moses went out from the presence of Pharaoh and he prayed to Yahweh. And Yahweh did as Moses said. And he removed the swarms of insects from Pharaoh, from his servants and from his people. Not one was left.

God answers Moses' prayer; literally, **'And Yahweh did according to the word of Moses.'** The same expression is used in verse 13 for God's compliance with another of Moses' requests.

The ending of this verse is abrupt: **'Not one was left.'** No particle or conjunction (such as 'and' or 'but') introduces the statement. It is stark and forceful as it stands alone. The flies do not diminish in number, or become progressively less troublesome; no, they simply disappear. Not only God's production of the plagues is miraculous, but their removal as well.

8:32. But Pharaoh hardened his heart this time also and he did not send out the people.

The Hebrew verb from which **'hardened'** derives is *kābēd*, which, as we noted earlier, means, 'to be heavy/weighty' (for the use of this term throughout the account of the plagues see the commentary on 7:14).

Application

For the first time a clear distinction is made between the Hebrews and the Egyptians (8:22-23). The Israelites are set apart, and they do not suffer any of the plague of flies. This is an early indication that God has chosen Israel from among the nations (Deut. 10:15). He is in the process of separating Israel from the rest of the world and making her a holy nation, a royal priesthood and a people for God's own possession (Exod. 19:6).

Election, merely seen in seed form in the plagues, applies to the church throughout the ages. Peter, in speaking to believers in the New Testament, comments: 'But you are a chosen race, a royal priesthood, a holy nation, a people for God's own possession, that you may proclaim the excellencies of him who has called you out of darkness into his marvellous light' (1 Peter 2:9). Just like the church in the Old Testament, we have been set apart, called from the darkness of the world by the power of the sovereign God of the universe.

The fifth plague: pestilence on the livestock (Exodus 9:1-7)

This section relates the fifth plague that God brings upon Pharaoh and Egypt. It is the fourth time that Moses goes to Pharaoh to pronounce the same message (see 7:15-16; 8:1,20; no audience occurred announcing the third plague).

9:1. And Yahweh said to Moses, 'Go to Pharaoh, and you shall say to him, "Thus says Yahweh, the God of the Hebrews, 'Send out my people that they might serve me.'"'

The message is repeated. Pharaoh is directed to let the people leave Egypt, or there will be serious consequences. An important addition to the command is the inclusion of the title for Yahweh, **'the God of the Hebrews'**. This epithet has not been applied since the first plague (7:16), and it serves as a reminder to Pharaoh who it is that he is battling against.

9:2-3. 'If you refuse to send them out and continue to hold them, then behold the hand of Yahweh will be on your livestock which is in the field, on the horses, on the donkeys, on the camels, on the herds, and on the flocks with a very heavy plague.'

The opening construction of the verse is frequently used to introduce an 'if … then' clause. The 'if' is stated in verse 2; the 'then' appears in verse 3. A condition is stated — that if

a certain circumstance occurs, then a necessary consequence will follow.

The supposition is that Pharaoh will **'refuse'** to yield to
God's demands. That verb is used habitually throughout
the plague account to describe Pharaoh's wilful negation
and denial of Yahweh's demands (see 4:23; 7:14; 8:2;
10:3,4). It is an outright rejection of what God requires.[35]

The consequence of Pharaoh's behaviour is that **'the
hand of Yahweh'**, not just 'the finger of Elohim', as the
magicians had said (8:19), will manifest itself and come in
clear power. Ancient Egyptian texts characteristically
describe Pharaoh's power in terms of his 'strong hand'.[36]
The Exodus account ironically employs that same characteristic to describe Yahweh as he humiliates Pharaoh
and Egypt (see commentary on 3:19).

The animals struck by this plague are the ones that
provide food, milk, clothing and transportation. Some have
argued that the appearance of **'camels'** in the list is
anachronistic because they did not commonly appear as
domesticated animals until the end of the second millennium. This is hotly debated. However, it does appear that
camels were used at least in a limited way as early as the
beginning of the second millennium.

This plague is also a polemic. Bull cults are known to
have flourished throughout the history of Egypt. Egyptians
viewed the bull as a fertility figure, the great inseminator
imbued with the potency and vitality of life. Apis was the
most important of the Egyptian sacred bulls. Other bull
cults included Buchis (sacred bull of Hermonthis) and
Mneuis (Heliopolis). In addition, bulls were understood as
embodiments of the great Egyptian gods Ptah and Ra.[37]
Numerous important female deities are pictured as livestock animals: Isis, queen of the gods, bears cow's horns
on her head; Hathor is given a bovine head for her task of
protecting the king. The biblical author is demonstrating
that these gods are impostors. Yahweh is sovereign over all
things.[38]

Verse 3 begins, **'Behold, the hand of Yahweh will be…'** The verb is a Qal feminine participle (in agreement with the feminine 'hand') of 'to be' and appears only once in Scripture in this form. The term is probably a word-play on the name Yahweh that stands directly before it. Yahweh also derives from 'to be'.

The severity of the plague is emphasized by the words *kābēd m^e'ōd*, which literally means, 'very heavy'. The use of *kābēd* is caustic, because Pharaoh's heart is spoken of so frequently as being *kābēd* (e.g., 7:14; 8:32). In other words, the plague is 'heavy' upon Egypt on account of Pharaoh's heart being 'heavy'.

9:4. 'But Yahweh will make a distinction between the livestock of Israel and between the livestock of Egypt. And not one shall die that belongs to all the children of Israel.'

A first proof that Yahweh is the source of this plague is the fact that he spares the herds of the Hebrews. The verb translated **'make a distinction'** is the same one that is used in 8:22. It simply means 'to set apart'. The point is that God treats his people differently from the Egyptians: the latter are cursed; the former are blessed.

The end of the verse literally reads, **'And it will not die from all of the sons of Israel a thing.'** The subject of the clause appears in the last position. While there is considerable freedom in the disposition of the parts of a sentence in Hebrew, this example is stark. No doubt it is emphatic to underscore the complete protection of anything that belongs to the Israelites.

The word for **'thing'** is *dābār*. That is probably a word-play on the use of the word *dēbĕr* ('plague') from the previous verse. One people is on the receiving end of a *dbr* in one way, and the other people in the opposite way.

9:5. And Yahweh set a time, saying, 'Tomorrow Yahweh will do this thing in the land.'

A second proof that God originates the fifth plague is that he sets a precise time for its arrival in Egypt. Yahweh had done the same thing for the fourth plague (8:23), and he does it again here to lay stress on the fact that the timing of the plagues belongs to him. Thus the miraculous nature of the pestilences is seen not only in their degree and intensity, but in their timing and duration.

9:6. And Yahweh did this thing on the next day. And all the livestock of the Egyptians died. But from the livestock of the children of Israel not one died.

Since the **'livestock'** appear again in the seventh plague (9:19-21), the question is how to understand the use of **'all'** in the present verse. In other words, how could all the livestock be killed in this plague and then still be alive to suffer the impact of later disasters? Some interpreters argue that the use of 'all' is hyperbole in order to under-score a contrast with **'not one'**.[39] Another position says that the word 'all' can be used in a collective sense, as opposed to an exhaustive meaning. Thus every type of domestic animal *without distinction* was struck by the plague, but not every single animal expired.

9:7. And Pharaoh sent out [messengers], and behold nothing from the livestock of Israel died, not even one. But Pharaoh's heart was hardened, and he did not send out the people.

Pharaoh investigates what has happened in the land. He is told that not even one animal belonging to the Hebrews has been affected by the plague. The lack of disease among the Israelite livestock is emphasized by the use of the Hebrew phrase **'up to one'**. That term is a proclitic preposition often joined to the noun it modifies by a *maqqef.* It expresses degree and measure, and it perhaps takes on a privative sense.[40] It is clear that not any — no, not a single one — of the Israelites' animals was struck by the malady.

Pharaoh's activity is shown as paradoxical. He **'sends out'** his servants to investigate Goshen, but he refuses to **'send out'** the people of God from Goshen.

Pharaoh's denial of the request for Israel to leave was because **'his heart was heavy'** *(kābēd)*. The verb *kābēd* is a stative verb, indicating the condition, or state of being, of Pharaoh's heart. It is not being used as an active verb, as if the heart were in the process of becoming heavy. It simply was in a state of heaviness.

Application

It may be appropriate at this point to consider how humanity normally views or understands so-called natural disasters. When calamities of nature strike, such as hurricanes, tornadoes, or diseases of cattle, people almost always see no reason or source behind the disaster. They regard it as merely a matter of chance — disorder breaking in on the normal order of nature. 'Mother Nature' is fickle and cannot be trusted. In other words, there is no purpose or meaning to natural calamities.

The Bible teaches something different. At the very heart and foundation of Scripture is the doctrine of the sovereignty of God. What this means is that God is the Creator of the universe, Lord and Master of all, and his will is the cause of all things. In other words, it is God who is on the throne of the universe, maintaining the creation, directing it and working all things according to his own will and purpose. The biblical picture is that everything that happens in heaven and on earth occurs because of God's decree, will and purpose.

B. B. Warfield gets to the core of the matter when he says, 'All things without exception, indeed, are disposed by Him ... and if calamity falls upon man it is the Lord that has done it.' Pharaoh and the Egyptians attempted to explain away the plagues as not originating with Yahweh — they looked for other explanations.

The sixth plague: boils
(Exodus 9:8-12)

This section relates the sixth plague that came upon Egypt. And just as in the case of the third plague, there is no audience before Pharaoh and no warning given to the Egyptians (see commentary on 8:16). That similarity probably means that the second cycle of plagues is drawing to a conclusion (see 8:20).

9:8. Then Yahweh spoke to Moses and to Aaron: 'Take for yourselves handfuls of soot from a kiln and toss it towards heaven before the eyes of Pharaoh.'

At first glance, this command seems to be strange. Why soot from a furnace? The answer is that it is poetic justice. The type of furnace spoken of here was probably a kiln for burning bricks. The furnace, then, was a symbol of the oppression of the Hebrews, the sweat and tears they were shedding to make bricks for the Egyptians. Thus the very soot made by the enslaved people was now to inflict punishment on their oppressors.

It is specifically stated that Moses was to throw the soot into the air **'before the eyes of Pharaoh'**. The King of Egypt would thus witness first-hand the miraculous nature of the plague and he would be left without excuse. He would be unable to explain away the nature of the pestilence: it comes from Yahweh working through his prophets.

9:9. 'And it will become like fine dust upon all the land of Egypt. And it shall become festering boils breaking out on mankind and on beast in all the land of Egypt.'

Part of the miraculous nature of this plague is the multi-plication of the handfuls of soot into a **'fine dust'** that covers the entire land of Egypt.[41] In addition, the divine nature is reflected in the transubstantiation, or the changing of one substance into another: soot is trans-formed into dust. Finally, the effect of dust in bringing disease upon creatures also points to the plague's super-natural constitution.

The type of disease is unknown. Some commentators contend that it was anthrax, an infectious and usually fatal disease.[42] Anthrax is characterized by malignant pustules (elevated blisters or boils). Others argue it was smallpox.[43] Much of the vocabulary used in describing the disease, however, is used elsewhere in the Old Testament of leprosy and its consequences (see Lev. 13:18-20). Whatever the disease was, it was dangerous and life-threatening.

The sixth plague became proverbial in ancient Israel. For instance, Moses later warns the Hebrews that if they disobey God's commands, 'The Lord will smite you with the boils of Egypt and with tumours and with the scab and with the itch, from which you cannot be healed' (Deut. 28:27).

9:10. So they took soot from a kiln and they stood before Pharaoh. And Moses tossed it towards heaven, and it became festering boils breaking out on mankind and on beast.

Moses and Aaron did exactly as God had commanded them. This is confirmed by the repetition of entire phrases from verse 8. The result of their activity was precisely what God had predicted.

9:11. And the magicians were not able to stand before Moses on account of the boils, because the boils were on the magicians and on all the Egyptians.

This is the final mention of the Egyptian magicians in the plague account. They appear more impotent than ever. Not only are they unable to rid the land of the disease, but they cannot even protect themselves. This final word demonstrates that they and their powers have been completely vanquished and subdued by the force of Yahweh.

The Hebrew verb for **'to stand'** is the same one that was used in the previous verse. It highlights a contrast: whereas Moses and Aaron could *stand* before Pharaoh and perform miraculous feats, the Egyptian magicians could not even *stand* before the Hebrew prophets. Here we have another proof of the power of Yahweh.

9:12. But Yahweh hardened the heart of Pharaoh, and he did not listen to them, as Yahweh had said to Moses.

Observe the active nature of God's work in hardening Pharaoh's heart so that the king would not relent or repent. God's direct agency has been seen before regarding Pharaoh's heart (see the commentary on 4:21 and 7:3). At other times, the text recounts that Pharaoh hardened his own heart (8:15,32). The reason for the alternation is perhaps to teach that Pharaoh was responsible for his own sin, yet, at the same time, God is sovereign and he had decreed Pharaoh's actions.[44]

Application

The sixth plague, like the previous ones, is repeated and intensified in the book of Revelation. John reports the beginning of the pouring out of the seven bowls of wrath upon the followers of Satan in the following way: 'And the first angel went and poured out his bowl into the earth; and it became a loathsome and malignant sore upon the men who had the mark of the beast and who worshipped his image' (Rev. 16:2).

As before, the plagues in Egypt serve to foreshadow the plagues that are to be directed upon the ungodly in the last days. However, the plagues in Revelation are much greater and more extreme — they confirm the nature of the final judgement against the followers of the devil.

The seventh plague: hail
(Exodus 9:13-35)

Here is the beginning of the third cycle of plagues. The nature of the plagues changes in this sequence: they now have to do with weather and matters of the sky. There is no symbiotic relationship between these three plagues and the previous ones; scholars who would argue for a natural progression of the plagues stumble at this point. The hailstones of the seventh plague have absolutely no relationship to the boils of plague number six.

The contest is heating up. This audience with Pharaoh contains an extended warning to him. The issue is coming to a climax. And, for the first time, some of the Egyptians listen to Moses and the alarms that he sounds.

9:13-14. And Yahweh said to Moses, 'Get up in the morning and stand before Pharaoh, and you shall say to him, "Thus says Yahweh, the God of the Hebrews, 'Send out my people that they might serve me. For this time I am sending out all my plagues against you and against your servants and against your people, in order that you might know that there is no one like me in all the earth.'"'

The beginning of the seventh plague has a familiar ring about it. The first two cycles of plagues each begin in the same way: plagues numbers one and four both open with Moses going to Pharaoh in the morning and taking a stand before him (see 7:15; 8:20). Thus it is evident that plague number seven marks the inception of a third cycle of plagues.

The command to Moses to **'stand before Pharaoh'** harks back to verse 11 of this chapter. There the magicians could not *stand* before the Hebrew prophets. Moses, however, now takes a firm *stand* before the King of Egypt.

The particle introducing the clause, **'For this time I am sending out all my plagues...'**, is a conjunction meaning 'because/for', or an emphatic adverb, 'indeed'. It therefore indicates the certainty of the statement that follows. It is not conditional; there is no 'if ... then' situation. It is going to happen.

What God is hurling at Egypt is a series of **'plagues'**. That noun is derivative of the verb that means 'to strike', 'to smite'. It is used of a devastating blow struck by God.

The use of the verb 'to send out' is a word-play on verse 13. In that passage God demands that Pharaoh *send out* the Hebrews. But because Pharaoh does not do so, God responds by **'sending out ... plagues'** on Egypt.

The plagues are principally targeted **'against you'**, or more literally, **'against your heart'**. The Egyptians believed that Pharaoh's heart was the all-controlling factor in both history and society.[45] Now the King of Egypt's heart is hardened against the Hebrews. Yahweh assaults his heart to demonstrate that only the God of the Hebrews is the sovereign of the universe.

The reason for the attack is stated. It is so that Pharaoh (and the Egyptians) might **'know'** that Yahweh stands alone as sovereign of the universe. As we have noted previously, back at the time of the very first audience in the Egyptian court, Pharaoh had declared, 'I do not know Yahweh' (Exod. 5:2). God will ensure by means of the plagues that Pharaoh and his servants acknowledge the hand of Yahweh over Egypt!

9:15. 'For if by now I had sent out my hand and struck you and your people with the plague, then you would have been wiped from off the earth.'

The idea here is that God has been long-suffering towards Pharaoh and his people, and he has sustained the King of Egypt. If God had put forth his hand in full power, the Egyptians would have perished long ago. The verb translated **'wiped off'** means 'to be destroyed', and it also bears the sense of becoming unknown or effaced. An antithesis with the previous verse is apparent: whereas Yahweh will become known throughout the earth, the King of Egypt and his people would become unknown if God so desired it.

9:16. 'But on account of this I have raised you up, so that I might show you my power and in order that my name might be proclaimed in all the earth.'

This verse opens with a strong adversative meaning **'but, however'**. It shows an emphatic contrast. God has not destroyed Pharaoh, as he could easily have done. Rather, Yahweh has, literally, **'caused you to stand'** (Hiphil causative stem). Pharaoh's standing is to be viewed in opposition to the inability of his magicians to stand in the presence of Moses and Aaron (see commentary on verse 11). And the only reason Pharaoh is able to stand is because Yahweh has so willed it.

The purpose of God's sustaining hand is directly stated. It is not because Pharaoh has earned, or merited, God's grace. It is not because he does not deserve the judgement of the plagues. It is for one reason, and one reason alone: so that God's name might be glorified in all the earth. The Hebrew verb for **'proclaimed'** appears here in the Piel stem. In that stem, throughout the Old Testament, the verb means to give a laudatory recital, great praise and a recounting of the greatness of God. It is a word associated with worship.

9:17. 'Yet you are setting yourself up against my people and not sending them out.'

This verse emphasizes Pharaoh's refusal to let the Hebrews leave Egypt. The verb translated **'setting yourself up'** is a Hithpael, or reflexive participle, that means 'exalting yourself' and comes from the verb 'to lift up'. This verb goes right to the heart of the matter: Pharaoh is playing the deity, he is exalting himself against the Holy One of Israel.

9:18. 'Behold, this time tomorrow I am going to cause a very heavy hail to rain down, such as there has not been in Egypt from the day it was founded until now.'

God has fixed a time for bringing the seventh plague. It will not merely take place 'tomorrow', as in plagues number two (8:10), four (8:23,29) and five (9:5). But it will be **'at this time, tomorrow'**, i.e., the very hour at which Moses is speaking to Pharaoh, one day later.

The hailstorm that is promised will be *kābēd mᵉʾōd* — that is, **'very heavy'**. Again, this adjective is the one that is employed to describe the state of Pharaoh's heart throughout the Exodus account. The severity of the storm mirrors the degree of the hardness of Pharaoh's heart! In addition, see the commentary on 9:3 in which the fifth plague is likewise called *kābēd mᵉʾōd*.

The intensity of the storm is further highlighted by the statement that such a hailstorm had never been seen in Egypt since its inception. That announcement, Cassuto has pointed out, reflects a common Egyptian expression of the time.[46] Pharaohs such as Thutmosis III would assert that they had done something greater 'than all the things that were in the country since it was founded'. Yahweh employs the same idiom to demonstrate his power over any natural phenomena that had ever been experienced in the land of Egypt.

It is critical to remember that the Egyptians believed their gods to be personified in the elements of nature. The catastrophe of the hail was therefore a mockery of the Egyptian heavenly deities, including Nut (the female representative of the sky and personification of the vault of heaven), Shu (the supporter of the heavens who holds up the sky) and Tefnut (the goddess of moisture).

9:19. 'Now send out! Bring into safety your livestock and all that belongs to you in the field. Every person and every animal that is found in the field and is not gathered to the house, the hail will come down on them and they will die.'

The beginning of the verse is a double imperative: **'Now send out! Bring into safety...'** God, through Moses, gives Pharaoh good advice so that the plague should not harm his countrymen or their livestock (and Pharaoh himself owned vast numbers of livestock). God urges him and directs him to submit.

The verb **'send out/forth'** has been used throughout the exodus incident of what God demanded that Pharaoh should do for the Hebrews. Here Pharaoh is called to *send out* his people in his own interest, but once again he does not heed God's word, as will be seen in subsequent verses.

9:20. Some of the servants of Pharaoh who feared the word of Yahweh caused their servants and their livestock to flee into the houses.

Some of the Egyptians did what Moses had commanded them. They obeyed because they **'feared the word of Yahweh'**. That verb often signifies a fear that is associated with reverence, respect and even worship. Its use in the exodus context perhaps suggests a remnant of believers among the Egyptian people. Even if that was the case, it was only a small number. Exodus 9:30 indicates that Pharaoh's servants as a group did not fear the Lord.

9:21. But whoever did not listen to the word of Yahweh left his servants and his livestock in the field.

The majority of Egyptians, literally, **'did not set their hearts to the word of Yahweh'**. Their hearts remained hardened, like Pharaoh's, to the truth and reality of God's proclamations and promises to them. The heart of the matter is the matter of the heart.

9:22. And Yahweh said to Moses, 'Stretch out your hand to the sky so that hail will be upon all the land of Egypt, on man and on beast and on every plant of the field in the land of Egypt.'

The next day God commands Moses to bring the plague on the land as he had foretold. The word for **'hail'** occurs twenty-nine times in the Old Testament, and twenty of them refer to this event in Egypt (see Ps. 78:47-48).[47] In the history of Egypt, not only was hail rare, but when it did fall it was not usually particularly menacing. Its severity in the seventh plague is quite striking.

9:23-24. And Moses stretched out his rod to the sky, and Yahweh gave thunder and hail, and fire came down to the earth. And Yahweh rained hail upon the land of Egypt. And so there was hail and lightning in the midst of the hail, very heavy; and there was nothing like it in all the land of Egypt since it became a nation.

The severity of the storm is highlighted by the accompanying lightning and thunder. The appearance of these physical manifestations in the Old Testament often indicates the presence of God (see Exod. 19:16; 20:18). The word **'thunder'** literally means 'voice'. It is a term commonly used in connection with a theophany (see Gen. 3:8; Ps. 29:3-9).

The writer comments that in the midst of the hailstorm, literally, **'fire was taking hold of itself'** (the verb is a Hithpael reflexive participle). The same expression is used in Ezekiel 1:4, also in the context of a great storm. The significance of the idiom is dubious, although it has been suggested that it refers to lightning that is incessant, with strikes that appear in close succession.[48]

The use of the word **'nation'** is important. Egypt was probably the earliest united kingdom in the ancient Near East, having been in existence since about 3100 B.C. The exodus event occurred some eighteen centuries after that time (see discussion of chronology in the introduction). To say that this hail was the most severe in all the history of Egypt is a grand claim indeed!

9:25. And the hail struck all the land of Egypt, all that was in the field, from man to beast, and every plant of the field the hail struck, and every tree of the field was shattered.

The extent of the destruction caused by the hailstorm was great. It **'struck all the land of Egypt'**. What the author means by that general expression is spelt out by a three-fold parallelism:

    all that was in the field
    all plants of the field
    all trees of the field.

The structure and vocabulary of each line are essentially the same (and it should be noted that each line in the Hebrew begins with the sign indicating the direct object). Cassuto comments appropriately: 'This is certainly not coincidental: we hear three mighty blows, as it were, one after the other.'[49]

9:26. Only in the land of Goshen, where the children of Israel were, it did not hail.

Once again, the region left unaffected by the severe hail was Goshen, the settlement area of the Hebrews. It remained untouched, safe, secure and tranquil. Some commentators have attempted to explain away this distinction by saying that storms hammering Egypt in the Nile Valley would have been trapped there and unable to strike Goshen. That interpretation is impossible to justify in the light of God's elective work, which is so evident in the plague account (see commentary on 9:4-7).

In the record of this seventh plague the word **'land'**, or 'earth', is used seven times.[50] The first six refer to the plague that strikes Egypt, and the seventh time relates to the calm that prevailed in the land of Goshen. It is, of course, suggestive of the creation account in which the seventh day is one of rest, peace and harmony.[51]

As an aside, it is important to note what Pharaoh does not do. He does not summon his magicians to repel or replicate the plague. Nor does he send messengers to Goshen to see if it has been affected. What had happened, or was going to happen, was all too obvious.

9:27. Then Pharaoh sent out and he called for Moses and for Aaron, and he said to them, 'I have sinned this time; Yahweh is the righteous one, and I and my people are the wicked ones.'

The King of Egypt calls for the Hebrew prophets and then makes a grand confession: **'I have sinned this time.'** Pharaoh's self-condemnation is not very convincing because he is not acknowledging his earlier, previous sins and arrogance. He is only speaking of the present situation. In support of this point is his use of **'this time'**, or 'now', which mirrors God's use of the same expression in verse 14. It would be a mistake to conclude that Pharaoh has seen the light and that he exhibits a repentant heart. He may be weakening but he still plays the snake — lying, manipulating and twisting.

Even so, it is striking that Pharaoh should make any such confession at all. The ancient Egyptians believed in the purity of their sovereign. Individuals who approached Pharaoh were commanded to prostrate themselves, 'smelling the earth, crawling on the ground', while 'invoking this perfect god and exalting his beauty'. God is attacking this notion of Pharaoh's character being pure and untainted. There is only one who is good and perfect.

9:28. 'Pray to Yahweh, for there has been enough of God's thunder and hail. And I will send you out, and you will stay no more.'

On the surface, Pharaoh's response appears to be unqualified. However, the tone or spirit of his statement is suspect.

First, he begins with the imperative, **'Pray,'** thus directing the prophets to undertake such activity.

Secondly, the reason Pharaoh gives for this command is, literally, **'because there has been too much of the voices of God'** (Elohim). He refers to the thunder and hail as belonging, not to Yahweh, but to Elohim. As we have noted elsewhere, the latter is a more generic name for deity in the ancient Near East.

Thirdly, at the close of the verse, Pharaoh declares, literally, **'You** [plural] **will not again have to stand...'** The point is that Pharaoh is telling Moses and Aaron they need no further audience with him. This is ironic in the light of verse 16, in which God has allowed Pharaoh to *stand* before him, but now Pharaoh will not let God's prophets *stand* before him. Pharaoh continues to play the part of deity.

This is the third time Pharaoh has asked the prophets to intercede for him. He is, of course, being deceitful and lying again.

9:29. And Moses said to him, 'When I go out of the city I will spread out my hands to Yahweh, the thunder will stop, and the hail will be no more, so that you might know that the earth belongs to Yahweh.'

Moses' response, **'I will spread out my hands to Yahweh'**, is an expression signifying the act of prayer (see 1 Kings 8:38; Ezra 9:5). The reason the prophet was willing to perform this intercession was not to placate Pharaoh. It was so that Pharaoh **'might know that to Yahweh belongs the earth'**.

> The earth is Yahweh's, and all it contains,
> The world and those who dwell in it
>
> (Ps. 24:1).

It is Yahweh who rules over the earth, not the Egyptian gods, and certainly not Pharaoh (who was considered ruler over the two lands of Upper and Lower Egypt).

9:30. 'But I know that you and your servants still do not fear before Yahweh God.'

Moses is very direct with Pharaoh. He knows that Pharaoh's confession and asking for prayer are mere empty, vain words. The King of Egypt is a liar, a white-washed sepulchre, one 'holding to a form of godliness although denying its power' (2 Tim. 3:5). The Egyptians may have feared the plagues and may have been afraid of some sort of divine power, but they did not yet fear Yahweh.

9:31-32. (Now the flax and the barley were destroyed because the barley was in the ear and the flax was in bud. The wheat and the spelt were not destroyed because they ripen later.)

These two verses are in the form of an antithetic parallelism. It appears as follows:

a		b	c
The flax and barley	and	were destroyed	because the barley was ears of grain and the flax was in bud;

a		b	c
The wheat and the spelt	and	were not destroyed	because they ripen later.

This literary feature is for the purpose of emphasizing the antithesis. The crops which were ripe, or almost ripe, were ruined, but those which were only at the stage of tender shoots were saved and untouched.

The reasons for the antithesis are threefold. First, the preservation of the young, tender plants shows the miraculous nature of the plague. It is normally that very stage that is devastated by hail, but on this occasion God excludes it from the destruction. Secondly, it shows God's grace in the midst of judgement. God still gives sustenance to Egypt, and allows them to survive despite the plague. Why? See the commentary on verse 16. And, finally, the fact that some of the crops are kept alive provides material to receive the onslaught of the next plague, the locusts.

9:33. **And Moses went out of the city from the presence of Pharaoh, and he spread out his hands to Yahweh. And the thunder and the hail stopped, and rain no longer poured down to the land.**

One of the main elements in the recitation of each plague is recapitulation — that is, a brief summary or overview of what had been previously stated or recorded. See, for example, 8:17,24; 9:6,10; etc. The primary purpose of recapitulation is to show that the event did happen — and that it occurred exactly as God had planned and foretold.

9:34. When Pharaoh saw that the rain and the hail and the thunder stopped, he sinned again, and his heart was hardened, he and his servants.

Pharaoh again refuses to fulfil his word. The danger has passed, and so there is no evidence of a change of heart. The text says that, literally, **'He added to/increased the sin.'** Once the threat is over it appears that he becomes still more hardened in his wickedness.

For the first time we see that the concept of a hardened heart is applied not only to the Egyptian king, but now also to his servants. Moses was right when he said in verse 30 that 'You [i.e., Pharaoh] and your servants still do not fear Yahweh God.'

The list of rain, hail and thunder is in the reverse order from that of verse 33. The two lists form a chiastic structure in order to emphasize the cessation of the plague.

9:35. So Pharaoh's heart was hard and he did not send out the children of Israel, as Yahweh had said by the hand of Moses.

The account of the seventh plague ends with this formula that is found, in one variation or another, at the conclusion of every plague thus far (7:22; 8:15,19,32; 9:7,12). It is a convention of this section of Exodus signalling the final end of a particular plague episode.

Application

We read in the Apocalypse of John the following description of the seventh bowl of wrath that will be meted out on unbelievers: 'And the seventh angel poured out his bowl upon the air; and a loud voice came out of the temple from the throne, saying, "It is done." And there were flashes of lightning and sounds and peals of thunder; and there was a great earthquake, such as there had not

been since man came to be upon the earth, so great an earthquake was it, and so mighty... And huge hailstones, about one
hundred pounds each, came down from heaven upon men; and
men blasphemed God because of the plague of the hail, because
its plague was extremely severe' (Rev. 16:17-21).

The similarities between this seventh plague in Revelation and
the seventh plague in Egypt are striking. First, it should be noted
that both plagues are accompanied by thunder and lightning.
Secondly, the extent of the two plagues is underscored: in Egypt
nothing like it had been seen in the land since it was founded as a
nation (9:24); in Revelation nothing like it had occurred since man
came to be on the earth. Both plagues were extremely severe, and
in both instances mankind's response to them was hardness of
heart or blasphemy.

The size of the hailstones in Revelation underscores the
absolute extremity and severity of the plague at the end times — it
is so much greater than the plague in Egypt. The disaster that
befell the Egyptians was simply a mere foretaste of the final
judgement. That ought to give us pause. And it ought to drive us to
share the good news of Christ that delivers people from such an
end.

The eighth plague: locusts
(Exodus 10:1-20)

We need constantly to keep in mind the truth that the exodus event is not merely a confrontation between Israel and Egypt. There is much more to it than that. We are witnessing a contest and conflict between the God of Israel and the gods of Egypt. The gods of Egypt include Pharaoh himself (as the incarnation of Ra and Horus) and the various other gods personified in the elements of nature. It is a heavenly combat!

The plagues are Yahweh's means of bringing Pharaoh and the other gods of Egypt to their knees. In the first seven plagues we have seen how God has attacked certain important deities of Egypt and how he has destroyed them. The Lord, however, has the ultimate goal of bringing glory and honour to himself through the plagues.

10:1-2. And Yahweh said to Moses, 'Go to Pharaoh, because I have hardened his heart and the heart of his servants in order that I might perform these my signs in their midst, and in order that you may recount it in the ears of your sons and your sons' sons how I dealt harshly with Egypt and how I performed my signs against them, so that you might know that I am Yahweh.'

The eighth plague begins, like many of the others, with God commanding Moses to seek an audience with Pharaoh. God then explains to the prophet that he has hardened Pharaoh's heart so that the king will not relent. The verb 'to harden' in this instance is the Hiphil (causative) of *kābēd*. Derivatives of this verb have been used earlier regarding the nature of Pharaoh's heart (see the commentary on 7:14).

Before the shape of the eighth plague is revealed, God communicates two reasons for the plagues being brought against Egypt. First, they are a judgement against Egypt. The verb 'to deal harshly' in the Hithpael stem bears a sense of mockery: Brown, Driver & Briggs translate this clause: 'how I have made a toy of Egypt'.[52]

Secondly, the plagues are to be a benefit to the people of Israel. They are to be used to educate the Hebrews and their posterity regarding the person and character of the Creator. In Exodus 18, Moses tells his father-in-law Jethro about the plagues and the deliverance from Egypt. Jethro's response is significant: 'Now I know that Yahweh is greater than all the gods...' (Exod. 18:11). Examples of such recounting to descendants are found in passages such as Psalm 78.

10:3. So Moses and Aaron came to Pharaoh and they said to him, 'Thus says Yahweh, the God of the Hebrews, "How long will you refuse to be humble before me? Send out my people that they might serve me."'

So Moses and Aaron confront Pharaoh again. This time it is in the form of a direct rebuke: Pharaoh refuses to humble himself before Yahweh, the Lord of the universe. The verb 'to humble' is used to demonstrate a striking contrast between the persons of Moses and the King of Egypt. In Numbers 12:3 we read, 'And the man Moses was more *humble* than any man who was upon the face of the earth.' Pharaoh is the antithesis of the Hebrew prophet. He falsely plays the role of humility, claiming that he is a sinner — but it is all pretence.

The rebuke of Pharaoh is also sardonic. The verb 'to humble' appears back in Exodus 1:11-12 where it is used to describe how Pharaoh attempted to *humble* the Hebrews by placing taskmasters over them. In both passages, 1:11 and 10:3, the Piel infinitive construction of the verb is employed. Poetic justice is at work here: Pharaoh's actions now come back to haunt him.

10:4. 'If you refuse to send out my people, then behold tomorrow I am going to bring locusts into your territory.'

The nature of the eighth plague is spelled out: God will bring locusts upon the land of Egypt. Locusts constituted a particularly nasty problem in ancient Egypt. On account of that danger, the ancient Egyptians worshipped the god Senehem, who was supposed to be the divine protector against ravages from pests. An identification problem exists, however, because Senehem seems to have been a minor deity in dynastic Egypt. Why Yahweh should concern himself with mocking a subordinate deity is not clear. Perhaps protecting against grasshopper attack was the function not merely of one god, but of the gods in general. A hint of that possibility appears in the Tanis Stele from the reign of Taharqa (Dynasty 25), which speaks of 'a fine field, which the gods protected against grasshoppers'.[53]

10:5. 'And they will cover the surface of the land, so that one will not be able to see the land. And they will consume the remainder of what escaped for you from the hail. And they will consume every tree that is sprouting for you in the field.'

The picture of the plague is graphic. The locusts **'will cover'** the land of Egypt. That verb is used throughout the exodus account: in the second plague the frogs *covered* the land (8:6); later, God *covers* the camp of Israel with quails for the Hebrews' sustenance (16:13); and the entire Egyptian army is destroyed by being *covered* by the waters of the Red Sea (14:28; 15:5,10). It is a verb that stresses the bounteous nature of the provision, whether it be for good or ill.

The text literally says that the locusts will cover **'the eye of the land'**. This is a Hebrew idiom that indicates the visible surface of the land — that is, all that the eye can see. In the book of Numbers Balak, King of Moab, has a great fear of Israel because the Hebrews 'cover the eye of the land' (Num. 22:5,11). That expression reflects a great multitude.

The consequences of the locust plague are enumerated. All vegetation will be destroyed. All trees, in various stages of growth, will be ruined. The author then defines for us exactly which plants he is talking about: literally, **'the escaped remnant from the hail'**. In other words, any vegetation that survived the seventh plague, the hail, will be demolished by the locust invasion.

10:6. 'They will fill your houses and the houses of all your servants and the houses of all the Egyptians — something which your fathers and your fathers' fathers never saw from the day they were upon the ground even to this day.' And he turned and he went out from the presence of Pharaoh.

The phrase, **'your fathers and your fathers' fathers'** recalls verse 2, which is addressed to the Hebrews and speaks of 'your sons and your sons' sons'. This is an important contrast. Egypt is being pointed to her past, to her time of great glory. But that celebrity and splendour are about to end. Israel, on the other hand, is being instructed about her future, about deliverance, about a promised land.

Moses gives Pharaoh no time to respond. He knows what Pharaoh has to say. With a hardened unbeliever there comes a time when dialogue must be concluded. Pharaoh is not changing his behaviour but wallowing in his sin.

10:7. And the servants of Pharaoh said to him, 'How long will this one be to us as a snare? Send out the men that they might serve Yahweh their God. Do you not yet know that Egypt is ruined?'

Pharaoh's counsellors step in to give the king advice. They voice disagreement with Pharaoh's unyielding stance. And, ironically, they ask the same question God had raised in verse 3: **'How long?'** However, it should be noted that even the court officials have no desire to accede fully to the demands of the Hebrew prophets. They recommend that Pharaoh let **'the men'** go, the word 'men' being a masculine plural noun. Throughout the account of the plagues God has directed Pharaoh to let 'my people' go, not merely the men. In verse 11, Pharaoh appears to have accepted this counsel of his courtiers.

There is a scornful note in the way the officials refer to Moses. They do not call him by name, but merely say **'this one'**. Pharaoh's courtiers obviously do not really fear Yahweh (see 9:30).

10:8. And Moses and Aaron were brought back to Pharaoh, and he said to them, 'Go, serve Yahweh your God. Who will be going?'

Pharaoh is still playing the part of the one in control. First, he has the two Hebrew prophets **'brought back'** to the court. The verb is in the rare Hophal stem, indicating that Moses and Aaron are being acted upon, or being caused to do something.[54] Secondly, the king commands the prophets with a double imperative: **'Go, worship!'** This is the same double command he gave to the foremen to order them back to work in 5:18. Finally, Pharaoh plays the controller by trying to ascertain who the Hebrews believe will be going out of the land. His question is in the form of a repeated pronoun, **'who and who?'**, and this is probably for an emphatic purpose.

10:9. And Moses said, 'We will go with our young and with our old, with our sons and with our daughters, with our flocks and with our herds we will go, because we are to hold a feast to Yahweh.'

Moses responds by rejecting any conditions or limitations set by Pharaoh. God has commanded that all his people should go, and indeed that is what Moses demands. The inclusive nature of the departure is emphasized two ways in this verse. First, the verb **'we will go'** is repeated in it. Secondly, Moses employs a figure of speech in which two opposites are all-inclusive. In other words, when he says that **'young and ... old'** will go, he means not only that the young and old are to depart, but also everyone in between!

The idea that the Hebrews will celebrate **'a festival to Yahweh'** is no ploy on the part of Moses. The word for 'festival/feast' is found throughout the exodus account as a term for the Passover (see 12:14; 13:6; 23:15; 34:18). A note of sarcasm is evident because the celebration will be at the expense of Pharaoh and the Egyptians.

10:10. And he said to them, 'Yahweh is thus with you — if I send you out with your children! Take heed because evil is before your face!'

Pharaoh's rejoinder is bitter and condescending. The sense of it is a denial of the existence of Yahweh and his being with his people. The king exclaims that the only evidence that such a deity is real will be if Pharaoh releases all the Hebrew people. But he proclaims that he will do no such thing. In the end, the deliverance of the Israelites proves Pharaoh's words to be true.

The verse ends with the warning: **'Take heed because evil is before your face.'** The Hebrew word for **'evil'** is *rāʿāh*. It may be a Hebraized form of the name of the Egyptian sun-god Ra.[55] That bilingual word-play is found also in Exodus 5:19; 32:12,22; Numbers 11:1; 20:5 and

Deuteronomy 9:18. These *double entendres* are for the purpose of ridiculing the chief deity of Egypt, who was understood to be incarnated in the person of Pharaoh.

10:11. 'Not so! Go, now, the men, serve Yahweh, because that is what you are seeking.' So he drove them out from before Pharaoh.

Pharaoh's directive here begins with a negative followed by a demonstrative adverb: **'Not so!'** Such a construction implies the opposite of what was said in the sentence with which a comparison is being made (cf. Ps. 1:4). Pharaoh is not going to release all the Hebrews.

Then he issues his royal command with another double imperative: **'Go ... serve!'** Pharaoh still restricts the ones who are allowed to leave — only the men may depart. In this regard, the king has accepted the advice of his courtiers in verse 7. The reason for such a restriction is obvious. Pharaoh is holding hostage the families of the Israelite men. He knows the Hebrew men would never abandon their families, and so he is still attempting to keep Israel in subjection.[56]

Many translations say, **'They were driven out from before Pharaoh.'** However, the last sentence is actually active, not passive (being a Piel imperfect). It should read, **'He drove them out,'** the 'he' obviously referring to the king. This verb has been used previously (6:1) of God commanding Pharaoh to drive all the Hebrews out of his land.

10:12. And Yahweh said to Moses, 'Stretch out your hand over the land of Egypt for the locusts, so that they will come up over the land of Egypt and that they will consume every plant of the land, all that remained from the hail.'

The Lord calls for Moses to stretch out his hand (presumably with the rod in it) and bring forth locusts to destroy the remaining vegetation of Egypt. The Hebrew preposition *b'* is placed before the word **'locusts'**, and it is used instrumentally; in other words, Egypt's flora will be destroyed **'by means of'** the locust plague.

10:13. So Moses stretched out his rod upon the land of Egypt. And Yahweh blew an east wind on the land all that day and all that night, and when it was morning the east wind had carried the locusts.

Yahweh employs a secondary agent, the east wind, to bring locusts into Egypt. Normally locusts approach Egypt from the south, and thus their coming from the east indicates an abnormal condition. An east wind is later used to divide the Red Sea (14:21).

The **'east wind'** appears throughout Scripture as a sign and means of God's judgement. The Lord shatters the ships of Tarshish with an east wind (Ps. 48:7); he scatters Israel in the same manner (Jer. 18:17; Ezek. 19:12) and he dries up the wells of Ephraim with it (Hosea 13:15). Consider also its use in Ezekiel 27:26 and Jonah 4:8. The point is that divine doom is coming upon Egypt.

10:14. And the locusts came up over all the land of Egypt and they settled down in all the territory of Egypt in great numbers. Never before had there been so many locusts, nor will there [ever] be.

The phrase translated **'in great numbers'** is literally 'very heavy' (Hebrew *kābēd m''ōd*). The previous plague of hail was similarly described (9:18,24). And, of course, Pharaoh's heart has been characterized as *kābēd* throughout the plague account. Again, the extent of the plague mirrors the state of Pharaoh's heart.

The final clause of the verse is also reminiscent of the seventh plague. The author commented in 9:18,24 that no hail had ever been as severe in the history of Egypt. That idea is present in the case of the locust plague as well. But more is added: no locust infestation in the future will ever surpass this one.

10:15. And they covered the surface of all the land. And the land was darkened. And they consumed every tree of the land and every fruit of the tree that remained from the hail. Nothing remained green on tree or plant in all the land of Egypt.

The locusts, literally, **'covered the eye of all the land'**. Regarding this idiom, see the commentary on Exodus 10:5.

The onslaught was so severe that the land was darkened. The locusts swarmed upon the land in such great numbers that they hid the land from the eye. The verb 'to darken' is often used in the context of judgement and curse (Isa. 5:30; Lam. 5:17; Ps. 69:23). So in a metaphorical sense the locust plague symbolizes the darkened state of Egypt, both physically and spiritually, and its position as a nation under the judgement of God.

The figure of a locust plague representing judgement is used by the later prophet Joel against the nation of Judah (Joel 2:1-2). And he further understands the plague to be a mere foretaste of the final judgement called the Day of Yahweh. That great locust plague finds its ultimate fulfilment in the book of Revelation (9:3-4).

10:16. And Pharaoh made haste and called for Moses and for Aaron, and he said, 'I have sinned against Yahweh your God and against you.'

Pharaoh again calls for Moses and Aaron, but a new word is added to the invitation: **'Pharaoh made haste.'** As the plagues intensify, so does Pharaoh's response. He appears now to be growing desperate.

This is the second time that the king acknowledges his own sin in the matter (see commentary on 9:27). Here, however, he makes a broader confession. Pharaoh admits that his sin has been directed against Yahweh and his prophets (he uses the second person masculine plural). Note that he does not acknowledge any wrongdoing against God's people in general, and thus his admission is still inadequate.

10:17. 'Now please forgive my sin only this once, and pray to Yahweh your God that he might only remove this death from upon me.'

The king apparently acknowledges his sin. But, truly, how remorseful is he? He does seek forgiveness. Yet, he says, **'only this once'**. In other words, Pharaoh is recognizing some responsibility for the present plague of the locusts, but he refuses to own up to any liability for the first seven disasters. The fact is that he is only admitting present culpability in order to cause removal of the present plague.

Pharaoh's admittance of sin is significant. The ancient Egyptians believed him to be divine and sinless during his lifetime, and at death he was not thought to face any judgement. He was simply transformed into the god Osiris, who presided over judgement and death. But in the exodus episode he is pictured as one who is deserving of facing judgement day and death.

10:18. So Moses went out from the presence of Pharaoh and he prayed to Yahweh.

There is no dialogue on the part of the Hebrew prophets. Their only response is to leave the presence of Pharaoh and then make supplication to Yahweh. Again, it should be observed that the prophets do not pray to the Lord in the presence of the Egyptian king.

10:19. So Yahweh changed the wind to a very strong west wind and it lifted the locusts and it drove them into the Red Sea. Not one locust remained in all the territory of Egypt.

The prevailing winds in Egypt come from the east, from the direction of the Red Sea. This verse literally says that **'Yahweh turned the very strong wind of the sea.'** In other words, the Lord made a major alteration in the direction of the wind in order to carry the mass of locusts into the Red Sea.

This event of destruction serves as a foreshadowing of what God later does to the Egyptian army. Yahweh hurls Pharaoh's forces into the sea 'and not one of them remained' (Exod. 14:28; the same Hebrew wording as in the present verse).

10:20. But Yahweh hardened Pharaoh's heart, and he did not send out the children of Israel.

The eighth plague has the same conclusion as the previous ones. (For comment upon Yahweh's role in the hardening of Pharaoh's heart and the use of **'hardened'**, see Exod. 4:21.)

Application

The drama of the exodus is beginning to reach fever pitch. Note that verse 1 of this section relates the hardness of the hearts of Pharaoh and his courtiers, and then the final verse (10:20) also tells of the hardness of Pharaoh's heart. This reprise of the opening theme emphasizes the absolute unyielding and unbending nature of Pharaoh and the other leaders of Egypt. No matter that all Egypt was falling apart around them, the unbelieving leaders still failed to comprehend what was happening to them. They had a distorted view of the operation of the universe. And that is true of the ungodly throughout the ages — they do not realize that a sovereign God is in control. Their hearts are hardened towards him.

Locust plagues are symbols of how God metes out judgement in the Scriptures (see Deut. 28:38; 1 Kings 8:37; 2 Chron. 7:13). One is used in the book of Revelation to represent the tormenting of unbelievers: 'And out of the smoke came forth locusts upon the earth; and power was given them, as the scorpions of the earth have power. And they were told that they should not hurt the grass of the earth, nor any green thing, nor any tree, but only the men who do not have the seal of God on their foreheads. And they were not permitted to kill anyone, but to torment for five months; and their torment was like the torment of a scorpion when it stings a man' (Rev. 9:3-5).

The locust plague in Exodus devours the grass, every green thing and the trees. But that is nothing compared with the locust plague at the end times, when the locusts will torture ungodly people.

The ninth plague: darkness
(Exodus 10:21-29)

The ninth plague comes without any audience before Pharaoh. It arrives without warning, just like the sixth and ninth plagues. So ends the third triad of plagues.

10:21. Then Yahweh said to Moses, 'Stretch out your hand to the heavens so that there will be darkness upon the land of Egypt, a darkness that may be felt.'

Yahweh's power over the gods of Egypt is clearly displayed in this image. The ancient Egyptians regarded Amon-Ra, the personification of the sun, as their chief deity. For them his rising in the east was the symbol of life and resurrection. He was the creator-god. However, when Amon-Ra sank in the west this was understood to represent death and the underworld. When Yahweh wills it, the sun is darkened, and Amon-Ra is hidden and unable to shine upon his worshippers. During the ninth plague Amon-Ra does not rise and does not give life; his realm is death, judgement and hopelessness.

The miraculous nature of the plague is not only in its timing but also in its severity. The verse refers to a darkness that may be **'felt'**, or 'handled'. This verb is a Hiphil, and it only appears in that form in only one other place in the Old Testament, Judges 16:26, in which Samson asks to be able to *feel* the pillars of the Philistine temple. The idea being conveyed regarding the darkness is its peculiar thickness, density and heaviness.

Some commentators want to explain the **'darkness that may be felt'** by arguing that this plague is really a sandstorm, or the khamsin from Arabia that brings thick dust or sand to Egypt. There is absolutely no justification for such a naturalistic explanation of the Scriptures.

See the commentary on 10:15 regarding 'darkness' as a symbol of judgement and the curse.

10:22. So Moses stretched out his hand to the heavens, and a deep darkness was in the land of Egypt for three days.

The Hebrew term for **'deep'** is actually another term for **'darkness'**. And thus the clause reads, literally, **'and a dark darkness was in the land...'** 'Deep' is also a word associated with the darkness that accompanies God's judgement. Often the noun is figuratively used of calamity brought on by Yahweh. Consequently, the use here of the word 'deep' emphasizes the judgemental nature of the ninth plague.

The Septuagint adds the word for 'storm/tempest' to the passage. This may be an attempt by early translators to provide a natural explanation for the plague of darkness. Again, there is no evidence from the Masoretic Text that the biblical author sees anything but a supernatural intervention.

The figure of **'three days'** as the duration of the plague may be significant. In the Old Testament the number three sometimes symbolizes completeness, finality and definitiveness (cf. Isa. 6:3). In the case of the ninth plague it may indicate the final defeat of Amon-Ra and the other gods of Egypt.

10:23. One could not see one's brother and one could not rise up from one's place for three days. But for all the children of Israel there was light in their dwellings.

The miraculous nature of the plague of darkness is emphasized here. First, a distinction is made between the Egyptians and the Hebrews: God's people have light and Pharaoh's people do not. Secondly, apparently the Egyptians could not even light lamps or candles to see, whereas the Hebrews could. Yahweh is truly the provider of light (not Ra!). It does not exist apart from him, and he bestows it upon whom he will.

The contrast also represents a profound metaphor. In the Old Testament, light signifies covenant blessings such as prosperity, peace and justice. Darkness, on the other hand, reflects judgement, curse and death.

10:24. Then Pharaoh called Moses, and he said, 'Go, serve Yahweh! Only your flocks and your herds will be left behind; also your children may go with you.'

Back in 10:8, Pharaoh had uttered the same opening words: **'Go, serve Yahweh!'** In that instance he had made a reservation that the Hebrew women and children would not be allowed to go with the men (10:10). Now we see that the king backs away from that pronouncement and allows them to depart.[57] Thus, he is made to regret his previous kingly edict.

Pharaoh is not humble, however. He does not accede to Yahweh's commands. He still refuses to let go. He orders the Hebrews to leave their flocks and herds behind. The Hebrew verb used for **'leave behind'** really means that the animals would be 'detained'. It is a strong verb that indicates a 'persistent overtone of wilful, deliberate, or intentional action'.[58] Pharaoh still has the desire to destroy the Israelites. How long could they survive in the wilderness without food or other necessities?

10:25. But Moses said, 'Indeed, you will give into our hands sacrifices and burnt offerings and we will make [a sacrifice] to Yahweh our God.'

Moses replies directly and assertively. His answer begins with the words, **'Indeed, you...'**; it is an emphatic particle followed by a personal pronoun. Moses now commands the King of Egypt!

Not only will the Hebrews take their own animals with them (see next verse), but Pharaoh will provide livestock from his own herds for the sacrifice of the Israelites. The verse literally says, **'Indeed, you, you will give sacrifices and burnt offerings...'** Thus Moses declares that the Hebrews will leave with their own animals in addition to those given them by Pharaoh. It is ironic that Egypt should provide the resources for the Hebrews' worship of Yahweh.

The most basic meaning of the verb used here for offering sacrifices is 'to do/make'. However, one of its various meanings is 'to observe/celebrate a festival' (see Exod. 12:47-48). That is clearly its meaning in the present context.

10:26. 'And also our livestock will go with us. Not a hoof shall remain. Because we shall take from them to serve Yahweh our God. And we will not know what we will use to serve Yahweh until we arrive there.'

Moses does not yield an inch to the Egyptian king. Here he employs a figure of speech called a synecdoche of the part to emphasize that not one animal of the Israelites will remain in Egypt. When he says, **'Not a hoof shall be left behind,'** a part (the hoof) is used to represent the whole animal. In other words, every single animal is leaving!

The prophet reasons with the monarch. His argument is basically that the Hebrews need their animals in order to worship God. They are not certain how many of their livestock they will need for worship; thus they must take them all. As we shall immediately see, such rationalization is wasted on Pharaoh.

10:27. But Yahweh hardened Pharaoh's heart, and he was not willing to send them out.

Yahweh again steps into the centre of the action. Note the sequence: Yahweh hardens Pharaoh's heart and then the Egyptian king refuses to let the Hebrews leave. The point is that God's volition is being exercised in the scenario. It is not Pharaoh who is in control, but God's will that is done.

10:28. And Pharaoh said to him, 'Go from before me! Guard yourself, that you do not see my face again, because in the day that you see my face, you will die.'

The king attempts to expel Moses from his presence with vindictive words and angry threats. There is a clear warning here: Pharaoh cautions Moses with a Hiphil imperative meaning, 'Take heed!' or 'Be on guard!' The base nature of Egypt's king is revealed in this verse. He simply has the desire to kill Moses.

Pharaoh's final statement sets up a scene of self-ridicule. Egypt is under the effects of the ninth plague — that is, total darkness upon the land. And now Pharaoh speaks of **'the day that you see my face'**!

10:29. And Moses said, 'As you have said, I will never see your face again.'

This verse plays on the wording of verse 28, and it literally reads, **'I will never again see your face.'** Moses thus pronounces Pharaoh's words from the previous verse as prophetic. The Hebrew prophet will not see Pharaoh's face because it is hidden in darkness, and the Hebrews will soon leave Egypt.

Application

This plague is also a forerunner of a catastrophe that appears in John's Apocalypse. We read in Revelation 16:10-11: 'And the fifth angel poured out his bowl upon the throne of the beast; and his kingdom became darkened; and they gnawed their tongues because of pain, and they blasphemed the God of heaven because of their pains and their sores; and they did not repent of their deeds.' The extremity of horror experienced in the final plague at the end of the ages is underscored by the actual physical pain that the ungodly will suffer because of it. The Exodus plague is terrible, but this one is overwhelming.

5. The tenth plague: Passover

(Exodus 11:1 - 13:16)

Announcement of Passover
(Exodus 11:1-10)

It seems clear from this section that Moses has remained in the presence of Pharaoh. It is not until verse 8 of this passage that Moses leaves Pharaoh's court. If that is the case, then verses 1-3 become problematic. Is there an actual revelation of God to Moses in the presence of Pharaoh and his court? Some translators have skirted the problem by translating the opening of verse 1 with 'Now the Lord had said to Moses', a translation indicating a pluperfect tense — as if God had told this to Moses at a previous time (i.e., before his current stand in Pharaoh's court). The problem is that no such tense is found in Hebrew narrative prose.

The verse literally opens with, **'And Yahweh spoke to Moses.'** The Hebrew appears to indicate that God spoke to Moses in the midst of his audience with Pharaoh. And why not? Even if it was an audible communication (and we do not know this for certain), it would have served as a sign to, and put fear into, Pharaoh and his servants. There was no need for solitude for divine communication to take place (as on previous occasions) since the plague account was now moving towards a grand climax.

Exodus 11:3 is a parenthesis, a historical insertion by the author into the midst of the audience with Pharaoh.

Verse 4 then returns to the conversation between Moses and Pharaoh.

11:1. And Yahweh spoke to Moses, 'Yet one plague I will bring upon Pharaoh and upon Egypt, and afterwards he will send you out from this place. When he sends you out from this place he will certainly drive you out completely.'

The origination and source of the plagues is announced. They are not mere natural occurrences but Yahweh has 'brought' them upon Egypt. This is the first time in the exodus account that this Hebrew term is used. In this form, **'plague'** is used almost exclusively to refer to a physical blow given by an overlord to a subject and, most often, it is used of the action of the Hebrew God in meting out chastisement. This is a direct claim of sovereignty, that nature is at Yahweh's beck and call, and it performs his will. It is a striking teaching in the light of Egyptian religion, which teaches that nature is the personification of the gods.

Yahweh declares that he will bring one final plague upon Egypt. It will result in the expulsion of the Hebrews. The idea that Pharaoh will drive them out **'completely'** probably refers to the Hebrew people in their fulness, altogether.[1] Remember that Pharaoh had previously said he would send the Hebrews out without their children (10:10), or at another time without flocks (10:24), and on an even earlier occasion that they could go provided they went not very far away (8:28). Now we see that the Israelites will leave Egypt in totality. Their departure will be without restriction or limitation.

The unqualified nature of the release is supported by a repetition of the Hebrew verb *garas* (the first a Piel infinitive absolute, followed by a Piel imperfect): **'He will certainly drive you out.'**

11:2. 'Speak now in the ears of the people, that they might ask, a man from his neighbour and a woman from her neighbour, for articles of silver and for articles of gold.'

This command refers back to a similar directive in 3:22. It probably alludes to the same event because the people are now nearing the time of departure. The Septuagint and other early manuscripts understand it in this way, as they add 'and clothing' in this verse in order to make it the same as the earlier passage (see commentary on 3:22).

Again, this episode is a fulfilment of God's promise to Abraham in Genesis 15:14. He had declared that his people would come out from Egypt 'with great possessions'. It is also a material judgement on Egypt for having enslaved the people of God for over four centuries.[2]

11:3. And Yahweh bestowed favour on the people in the eyes of the Egyptians. Also the man Moses was very great in the land of Egypt in the eyes of the servants of Pharaoh and in the eyes of the people.

Just as God controls Pharaoh by hardening his heart, the Lord causes grace or favour to be bestowed on the Hebrews by the Egyptians. The verse literally says, **'He gave the people grace in the sight of the Egyptians.'** It is a telling fact that the very people who had been hated and despised by the Egyptians (see commentary on 1:12) now come to be respected by them. God is at work, changing the spirit of the Egyptians towards the Hebrews.

The second half of the verse then speaks of Moses' standing in Egypt: **'Also the man Moses was very great in the land of Egypt.'** How could it be otherwise? What power he had been given! What wonders were wrought by his staff and his hand!

Consider who it was that believed Moses to be so great. First, it was **'the servants of Pharaoh'**, which probably refers to the Egyptians. And, secondly, **'the people'** stood

in awe of him. This perhaps refers to the Hebrews, as it
does earlier in the verse. The only one not mentioned is
Pharaoh. His heart remained hard.

11:4. And Moses said, 'Thus says Yahweh, "In the middle of
the night I am going out in the midst of Egypt."'

Moses now utters the very words of God, introducing them
with the divine formula, **'Thus says Yahweh...'** He conveys them in the form of Yahweh speaking in the first
person. God says, **'I am going out'** through Egypt. This
verb is used commonly in the exodus account in relation
to Israel's departure from Egypt. Because Pharaoh will not
let God's people go out *of* Egypt, God will go out *in* Egypt!

Although many translations say this will take place **'at
midnight'**, the Hebrew simply signifies 'in the middle of
the night'. Night-time was an especially fearful time for the
Egyptians. In the 'Hymn to the Aton', the author describes
the dread of night because the sun-god has departed to
the underworld and is no longer protecting the Egyptians.
For the Hebrews, on the other hand, there is no fear, for
'He who keeps Israel will neither slumber nor sleep' (Ps.
121:4). Yahweh is awake, working, sustaining and protecting his people.

11:5. 'And every first-born in the land of Egypt will die, from
the first-born of Pharaoh who sits on his throne to the first-
born of the slave girl who is behind the millstone, and every
first-born of animals.'

God will bring a final, horrible plague upon Egypt. It will
result in many deaths. Who is to die? All the first-born,
from Pharaoh's son, who presumably was prince of Egypt
and next in line of succession, to the girl slaving away in
the mill. This is a merism, two opposites that are all-
inclusive. Pharaoh, of course, had the greatest stature in
Egypt, whereas the mill-worker had the least. Cassuto

argues that in Egyptian literature the mill-worker is a common symbol for the poorest of the poor.[3] In any case, all Egypt will be greatly affected by the plague of death.

The first-born of animals will also die. Egyptians attributed divine character to animals, and so they will be destroyed to show that Yahweh discharges judgements against the gods of Egypt.

11:6. 'And there will be a great cry in all the land of Egypt, the like of which has never been, nor will ever be.'

The intensity and severity of the final plague are expressed in a similar fashion to those of other plagues (see 9:24; 10:14). The extent of the plague will result in **'a great cry'** throughout the land of Egypt. This 'great cry' will not be one of weeping or wailing, but rather a loud call for help under distress and duress. Egypt will call upon its gods for aid, but they will remain silent. The same verb, 'to cry', was used in relation to the Hebrews as they called on Yahweh for deliverance from Egyptian oppression. Unlike the Egyptian gods, Yahweh answered them.

11:7. 'But for all the children of Israel not a dog will growl against a man or an animal, in order that you might know that Yahweh makes a distinction between Egypt and between Israel.'

Whereas God will destroy the first-born of both man and beast in Egypt, not even **'a dog will sharpen its tongue'** against the Hebrews or their animals. That expression signifies angry growling.[4] There will be no such hostility in Goshen.

A debatable point is whether the author is here making a subtle reference to the impotence of Anubis, the god of the dead and embalming. On this interpretation Anubis, who had a canine form, is seen to have no power of life or death over the Hebrews, who were protected by Yahweh.[5]

The reason for such a contrast is stated clearly. It is so that the Egyptians might know (the ending on the verb signifying **'you'** is in the plural) that Yahweh makes a distinction between Israel and Egypt. The verb means 'to treat differently/to discriminate' (see its use in 9:4). This is the wonderful doctrine of election in which God sets apart a people by his own will and desire. Israel, by no means of its own merit or goodness, is the recipient of Yahweh's favour and grace.

11:8 'And all these your servants will come down to me, and they will bow down to me, saying, "Go out, you and all the people who are following you!" And afterwards I will go out.' Then he went out from the presence of Pharaoh in a rage.

Moses announces that all the servants in the Egyptian court will bow down before him, rather than before Pharaoh. It is Moses (and ultimately Yahweh) who has the upper hand now. In support of this is the fact that Moses does not wait to be dismissed by Pharaoh but he up and leaves of his own accord. And he does so in great anger or, literally, **'with a hot/scorching nose'**.

11:9-10. Then Yahweh said to Moses, 'Pharaoh will not listen to you, so that my wonders might be multiplied in the land of Egypt.' And Moses and Aaron did all these wonders before Pharaoh. But Yahweh hardened Pharaoh's heart, and he did not send the children of Israel out from his land.

Here is a summary statement of the setting in Egypt after the nine plagues have occurred. From the very outset of the plagues God has said that Pharaoh would not listen to Moses. The reason is stated here: so that God's **'wonders'**, or 'miracles', would be multiplied in the land. And such marvellous, terrifying events testify to the reality of Yahweh, and to his sovereignty and majesty.

Thus, the situation (particularly regarding Pharaoh's heart) has not changed from the beginning of the plagues in chapter 7 right up to the ninth plague. However, starting with the next section, it will be narrated how the entire scene changes dramatically when Yahweh brings the tenth plague on Egypt.

Application

This section announces the climax of the plague account. It is a proclamation of death in Egypt. But even with that declaration of impending doom, Pharaoh refuses to yield or repent. One would think that such a pronouncement from a deity who already has acted by destroying Egypt with nine plagues would elicit a positive response from the Egyptian king. It does not happen.

Frankly, we should not be surprised. Even in the ultimate culmination of the plagues in the Apocalypse of John — which, as we have seen, is far harsher and more painful than the plagues in Egypt — people respond in hardness. In the plague account recorded in Revelation 16, it says that men 'blasphemed the name of God who has the power over these plagues, and they did not repent, so as to give him glory' (Rev. 16:9). Pharaoh thus epitomizes unbelieving mankind and the seed of the serpent.

Apart from God's grace (see Exodus 11:3) all men are akin to Pharaoh. They are hardened, unseeing and unrepentant. Paul comments regarding this: 'For he says to Moses, "I will have mercy on whom I have mercy, and I will have compassion on whom I have compassion." So then it does not depend on the man who wills or runs, but on God who has mercy. For the Scripture says to Pharaoh, "For this very purpose I raised you up, to demonstrate my power in you, and that my name might be proclaimed throughout the whole earth." So then he has mercy on whom he desires, and he hardens whom he desires' (Rom. 9:15-18).

Institution of the Passover
(Exodus 12:1-28)

This section of the book relates the detailed instructions relating to the first Passover and the command to observe the Passover event throughout subsequent history.[6] It gives various laws relating to the Passover meal (12:1-11), the placing of blood on the doors of houses (12:7,21-22) and the manner of celebrating the Feast of Unleavened Bread (12:14-20). Finally, the passage provides the divine rationale and purpose for the Passover event.[7]

12:1-2. And Yahweh spoke to Moses and to Aaron in the land of Egypt, saying, 'This month shall be the first of the months for you; it is to be the first month of the year for you.'

Laws concerning the Passover were given **'in Egypt'** (12:1). The designation of the location is for the purpose of not ascribing all Hebrew laws to Mount Sinai (Exod. 20 onwards). In other words, the Israelites were not a lawless society prior to the giving of the codified law at Sinai. It is also interesting to note that the laws given at Sinai rarely deal with the Passover in detail (except Deut. 16) — the reason is clear: the Passover laws were already set down in Egypt.

This announcement does not mean a change in the Hebrew calendar. The text literally reads, **'This month is for you the first month.'** Thus it is at the time of the Hebrew new year that the Passover occurs. And now the Israelites truly have something to celebrate — a new beginning that is born of redemption from Egypt!

Other texts inform us that the opening month is Abib (see Exod. 13:4; 23:15; 34:18). In the later Jewish calendar from the Babylonian exile it is referred to as Nisan (Neh. 2:1; Esther 3:7). The new year generally corresponds to the months of March and April.

12:3. 'Speak to all the congregation of Israel, saying, "On the tenth of this month, they shall take for themselves — a man shall take a lamb for his family, a lamb for his household."'

This is the first reference in the Bible to **'the congregation of Israel'**. The word *'dh* means 'a gathering'. The Septuagint, the Vulgate and multiple medieval manuscripts prefer the reading, 'the sons of Israel'. There is, however, no necessity for such an emendation. We are viewing for the first time the establishment of the Hebrews as a corporate entity.[8]

Each **'family'** is to secure a lamb. That term is literally 'house of the fathers', and it corresponds to an extended family, a sub-unit of a clan. The lamb is to be procured on the tenth day of the first month. That specific day is important: Yom Kippur (the Day of Atonement) occurs on the tenth day of the seventh month (Lev. 23:27), and the Israelites cross the Jordan River into the promised land on the tenth day of the first month. The number ten often symbolizes completion in the Bible: for example, the Ten Commandments, the ten plagues, etc. Here it may signify the complete redemption of Israel out of Egypt.

12:4. 'If a household is too small for a lamb, then he and his neighbour, closest to his house, shall take one according to the number of persons. According to what each person will eat, you will divide the lamb.'

Verse 4 opens with a particle introducing an 'if … then' clause in Hebrew. If there are not enough members in a family to consume the entire lamb then two neighbouring

('near') families may join in the feast. It would also allow
two families to share the expenses of the meal.

According to Josephus (Sarna tells us): '...a minimum
quorum of ten participants was required for this ritual in
Second Temple times. The actual slaughtering of the
animal was performed in groups of no fewer than thirty.'[9]

Why the entire sacrifice is to be consumed is not stated
in the text. Perhaps it is to signify complete and total
redemption from the land of Egypt.

12:5. 'An unblemished male lamb, one year old, shall be for
you; from the sheep or from the goats you may take it.'

The characteristics required of the animal to be sacrificed
and eaten are now spelled out. First, the beast shall be
'complete', 'perfect', or **'unblemished'**. The purity of sacrifice is thus demanded. It is also to be a one-year old male,
which according to later law at Sinai is a clean animal.
Therefore, the animal may be offered as a sacrifice and
eaten.[10]

The animals sacrificed may be either sheep or goats.
The Hebrew term includes both kinds.

Later prophets use the imagery of a sacrificial lamb for
the work of the coming Messiah. Isaiah 53:7 says, 'He was
oppressed and he was afflicted, yet he did not open his
mouth; like a lamb that is led to slaughter, and like a
sheep that is silent before its shearers, so he did not open
his mouth.'

12:6. 'Keep watch over them until the fourteenth day of this
month, when all the community of the congregation of Israel
shall sacrifice them at twilight.'

Each family is to 'guard' or **'keep watch over'** the sacrificial animal for four days — it is to be protected from any
defect or unholy intrusion. Then on the fourteenth day of
the first month the people are to slaughter the

lambs/goats simultaneously. The sacrifice is a united act of worship.

The term **'community'** is found for the first time referring to the people of God. It literally means 'assembly': the people of Israel are congregating for a communal worship service. This act of redemption is solidifying the Hebrews as one covenanted people before Yahweh.

The time of the community sacrifice is unclear. A direct translation of the Hebrew says, **'between the two sunsets/evenings'**. Some scholars have suggested this means 'twilight', that is, between sunset and dark.

12:7. 'Then they shall take from the blood and put it on the two doorposts and on the lintel of the houses in which they are eating.'

Each family is to take blood from the sacrificed animal and put it **'on the two door-posts and on the lintel'** of the entrance to the house. Every part of the entrance is to have blood smeared on it. The purpose of this act is stated later in verse 13: it is an external sign that those within are those numbered among the people of Yahweh. In other words, it is a pointer to their having been set apart as part of the community of God.

Why use blood as the sign? Throughout the Old Testament, the shedding of blood often signifies entrance into, and being part of, the covenant with God (see, for example, Gen. 15:9-17; 17:9-14). Blood is the essence of life, and thus it symbolizes the extremity of the covenant relationship extending to life and death. The Hebrews bear the sign of God and live; the Egyptians have no sign and many die.

12:8. 'And they shall eat the flesh on that night, roasted in fire, and unleavened bread with bitter herbs they shall eat with it.'

The Hebrew people were to eat the animal roasted or fully cooked. This was an innovation because in the ancient Near East spring rituals of pagans included eating a raw or half-cooked sacrifice.[11] The Lord was abolishing such bloody festivals of idolatry.

'Unleavened bread' *(mātsāh)* was also to be eaten at the Passover meal. It signifies the Hebrews' quick departure from Egypt. They did not have time to allow the bread to leaven, but they left with unleavened bread bound up in clothes over their shoulders (see 12:34).

'Bitter herbs' were included in the feast. These are symbolic of their bitter lives under slavery in Egypt (see Exod. 1:14). But now they would be freed from that bitterness!

12:9. 'Do not eat any of it raw or boiled in water, but only roasted in fire, its head, along with its legs, and along with its inner parts.'

Reiteration of the requirement for roasting the animal serves to stress the method of cooking. The text adds that the various parts of the animal are to be roasted at the same time: no parts are to be withheld from the fire. This prescription was kept throughout Israel's history of the Passover, as confirmed by 2 Chronicles 35:13: 'So they roasted the Passover [animals] on the fire according to the ordinance, and they boiled the holy things in pots, in kettles, in pans, and carried them speedily to all the lay people.'

12:10. 'Do not leave any of it until morning, but what remains of it until the morning you will burn with fire.'

Hebrew *lō'*, the negative, with an imperfect verb, is common in legislative texts of the Old Testament (eight of the Ten Commandments are so structured). It is a prohibition in legal literature. That is what appears at the beginning of the verse: here is a law that Israel must keep.

The sacrifice was to be eaten in totality. However, if that was not possible what remained was to be burned up. The meat of the animal had been set apart for the Passover celebration; it was too sacred to be used at any other time. The Hebrews were not to save any meat for later. In addition, the full consumption of the sacrifice points to its completeness and efficacy. It signifies a full-scale redemption.

12:11. 'This is how you shall eat it: your loins girded, your sandals on your feet and your staff in your hand. And you shall eat it in haste. It is the Passover of Yahweh.'

Each person who consumes the sacrifice must be arrayed in the following way: fully clothed, with a belt around the waist, sandals on the feet and a staff for walking in the hand. This manner of dress implies that the Israelites must be ready to depart Egypt at a moment's notice during the night-time festivity. While fully dressed, the participants are to eat the meat **'in haste'**. This term in the original Hebrew does not only mean 'quickly', but it bears a great sense of alarm/trepidation/danger.[12]

The word for **'Passover'** is *pĕsāh*. This is the first time it is used in the Bible. The precise meaning of the word in the original is much disputed.[13] In any event, *pĕsāh* is the principal term throughout Scripture that designates the celebration of the redemption of Israel out of Egypt (see Exod. 12:21,27,43,48; 34:25; etc.). There is no evidence or reason to believe that this was an established term or concept appropriated by the Hebrews at this time.

The Passover is not primarily about the deliverance of Israel out of Egypt. Nor is it mainly about the humiliation of Pharaoh and Egypt. Rather its essential purpose is the glorification and exaltation of Yahweh: **'It is Yahweh's Passover.'**

12:12. 'And I will pass through the land of Egypt on this night and I will strike every first-born in the land of Egypt, from mankind to animal. And I will bring judgement against all the gods of Egypt. I am Yahweh.'

The theme of the exodus event is here declared. God will demonstrate his superiority over **'all'** the false gods of Egypt (which has already been demonstrated by the plagues against specific gods). Pharaoh is included. All of these are non-gods. This is a great statement of monotheism.

Antagonism is confirmed by the adversative use of the preposition *beth* in the verse: **'And I will bring judgement against all the gods of Egypt.'**[14] The contest of deities is about to reach a climax.

12:13. 'And the blood will be a sign for you on the houses in which you are. And I will see the blood, and I will pass over you. And no plague will be upon you for destruction when I strike the land of Egypt.'

In the tenth plague, God will again make a distinction between his people and Pharaoh's people. Those who belong to Yahweh will bear upon their houses the sign of blood, and they will not be struck by the plague. Those who do not mark their homes with blood will suffer the plague.

It should be observed that the blood is merely **'a sign'**. It is a physical symbol that points to a spiritual reality; that is, the people inside the houses covered with blood belong to Yahweh. The blood does not cause the people to be Yahweh's, but simply acts as a billboard proclaiming the fact.[15]

The verb **'I will pass over'** is *psh*. Derived from this verb is the Hebrew name for the Passover, *Pesach*. Yahweh's act of passing over the covenant people in this final plague is why the feast is called Pesach, or 'passing over'.

12:14. 'This day is a memorial for you, and you will celebrate it as a feast to Yahweh throughout your generations. You are to celebrate it as a lasting ordinance.'

Passover is to have an abiding character, i.e., it is to be celebrated **'throughout your generations'**. Thus it is not only for the Hebrews in Egypt, but for their posterity, so that future generations might understand and remember the great deliverance of Yahweh when he brought the children of Israel out of Egypt.

This verse uses three terms to define the Passover. First, it is **'a memorial'**. That noun derives from the verb that means 'to remember/remind'. Passover, therefore, is to serve as a reminder to the Hebrew people of their lives of slavery and of the events of their redemption.

Secondly, Passover is **'a feast'**. A 'feast of gathering' or a 'pilgrim-feast' is what is especially signified by this word.[16] The Hebrews are being called together and appear before Yahweh; it is a communal celebration (see Exod. 23:14-17).

Finally, Passover is **'a lasting ordinance'**. The Hebrew term for 'ordinance' means 'law/rule/statute'. And thus we see a law given to Israel by God that precedes the laws revealed at Sinai. Israel is not lawless before the meeting at the mount. Note, in addition, the continuous, binding nature of the ordinance: bound to 'law' is a masculine adjective which means various things, but in the context of our passage probably signifies 'in perpetuity/in continuous existence'.

The command to keep the Passover is emphasized by the reiteration of this law in Exodus 12:24 and 13:10.

12:15. 'Seven days you will eat unleavened bread, but on the first day you will remove all leaven from your houses. Because anyone who eats leaven — his life will be cut off from Israel, from the first day to the seventh day.'

Further regulations and details of the Passover celebration
are now set out.[17] Three ordinances are set forth in this
verse. First, the Hebrews are allowed only to eat bread
without yeast during the festival period. Secondly, they are
to **'remove all leaven from [their] houses'** — apparently
this directive would keep them from accidentally using
leaven in their food. And, finally, the feast is to last for
seven days (the number seven, of course, often reflects the
idea of completion).

The sanction of being **'cut off'** from Israel is a common
penalty in the Torah (see, e.g., Lev. 17:10; 20:3,5,6). In a
general sense, it means that one is no longer considered
part of the covenant community of Israel or receives any of
the blessings associated with membership of that community. A person is simply denied fellowship with, and
standing in, the people of Israel. It is a very serious consequence, and it underscores the gravity and importance of
the Passover ordinances.

12:16. 'And on the first day will be a holy convocation and on
the seventh day there will be a holy convocation for you. No
work shall be done on them, except that which is eaten —
that alone may be made by you.'

On the first day and on the last day of the feast the Hebrews are to have **'a holy convocation'**, a gathering
together of the people of God. The term 'sacred assem-
bly/holy convocation' is used seventeen times in the Torah
(eleven times in Lev. 23, four times in Num. 28-29, and
twice in Exodus). This is its first appearance in the Bible. It
is a technical term for a religious gathering on the Sabbath
or on other sacred, set-apart days.

The prohibition against any work on these two days is
relayed in the strongest possible form in the Hebrew.
When the negative is used with 'all/any' it expresses
absolute negation, absolutely none whatsoever.[18] In this
sense, the first and last days of Passover operate in much
the same way as the later Sabbath (see Exod. 20:8-11).

12:17. 'Keep the feast of unleavened bread, because on this very day I brought out your hosts from the land of Egypt. And you shall keep this day throughout your generations as a lasting ordinance.'

The opening phrase of the verse literally says, **'Keep** [or 'guard'] **the *mătsōt***', i.e., the unleavened bread. This has received various interpretations. Some, such as the NIV translators, argue that there is an ellipsis here; that is, the term for 'feast' has been omitted (probably through a later scribal error). The translators of the Septuagint and the Samaritan Pentateuch believe the word *mătsōt* was somehow copied incorrectly and should really be *mīts'vāh* (Hebrew for 'commandment'), so that the phrase should read, 'Keep the commandment,' referring to the previous Passover commands. Some rabbinical interpretation takes the statement at face value and says it literally means to guard and protect the bread of the Passover so that no impure element (such as leaven) should get into the food.[19]

The description of the way God is bringing the Hebrews out of Egypt, according to **'hosts'**, or divisions, has military overtones (see commentary on 6:26).

The final clause says that the Passover celebration shall be **'a lasting ordinance for the generations to come'**. These precise words occur earlier, in verse 14. That repetition is to underscore the importance and benefit of the Passover to future generations, to the posterity of the Hebrews.

The verb used in this verse, **'I brought'**, is a Hiphil perfect. The perfect tense/aspect in Hebrew signifies completed action. But how can this be if the events of deliverance have not yet occurred? Perhaps it is what Gesenius calls the *perfectum confidentiae*; that is, it expresses facts which are undoubtedly imminent.[20] Because God is speaking these words they will indeed come to pass!

12:18. 'On the fourteenth day of the first month, in the evening, you will eat unleavened bread until the twenty-first day of
the month, in the evening.'

Holy, set-apart days and weeks begin and end in the
evening. Leviticus 23:32 says, 'From evening until evening
you shall keep the Sabbath.' This custom may perhaps
reflect the creation week of Genesis 1 in which the creation
days apparently commenced in the evening: '... and there
was evening and there was morning, day one' (1:5).

12:19. 'Seven days no yeast will be found in your houses,
because whoever is eating leaven — that person shall be cut
off from the congregation of Israel, whether he is an alien or
a native of the land.'

The yeast laws and their sanctions apply not only to the
native citizen of the people of God (**'the congregation of
Israel'**) but also to the **'alien'** or 'sojourner'. The Hebrew
word refers to a resident alien, a person to be distin-
guished from a foreigner. It is someone who has taken up
permanent residence in Israel but is not an Israelite by
birth or inheritance. In Israel, the alien had a special
status and had various rights, such as religious
participation.

In this verse, the Passover statutes apply to both the
alien and the native. However, a further restriction for
alien participation in the feast is given: the *ger* may not eat
the lamb or celebrate the festival unless he is circumcised,
as was the native Israelite. He must wear the physical sign
of belonging to the people of God or he is not included in
the celebration.

For the consequence of disobedience, see the commentary on 12:15.

The Hebrew preposition *b'* (or *beth*) is attached to both
'alien' and 'native-born'. Its use here is that of specification

and it serves to qualify the realm of the verbal action.[21] In other words, it has the sense of 'with regard to'.

12:20. 'You shall not eat any yeast. In all your dwellings you shall eat unleavened bread.'

The conclusion to the prohibition of eating leavened food and the directive to eat *matsah* is emphasized in this verse. Its structure is in the form of an antithetic parallelism with an internal chiastic structure. The verse looks like this (direct translation from original):

	a	b		
Anything	leavened[22]	you shall eat.[23]	not	
	c	b^1		a^1
In all your houses	you shall eat		*mātsōt.*	

This type of structure in a narrative serves to accentuate, or to bring to a climax, the preceding prose section.

12:21. Then Moses called for all the elders of Israel, and he said to them, 'Go at once and take for yourselves lambs according to your families and slaughter the Passover lamb.'

Moses now instructs the people to begin preparations for the initial Passover. Additional particulars are added in this section to the general statutes already given by the prophet. In this verse, we are told that the elders of Israel are the ones to prepare and administer the feast/sacrament of Passover. The elder is to care for the families that have been placed under his charge and authority.

'Go at once' is an imperative in Hebrew that means 'Proceed/lead'. It is the elders as the leaders in Israel who are to obey God's statutes first, and then the community will follow.

12:22. 'You shall take a bunch of hyssop and you shall dip it in the blood which is in the basin, and you shall touch the lintel and the two doorposts with the blood which is in the basin. And none of you shall go out of the door of his house until morning.'

Now Moses explains to the elders the method and manner of applying the blood-sign to the Israelites' homes. The elders are to use hyssop to smear the blood on the dwellings. Hyssop is a plant with many stalks, and its use prevents the blood from coagulating. It is employed in the administration of other rites in the Old Testament, primarily in regard to purification (see Num. 19:18). Hyssop later developed into a symbol of purification, as we read in Psalm 51:7: 'Purge me with hyssop, and I shall be clean; wash me and I shall be whiter than snow.'

The Hebrew term translated **'basin'** has two distinct meanings.[24] On the one hand, it can be translated as 'basin' or 'goblet' (see, for example, 2 Sam. 17:28; 1 Kings 7:50). But the word is more often used as a noun masculine for 'threshold' or 'sill' (see, for example, Judg. 19:27; Ezek. 43:8; etc.). If the latter translation is correct for verse 22, it implies that the entire structure of the door — lintel, doorposts and threshold — is to be covered with blood. It would then demonstrate a complete covering of the people inside.

12:23. 'And Yahweh will pass through to strike Egypt, and he will see the blood on the lintel and upon the two doorposts. And he will pass over the door, and he will not allow the destroyer to come to your houses to strike.'

The identity of **'the destroyer'** is a matter of disagreement among commentators. Some define it in an impersonal way. Sarna, for instance, argues that 'The plague, although personified, is not an independent demonic being. It can only operate within the limits fixed by God.'[25] While I would agree that the destroyer is not an 'independent demonic being', I would disagree regarding its impersonal nature. Rather, the figure is probably to be identified with an angel of Yahweh. In 1 Chronicles 21:9-17, an angel of the Lord serves as a destroying force against David and Jerusalem because of an uncalled-for census.

12:24. 'You shall keep this event as an ordinance for you and for your children for ever.'

As in verse 17 (where the verb **'keep'** occurs twice), the binding nature of the Passover ordinances is emphasized in the present verse. It is also a rite that must be carefully taught to children so that its meaning and significance would pass from generation to generation. The posterity of the Hebrews would be prime beneficiaries of the Passover event. It is thus **'a lasting ordinance'** (NIV), one that is to be honoured and observed in perpetuity.

12:25. 'And it will be when you come to the land which Yahweh is giving to you as he said, then you will keep this ceremony.'

The land that God had promised the Hebrews is Canaan, and it was given to Abraham and his seed many centuries before (see Gen. 12:7). The Israelites are to make certain that they keep the Passover ritual in the land flowing with milk and honey. They are not to forget what God has done for them as a people. One of the first acts of the Hebrews after entering the land was in fact the observation of the Passover (Josh. 5:10).

The Hebrew word for **'ceremony'** is the common term for labour/service. Used earlier of the Hebrews' slavery under Pharaoh (Exod. 1:14), it here reflects who it is that the Israelites truly serve. And the contrast is clear: the hard and cruel service they rendered to Pharaoh is now replaced by a compassionate, loving service to Yahweh.

12:26-27. 'And when your children say to you, "What does this ceremony mean to you?", you will say, "It is the Passover sacrifice to Yahweh, when he passed over the houses of the children of Israel in Egypt, when he struck Egypt but he delivered our houses."' And the people bowed down and worshipped.

Here at the conclusion of his instructions to the people, Moses reiterates the pedagogic aspect of the Passover ritual. When children see the events of the Passover celebration they will naturally be curious. Parents are to seize the opportunity to share with their children the story of redemption from Egypt, and continually to remind them of the God who acts.

The response of the people was, literally, that **'They bowed down and prostrated themselves.'** This is a Hebrew idiom reflecting a scene of worship, praise and adoration. It was used earlier in the book of Exodus (see commentary on 4:31).

12:28. And the children of Israel went and did as Yahweh commanded Moses and Aaron, thus they did.

Worship of Yahweh is soon followed by action. Obedience is born out of obeisance. What the Hebrews did was to make preparations for the Passover; that is, they complied with all the instructions and ordinances that Moses had just given to them.

The fact of their submission to the Torah commands is confirmed by the repetition of the verb 'to do'. The verse literally reads, **'The sons of Israel did what Yahweh commanded Moses and Aaron, thus they did.'** That same grammatical construction was earlier used of Moses and Aaron when they obeyed God's directives right down to the very details (see commentary on 7:6).

Application

A critical teaching of this foregoing section is the temporal application of the Passover commands. Passover is to be observed
by the people of God throughout history, from one generation to
the next. This injunction is intensified by its appearance three
times in the passage under consideration (vv. 14,17,24). The
continuous, binding character of the Passover celebration raises
a question for the church: how does the church keep this
command? Do we celebrate Passover?

The Lord's Supper in the New Testament is a Passover
commemoration (see Matt. 26:17-19). Every Passover meal
included two elements: wine and unleavened bread. The wine
symbolized the blood of the lamb that was shed for the Israelites
to protect them from the avenging angel. The bread signified the
bread that the Hebrews carried on their backs when they left
Egypt in haste. Jesus reinterprets those two elements and
pronounces the Passover event a type of foreshadowing of
himself and his ministry. In Matthew 26:26-28, Jesus says that
the wine is a figure of the blood of Christ that takes away the sins
of his people, and the bread is a figure of his body that is hung
on the cross for sinners. In short, what Jesus is proclaiming is
that he is the Passover Lamb, who by the shedding of his blood
is a substitute for his people, protecting them from the wrath and
judgement of God. In other words, as Israel is covered by the
blood of the Passover lamb, so the new Israel is covered by the
blood of the Messiah (see John 1:29; 1 Peter 1:19; 1 Cor. 5:7).

The fact of the matter is that when Christians celebrate the
Lord's Supper they are keeping the Passover that God commanded his people to honour in perpetuity. The *Scots Confession* of 1560 puts it this way:

> As the fathers under the Law, besides the reality of the
> sacrifices, had two chief sacraments, that is, circumcision
> and the Passover, and those who rejected these were not
> reckoned among God's people; so do we acknowledge
> and confess that now in the time of the gospel we have
> two chief sacraments, which alone were instituted by the

Lord Jesus and commanded to be used by all who will be counted members of his body, that is, Baptism and the Supper or Table of the Lord Jesus, also called the Communion of His Body and Blood.

The reason that Christians celebrate the Passover in this way is, first, to remind themselves of the work of Christ in delivering his people from death and darkness. It is, furthermore, a sign that believers are the people of God and the covenant, and that God dwells in their midst. And, finally, it is a sign of the continuity of the people of God from the Old Testament to the New Testament and beyond.

Death of the first-born (Exodus 12:29-36)

This section records the historical event of the first Passover. Everything that God has told Israel to prepare for now comes to pass. Included in the account is the death of the first-born, the expulsion of the Hebrews from the land by Pharaoh and the despoiling of the Egyptians.

12:29. And it came to pass at midnight that Yahweh struck all the first-born in the land of Egypt, from the first-born of Pharaoh who was sitting on his throne to the first-born of the prisoner who was in the dungeon, and all the first-born of the animals.

What took place at the first Passover is now described by the biblical author. All the Egyptians without exception are struck by the plague. The all-embracing nature of the disaster is accentuated by the use of two all-inclusive opposites: the plague strikes the family of Pharaoh, who sits in luxury on his throne, and it also hits the families of prisoners, those **'dwelling in the house of the pit'**. It spans all, from the one who enjoys the greatest comfort to the one in the situation of least comfort (cf. 11:5 in which a different image is used to reflect the idea of hardship).

The first-born of Egyptian animals are also destroyed, as Moses had prophesied in 11:5 (see commentary on that verse).

12:30. And Pharaoh arose that night and all his servants and all Egypt. And a great cry was [heard] in Egypt because there was not a house in which there was not one who died.

The extent of the final plague is stressed by this verse. It concludes with a statement of result or consequence: **'because there was *not a house* in which there was *not one* who died'**. That clause carries a double negative, a particle that means non-being or non-existence.[26] Thus, the plague is exhaustive in its outcome for the land of Egypt.

The serious nature of the plague is also highlighted by the singling out of Pharaoh in the passage. First, he is humiliated by being forced to rise from his bed in the middle of the night, a procedure that is clearly not one normally associated with royalty.[27] And, more critically, the king's house is subject to the consequences of the plague. It is a true statement that the final plague is primarily directed against Pharaoh as a god of Egypt and against the Egyptian royal succession. Numbers 33:4 links the Passover with the judgement upon the deities of Egypt.

12:31. **And he called for Moses and for Aaron at night, and he said, 'Rise up, go out from the midst of my people — both you and the children of Israel! Go, serve Yahweh as you have said!'**

As a result of the tenth plague, Pharaoh was desperate to rid his land of the Hebrews. The urgency to expedite Israel's departure is emphasized in this verse. First, Pharaoh employs four imperatives: **'Rise up, go out... Go, serve!'** The first two imperatives are found elsewhere in Scripture to indicate great haste. In Genesis 19:14, Lot urges his sons-in-law with these imperatives to flee for their lives from Sodom.

The King of Egypt is humbled. He is forced to summon to the palace the very men he had banished from it earlier (see 10:28). He also, for the first time, calls the Hebrews by the name, **'the children of Israel'**, or Israelites. This appears to be an acknowledgement of their status as a people — not yet a nation but in the process of becoming one.

Finally, the answer to the question of whom the Hebrews will serve/worship is given out of Pharaoh's very own mouth: **'Go, serve Yahweh!'**

12:32. 'Take your flocks and your herds, as you have said, and go! And also bless me.'

Pharaoh now concedes all the demands of the Hebrew prophets and withdraws all his previous limitations and restrictions. All the children of Israel may leave Egypt, and all their flocks with them. In addition, Pharaoh gives no time-frame for their departure and places no restrictions on how long they may be gone. Apparently, at least for the moment, the King of Egypt has been defeated.

The ultimate humiliation of Pharaoh is seen in his seeking the blessing of the prophets even after his defeat. Childs remarks that Pharaoh 'even seeks from Moses a blessing which serves to underline Moses' complete victory'.[28] Was this request honourable? Was it a sign of true remorse? Or was it sarcasm? What we can say with certainty is that there was no real repentance on the part of the king. He gave no recognition of any personal responsibility — he wanted the blessing without the liability, the shame, or the consequences. He simply desired the plagues to be gone. We know this to be the case, because once the immediate shock following the final plague had subsided, the Egyptian king pursued the Hebrews in order to destroy them.

12:33. The Egyptians urged the people to make haste, to send them out from the country, because they said, 'We shall all die.'

A literal rendering of the opening of this verse reads, **'And the Egyptians pressed/made strong upon the people.'** Ironically, the verb is the same one that is used of God hardening or making strong Pharaoh's heart (see 7:13,22;

8:15). Thus, previously the Egyptian hearts were hardened not to let the Hebrews go (9:34), but now they are equally determined to force them to leave.

The act of strengthening is so that the Hebrews would be *sent out*— this is the Hebrew verb so frequently used in the exodus account. The opening salvo between the Hebrew prophets and Pharaoh focused on that verb: 'Thus says Yahweh, God of Israel, "Send out my people..."' (5:1). Now the Egyptians are causing the Hebrews to be sent out!

The Egyptians are worried and faltering. They want the Hebrews to depart, literally, **'because all of us are dying'**. The latter is a participial form, and 'the participle is the form which indicates continued action...'[29] From the perspective of the Egyptians, if the Hebrews stay in the land Pharaoh's people will indeed all perish.

12:34. So the people lifted onto their shoulders dough [which] had not yet been leavened, in kneading bowls wrapped in clothes.

Prior to departing from Egypt the Hebrews perform two further acts. The first is stated in this verse. They place dough in **'kneading bowls'** (this term is used earlier in 8:3), and carry them upon their shoulders wrapped in garments. They had no time to leaven the dough or to cook it in Egypt. Great haste was the order of the day. It is in commemoration of this event that unleavened bread has been part of the Passover celebrations throughout history. Deuteronomy 16:3 says in regard to the instructions for Passover: 'You shall not eat leavened bread with it; seven days you shall eat with it unleavened bread, the bread of affliction (for you came out of the land of Egypt in haste), in order that you may remember all the days of your life the day when you came out of the land of Egypt.'

A temporal adverb is found in this verse: it has an adversative affect, meaning 'not yet'. Also, when it is followed by an imperfect verb, as it is in this case, the verb is in the pluperfect tense.[30] The correct reading of the clause is therefore: **'And the people lifted ... dough, [which] had not yet been leavened...'**

12:35-36. And the children of Israel did as Moses said, and they asked the Egyptians for articles of silver and articles of gold and clothing. And Yahweh gave favour to the people in the eyes of the Egyptians, so they gave them what they requested. Thus they plundered the Egyptians.

This event is the fulfilment of the commands that God had given to the people in 3:21-22 and 11:2-3 (see the commentary on both those passages).

Application

It is important to realize that the Passover event was a historical incident, that it was set and fixed in time and space. It was not merely an idea or a belief that found its reality in future celebrations, but it really did happen. The same can be said for the significance of the Lord's Supper. That Christian ritual truly represents the historical episode of the death and resurrection of Jesus Christ. The apostle Paul underscores the gravity and weight of the historicity of those events in the following passage: 'Now if Christ is preached, that he has been raised from the dead, how do some among you say that there is no resurrection of the dead? But if there is no resurrection of the dead, not even Christ has been raised; and if Christ has not been raised, then our preaching is vain, your faith also is vain' (1 Cor. 15:12-14).

The very essence of biblical religion and faith is the fact that what the Bible records actually occurred in history.

Initial journey: Rameses to Succoth
(Exodus 12:37-42)

This next section relates the very outset of the Hebrews' escape from the land of Egypt. It provides us with some interesting data regarding geography, chronology and the numbers of people that left Egypt.

12:37. And the children of Israel journeyed from Rameses to Succoth, about six hundred thousand men on foot, besides children.

The opening leg of the journey begins at **'Rameses'**, which was one of the cities the Hebrews had helped to build (see commentary on 1:11 for information regarding its location). The first stop in their travels was **'Succoth'**. Some researchers suggest that Succoth is to be found at Tell el-Maskhuta.[31] The name Succoth, perhaps derived from Egyptian *tkw* (Tjeku), has been discovered on numerous monuments at Tell el-Maskhuta. The problem with this identification is the fact that urban occupation did not begin at Tell el-Maskhuta until the seventh and sixth centuries B.C. E. L. Bleiberg has attempted to solve this problem by asserting that Tjeku (Succoth) was originally a region in the Wadi Tumilat area of Egypt and it was later located specifically at Tell el-Maskhuta.[32]

The number of people leaving Egypt was **'six hundred thousand men on foot, besides children'** (note that there is no mention of the word 'women' in the original). The term for **'men'** distinguishes this group from women, children and non-combatants.[33] For that reason, interpreters often estimate the size of the population of Israel at the exodus to have been between 2,000,000 and 3,000,000 people. In favour of taking these numbers at face value is that they coincide with the data given about the population size in the wilderness from the book of Numbers (see Num. 1:46-47; 2:32; 26:51).[34] In addition, according to Exodus 1, the Israelites were experiencing a great period of growth and increase (see analysis of 1:6-7).

Others argue that the figures are hyperbolic.[35] Some insist that the word for **'thousand'** (Hebrew *'ēlĕph*) actually means 'a clan', and thus six hundred clans left Egypt. *'Ēlĕph* is used that way in Judges 6:15. Others say that *'ēlĕph* is a military unit of men levied for war.[36]

12:38. And also a mixed multitude went up with them, and flocks and herds, a great number of livestock.

The verse begins by saying that '**A mixed multitude went up with them.**' 'Mixture' is a Hebrew word which is used of miscellaneous peoples who attach themselves to a group to which they do not naturally belong (see Jer. 25:20; 50:37; Neh. 13:3). Many English translations render the word as 'foreigners'. The point is that various kinds of people who were not part of Israel joined themselves with the people of God. Perhaps some of them were Egyptians who came to believe and fear the word of God (see Exod. 9:20-21).

The Hebrews left Egypt with, literally, **'a very heavy flock'**. As has been noted previously, the word for 'heavy' (Hebrew *kābēd*) has defined what God has done to Pharaoh's heart throughout the account of the exodus. As God made Pharaoh's heart *heavy,* or hard, thus he makes Israel *heavy* in material possessions.

12:39. And they baked the dough which they brought from Egypt into cakes of unleavened bread because there was no

yeast when they were driven from Egypt; they were not able
to wait and also they did not make provisions for themselves.

On the first leg of the journey, the Hebrews cooked unleavened bread for their sustenance. The reasons for their
having to resort to it were twofold: first, **'They were not
able to wait/linger/tarry'** in Egypt long enough for their
bread to rise. Secondly, the text reports that **'also they did
not make provisions for themselves'**. The Hebrews were
unprepared for the spontaneous nature of their departure.

12:40-41. And the length of time that the children of Israel
dwelt in Egypt was 430 years. And it was at the end of 430
years, on this very day, that all the hosts of Yahweh came
out from the land of Egypt.

Israel's period of enslavement lasted over four hundred
years. This was a fulfilment of God's prophecy to Abraham
in Genesis 15:13, where he says, 'Know for certain that
your seed will be strangers in a land that is not theirs,
where they will be enslaved and oppressed four hundred
years.' The discrepancy between the two figures may easily
be explained by the Genesis figure simply being a round
number, or one that is the minimum figure, that is, *at
least* four hundred years.[37] The number in the present
verses would then be the specific figure for the length of
the sojourn. The fact that 430 years is the specific figure is
confirmed in verse 41 where it says the Hebrews left Egypt,
literally, **'on this selfsame day'**.[38]

The opening word of verse 40 is literally **'dwelling'**. It is
a derivative of the verb used later in the verse (**'lived'**). This
is a unique usage of the noun form because it apparently
means in the context 'dwelling-time', length of stay.

12:42. It is a night of watching by Yahweh to bring them out
from the land of Egypt; this night is for Yahweh to be

watched by the children of Israel throughout their generations.

The final verse of the section begins by saying that Passover is **'a night of watching by Yahweh'**. Protection of his people is the main idea behind it. It is night-time, and the God of Israel neither slumbers nor sleeps (Ps. 121:4). He is the keeper and guardian of Israel.

In contrast, Pharaoh has to be aroused and awakened in the middle of the night to be told of the plague (12:30). The sun-god Ra is in the nether regions, and unable to come to the aid of his people. Where are the gods of Egypt?

Application

I once heard a missionary Baptist pastor from the Delta region of Mississippi preach on this text. The title of his sermon was 'God Works the Night-Shift'! The point of his sermon needs to be driven home to the church today — and that lesson is the constant, ever-working providence of God. He continually maintains and sustains the universe, and he has ceaseless and endless care and compassion for his people. The *Westminster Confession of Faith* speaks directly to this latter observation: 'As the providence of God doth, in general, reach to all creatures, so, after a most special manner, it taketh care of his Church, and disposeth all things to the good thereof' (Chapter V).

As the people of God, we can take great comfort from this doctrine: God's care of his church is uninterrupted and incessant. It has no end.

Reiteration of Passover commands (Exodus 12:43 - 13:10)

A third rehearsal of the Passover laws is found in this section, especially in Exodus 13:3-10. There we see the general laws, barring yeast from the festival, giving the directive to teach the meaning of Passover to children and issuing the command to keep this feast in perpetuity. New, more detailed instructions are set out in Exodus 12:43-49, in which those who are allowed to participate in the feast are listed and described.

12:43. **And Yahweh said to Moses and to Aaron, 'This is the ordinance of the Passover: any son of a foreigner shall not eat of it.'**

One of the principal teachings of this next section relating to the Passover is to define who may or may not partake of the festival. Regulations begin with a negative injunction: **'Any son of a foreigner may not eat of it.'** The title 'son of a foreigner' signifies a non-Israelite who temporarily dwells with the people of God (see Deut. 23:20). That person does not profess the religion of Yahweh and is not a member of the covenant. Passover participation is restricted to Israelites.

The verb **'eat'** is followed by the preposition *b'* and the pronominal suffix **'it'**. It is the partitive use of the preposition which implies the 'idea of an action as extending to something, with at the same time the secondary idea of participation in something'.[39] Thus, part of the restriction is that no foreigner is to participate in any part of the Passover communal event.

12:44-45. 'Any slave, one who has been bought with silver, after you have circumcised him, then he may eat of it. A temporary resident and a hired worker may not eat of it.'

The statute of verse 43 is now spelt out in further detail in these two verses. The general principle is: 'Any son of a foreigner may not eat of it' (i.e., the Passover, 12:43). However, there is one exception to the rule: the slave in Israel who has been circumcised is now part of the covenant people, and he may therefore participate in the Passover. This privilege is in accord with the circumcision commands of Genesis 17:12-13.

Two groups who do not have covenant status are the **'temporary resident'** and the **'hired worker'**. The first is a person who has a very temporary relationship with Israel, much more so than the 'alien' or 'sojourner' referred to in 12:19. The second is, strictly speaking, a mercenary worker who has been hired to work in Israel. These groups have no religious commitment to Yahweh, and they are thus denied access to the festival.

12:46. 'In one house it must be eaten; anything from the flesh shall not be brought out of the house to the outside. And you shall not break any bone of it.'

The prohibition of breaking any of the bones of the Passover sacrifice has received various interpretations. R. de Vaux, for instance, argues that in 'the Passover sacrifice the bones would not be broken in order that God might restore the victim to life, i.e. ensure the fertility of the flock'.[40] He draws this conclusion on the basis of apparent modern Arab parallels. Sarna comments that the law prevents the Hebrews from breaking bones in order 'to suck out the marrow'.[41] The meat of the animal should

have been completely satisfying. There is not much supporting evidence for either of these explanations.

G. A. Barton suggests that some parallels to this activity
are known from ancient Egypt.[42] His argument is not very
convincing.

M. Noth has the most balanced understanding of this
restriction.[43] The wholeness of the victim symbolizes the
communal character of the sacrifice; that is, it emphasizes
the cohesion of the family unit at worship.

The end of the verse is quoted in John 19:36 at the
crucifixion of Christ. The point is simply that Jesus is the
paschal lamb (cf. 1 Cor. 5:7). Leon Morris put it this way:
'When that sacrifice was instituted the command was
given that not one bone was to be broken. If this is the
allusion then John is viewing Jesus as the perfect Passover offering.'[44]

12:47. 'The whole congregation of Israel shall do it.'

In contrast to the foreign groups mentioned in verses 43
and 45, the entire **'congregation of Israel'**, without
exception, is to partake of the Passover feast. Apparently
that term signifies all who are circumcised (i.e., bearing the
sign of the covenant), and their wives and children, as-
sembling together for worship. The Septuagint translates
this word as 'synagogue', and it has a similar meaning.

12:48. 'And when a stranger sojourns with you, and he
celebrates the Passover to Yahweh, every one of his males
must be circumcised; and then he may draw near to celebrate it. And he shall be like a native of the land. And anyone
uncircumcised may not eat of it.'

The opening words of the verse involve a word-play in the
Hebrew: **'And when a sojourner sojourns with you...'** A
'sojourner' is different from the 'foreigner' of verse 43. The
former has lived in the land with the people of Israel for

some time. He has settled in the land and therefore he has privileges. The sojourner 'as a resident enjoys the rights of assistance, protection, and religious participation. He has the right of gleaning (Lev. 19:10; 23:22), participation in the tithe (Deut. 14:29), the Sabbath year (Lev. 25:6), and the cities of refuge (Num. 35:15).'[45] He could not, however, participate in the Passover unless circumcised.

This verse is for the future. It envisages what was stated back in verse 25, that is, the settlement of the Israelites in the land of milk and honey.

The word for **'circumcised'** is an infinitive absolute in Hebrew. It is being employed here as a legislative, jussive form; in other words, it is volitional, a word of command.[46]

12:49. 'One law shall be for the native and for the sojourner who sojourns in your midst.'

This sentence literally begins with the words: **'One Torah shall be for...'** The term **'Torah'** simply means 'instruction/teaching/law'. In the grammatical construction of the sentence 'one Torah' precedes the verb for the sake of emphasis.

The one law is that circumcision is a requirement for participation in Passover. It applies to the **'native'** Israelite as well as to the **'sojourner'**. Often in the Pentateuch these two terms are used in opposition to one another for the purpose of inclusiveness (Lev. 16:29; Num. 9:14; 15:29).

'One Torah' is a feminine noun qualified by a feminine adjective. However, in this verse it takes a masculine verb. Some would argue that the 'instances in which the gender or number of the following predicate appears to differ from that of the subject are due partly to manifest errors in the text'.[47] That conclusion is probably incorrect. Rather, this 'priority of masculine gender is due in part to the intensely androcentric character of the world of the Hebrew Bible'.[48] It is what grammarians sometimes call 'the prior gender'.

12:50. And all the children of Israel did just as Yahweh commanded Moses and Aaron.

This verse contains verbal reiteration for the purpose of emphasis. It reads, literally, **'All the children of Israel did as Yahweh commanded Moses and Aaron, thus they did.'** The very construction and vocabulary of the verse constitute an expression idiomatic in the book of Exodus (see 7:10; 12:28 and commentary on 7:6). This characteristic style signifies absolute obedience to the Word of God.

12:51. And it came to pass on this very day that Yahweh brought out the children of Israel from the land of Egypt according to their hosts.

See analysis of verses 40-41.

13:1-2. And Yahweh spoke to Moses, saying, 'Consecrate to me every first-born. The first opening of the womb among the children of Israel, whether man or animal, belongs to me.'

A general principle is now stated by direct word of God to Moses. Every first-born male, human or animal, is to be **'consecrated'** to God. This verb literally means 'to set apart'. In this verse it is in the Piel imperative form, so it is a command to put something into action.

Perhaps this activity is a polemic against other ancient cultures of the Near East. Preferential status is known to have been accorded to the first-born son in Nuzi, Assyria, Syria, Babylonia and Palestine.[49] Special treatment and privileges were considered inherent in the position of first-born. In other words, the eldest male is born with certain rights, and thus he is set apart from birth. In this verse we see that the rights of the first-born are not intrinsic, but rather something bestowed by the hand of God.[50]

The first two verses of chapter 13 appear to be out of place. Subsequent verses 3-10 revert to a discussion of

Passover regulations. It is not until verse 11 that the author gives detail to the laws of the first-born. However, there is a significant connection between Passover and the consecration of the first-born. In Egypt, God had destroyed the first-born of the Egyptians, both man and beast; now he redeems Israel's first-born and they belong to him!

13:3. Then Moses said to the people, 'Remember this day on which you came out from Egypt, from the house of slaves, because by a strong hand Yahweh brought you out from this [place]. Yeast shall not be eaten.'

Now begins the third time that Moses gives regulations regarding the Passover.[51] This is an example of repetition for the purpose of emphasis. Passover was the most remarkable day in the history of Israel. It was the birth of a nation no longer under the rod of oppression. *Pesach* symbolizes for the Hebrews the concepts of freedom, deliverance and redemption.

Moses' statement begins with the command to **'remember'**. The Hebrew word is an infinitive absolute which is being used as an emphatic imperative.[52] In such constructions, 'It predominantly expresses divine and/or prophetic commands.'[53]

The land of Egypt is called **'the house of slaves'**. Sarna makes an interesting comment about that nomenclature: 'It may derive from the Egyptian practice of settling the labour gangs in workmen's villages in proximity to the site of the project for which they were conscripted. These villages were wholly enclosed by walls. One such has been uncovered at Deir el-Medinah, near Thebes. It served the labourers engaged in the construction of royal tombs in the Valley of the Kings. To the Israelite conscripts, such a village may have appeared to be a gigantic 'slave house'.[54]

13:4. 'Today, in the month of Abib, you are leaving.'

The month in which the exodus took place is called **'Abib'**. This is a word used earlier of a barley crop being 'in the ear', that is, ripe for harvest (see 9:31). The Palestinian inscription called the Gezer Calendar (from *c.* 925 B.C.) also employs that term for the month of barley harvest.[55] Historically, barley harvest in Palestine occurs during the month of April.

Verse 4 begins with the word **'today'**. The Samaritan Hebrew Pentateuch would rather place it at the end of verse 3, which would then read, 'And no yeast shall be eaten today.' That emendation of the text is unnecessary because 'today' has been used elsewhere in the story precisely for the day of departure (12:41; 13:3).

13:5 'And it will come to pass when Yahweh brings you to the land of the Canaanites and the Hittites and the Amorites and the Hivites and the Jebusites, which he swore to your fathers to give to you, a land flowing with milk and honey, then you are to celebrate this service in this month.'

This is a basic reiteration of the promise of Exodus 3:8,17. God is in the process of fulfilling his purposes that he had earlier given to his people.[56] The only substantive difference between the present verse and the earlier ones is that the group called Perizzites is missing on this occasion. It is really not a problem, however, because the list is being used as a formula and it is unnecessary that every group be included each time it is quoted (see commentary on 3:8).

The words in Hebrew for **'you are to celebrate this service'** are a construction that can be translated literally, 'and you are to serve the service'. Perhaps this is a word-play on verse 3 which calls Egypt 'the house of servants/slaves' (using a variation of the same words as here in verse 5). Again, one of the great issues of the book of Exodus is underscored: the Hebrews are no longer to serve the Egyptians, but now they are to serve Yahweh, and him alone.

13:6. 'Seven days you are to eat unleavened bread, and on the seventh day there will be a feast to Yahweh.'

The Septuagint and the Samaritan Hebrew Pentateuch both read, '*Six* days you shall eat.' Apparently this translation was to keep the number of days in line with Deuteronomy 16:8 which says, **'Six days you shall eat.'** However, elsewhere in the Torah the text stipulates seven days for not eating *mātsāh* (see Lev. 23:6). This discrepancy is really not a problem. The difference simply revolves around whether or not the seventh day is to be included in the stricture against eating leavened bread. Obviously it is (see next verse), and at times that is assumed by the Torah while at other times it is not.

The number seven in Hebrew often symbolizes completeness. Here the Passover reaches its climax or crescendo on the seventh day. It is a festival day in which all the people gather for a sacred assembly (see Deut. 16:8 where the term 'sacred assembly' is used of the Passover event).

13:7. 'Eat unleavened bread seven days. And yeast shall not be seen by you, nor any leaven seen by you in all your borders.'

See commentary on 12:15. The only addition to earlier regulations regarding unleavened bread is that previously the command was to keep yeast out of their homes. Here we see a further directive that prevents it from even being allowed within the **'borders'** of the nation. This term is primarily used in the Old Testament of the outer boundaries of the territory that God gave to Israel in the land of Canaan (e.g., Josh. 12:2; 16:2-8).

13:8. 'You shall tell your son on that day, saying, "[This is] on account of what Yahweh did for me when I came out from Egypt."'

Redemption from Egypt must not only be recounted to children, but must also be explained to them.[57] Here is a simple justification for the celebration of the Passover throughout history: it is to recall what God had done for the Hebrews by rescuing them from Egypt. The catechism need not be more complex than this for children — the answer goes to the very heart of the issue: salvation.

Some grammarians see a textual corruption in the verse because of the use of the telic particle **'on account of/so that/because'** as a relative pronoun.[58] Although such usage is unusual, it is hardly a sign of a need for textual emendation. The verse makes perfectly good sense as it stands.

13:9. 'It shall be for you as a sign on your hand and for a reminder between your eyes, so that the law of Yahweh will be in your mouth — because by a strong hand Yahweh brought you out from Egypt.'

According to Talmudic interpretation this is a reference to the precept of wearing phylacteries,[59] that is, leather straps worn on the arms and head of a worshipper which contain copies of Exodus 13:1-10 and various other passages. Phylacteries are fitted on the person during morning prayers. Evidence for this practice derives from the Second Temple period, there being no confirmation of it from Old Testament times.

The command is probably to be understood metaphorically. Passover is thus to be before the eyes and upon the hands of the Hebrew. It has an ever-present status and significance.

13:10 'You must keep this ordinance according to its time from year to year.'

The final verse of the section enjoins the Hebrews to celebrate the Passover in perpetuity. It literally says they should keep the feast **'from days to days'**. On the last word is a directional ה in Hebrew, and in this instance 'The particle can mark forward progression through time.'[60] (Compare a similar usage in Judges 11:40.)

Application

In this section we are introduced for the first time to the concept of the first-born of Israel having been set apart, or consecrated, to God. They belong to him because he spared them in Egypt when he destroyed the first-born of the Egyptians (see discussion below in verses 10-16).

In the New Testament Jesus, Mary's first-born son, is set apart, or sanctified, according to the commands laid down in Exodus: 'And when the days for their purification according to the law of Moses were completed, they brought him up to Jerusalem to present him to the Lord (as it is written in the Law of the Lord, "Every first-born male that opens the womb shall be called holy to the Lord"), and to offer a sacrifice according to what was said in the Law of the Lord' (Luke 2:22-24). Luke even quotes Exodus 13:2 in his description. Elsewhere Christ is called 'the first-born among many brethren' (Rom. 8:29).

Also in the New Testament, believers are accounted as first-born by virtue of their union with Christ. It is the church of the first-born that is set apart to God (Heb. 12:23). In fact, the name the New Testament writers often give to Christians is 'saints' (e.g., Rom. 1:7; 1 Cor. 1:2; Eph. 1:1). That word in Greek literally means 'the set-apart ones'. Thus, Christians are in a special, set-apart relationship with the Creator. We are the first-born of Israel.

Law of the first-born (Exodus 13:11-16)

This passage provides an explanation of the command of verse 2 that all the first-born in Israel, whether man or beast, are to be consecrated to Yahweh. In addition, it describes the means by which the first-born are redeemed from Yahweh; that is, how they are ransomed from him. Rationale for this peculiar ritual is also given by the author.

13:11-12. 'And it shall be when Yahweh brings you to the land of the Canaanites which he swore to you and to your fathers, and he gives it to you, then you shall give over every first-born of the womb to Yahweh and every first offspring of animals which belong to you; the males belong to Yahweh.'

Verse 11 is a reiteration of verse 5. These are laws for the future of the people of Israel as they reside in the land of Canaan.

Verse 12 literally begins with: **'And you shall pass over every first-born of the womb to Yahweh.'** The verb 'to pass over' is employed in surrounding chapters regarding the feast and celebration of Passover (12:13,23). So here we have a verbal word-play: as Yahweh passed over the Hebrews during the tenth plague, the Hebrews are now to pass over their first-born to him.

The verb 'to pass over' is also a commentary on pagan child sacrifice. Pagans of the ancient Near East would take a child and pass him over/through the fire as a form of devotion and sacrifice (Deut. 18:10; 2 Kings 16:3). Yahweh does not require such barbarism. He wants the first-born set apart and devoted to his service. Thus the Israelites are not to pass over their first-born in the fire, but pass them over to the Lord.

This law applies to both humans and animals. The terms for **'first-born'** and **'males'** are unusual words in Hebrew that include the offspring of both.

13:13. 'Redeem every first-born donkey with a lamb; but if you do not redeem [it], then you shall break its neck. Redeem every first-born male among your sons.'

Neither donkeys nor human children will be sacrificed to Yahweh; instead they will be redeemed — that is, bought back for a price. In other words, God is permitting a substitutionary payment in place of the first-born of donkeys and humans. The only animal mentioned as being in need of redemption is the **'donkey'**, or male ass. Perhaps the reason for this is that the donkey was the only unclean domestic animal used by the Hebrews in Egypt.[61] The value of that animal for transportation or for packing is obvious, and so God allowed for its redemption by the substitution of a clean animal, namely, a lamb.[62]

If, however, a man does not want to substitute a lamb for his donkey, then he must kill the donkey by breaking its neck. Since man is depriving God of his due, then man is denied use of the animal. Breaking the donkey's neck instead of killing it with a knife or by some other means is probably in order to divorce it from any sacrificial act or intent.

The first-born of man is also to be redeemed. No mode of redemption or price to be paid is given here. Later, in Numbers 18:16, the valuation is provided: it is to be five shekels, according to the shekel of the sanctuary.

A connection is made between this redemptive act and the act of deliverance of the people from Egypt by the use of the verb 'to redeem'. It is a form used throughout the Bible to refer to God's saving act in Egypt (see, for example, Deut. 7:8; 13:5).

13:14. 'And it will come to pass in days to come, when your son asks you, saying, "What is this?" that you shall say to him, "With a strong hand Yahweh brought us out from Egypt, from the house of slaves."'

Children will be curious regarding the singular ritual associated with the redemption of the first-born. It must be explained to them (see comment on verse 8). Once again, the importance of the didactic value of the exodus event is underscored.

The beginning of an answer to the question is stated. The law of redemption is tied to the deliverance of the Hebrews out of Egypt by the power of Yahweh. The following two verses will spell out clearly the precise relationship between the two events.

'In days to come' is literally 'tomorrow'. The Hebrew can bear the idea of an indefinite future time period (see, for example, Deut. 6:20).

13:15. 'And it came to pass when Pharaoh was stubborn about sending us out that Yahweh killed all the first-born in the land of Egypt, from the first-born of man to the first-born of animals. Therefore, I sacrifice to Yahweh every first-born of the womb, the males, but every first-born of my sons I will redeem.'

The answer to the child's question from verse 14 continues. The principal reason for the redemption of first-born humans and animals is because God had killed the first-born of mankind and animals in Egypt. God had spared the first-born of the Hebrews, so now they belong to him.

The clause, **'This is why I sacrifice to the LORD'** is actually centred on a participial form which denotes 'a durative circumstance involving repeated actions'.[63] In other words, because of the events in Egypt, Israel throughout her history is continually to perform the redemption of the first-born.

13:16. 'And it shall be as a sign upon your hand and as a symbol between your eyes, because by a strong hand Yahweh brought us out from Egypt.'

The devotion and consecration of the first-born constitute a physical sign, or symbol, of God's redemptive act of rescuing Israel from Egypt. As the celebration of Passover is to serve as a pointer to the exodus (13:9), so too is the rite of redemption of the first-born (see commentary and bibliography relating to 13:9).

A major distinction between verse 9 and the present one is the replacement of the term 'reminder' (used in the earlier verse) with the word **'symbol'**. The latter term in Hebrew probably means 'bands/frontlets' (see its use also in Deut. 6:8; 11:18). Apparently it is a physical object that is being used figuratively in the sense of perpetual remembrance. Later Jews interpreted it literally, and thus came about the custom of wearing phylacteries.

Application

The redemption of the first-born in Israel by the blood of a lamb is a pointer to the fact that the Christian has been saved by the blood of Christ. The latter's work is also one of a substitutionary payment as he acts as a sacrificial lamb. In 1 Peter 1:18-19, the apostle, speaking to the church, comments: '...knowing that you were not redeemed with perishable things like silver and gold from your futile way of life inherited from your forefathers, but with precious blood, as of a lamb unblemished and spotless, the blood of Christ'. The author of the epistle to the Hebrews speaks of the Messiah's work in a similar fashion: 'and not through the blood of goats and calves, but through his own blood, he [Jesus Christ] entered the holy place once for all, having obtained eternal redemption' (Heb. 9:2).

It should further be observed that the act of redeeming the first-born in Israel was a mere shadow of the work of Christ. The result of the tenth plague was a deliverance of Israel that was physical, earthly and temporal. The redemptive work of Christ in his death is much greater: it is also eternal and spiritual. Thus, the Old Testament act of redemption reaches its apex and its fulfilment in the work of the great Redeemer in the New Testament.

6. Salvation at the sea

Exodus 13:17 - 15:21

God as guide (Exodus 13:17-22)

Here we witness the Israelites fleeing from Egypt. They are not leaving in great fear, however. The style of this paragraph is poetic and elevated.[1] It demonstrates the joy and passion with which the Hebrews left Egypt, the land of death and darkness — and why not? God was guiding them in his appearances as a pillar of fire and a pillar of cloud; it was the Lord who was leading this expedition and there was no room for fear.

13:17. And it came to pass when Pharaoh sent forth the people, that God did not lead them by way of the land of the Philistines, even though it was near, because God said, 'Lest the people change their minds when they see war, and they return to Egypt.'

The writer returns to a description of the travel itinerary of the Hebrews in their escape from Egypt. He explains, firstly, that God did not lead them to the promised land by the shortest route possible. That most direct route would have been the *Via Maris* (the Way of the Sea) that extends from the Nile river across the northern Sinai into the coastal plain of Palestine. This was an extensively travelled

road in ancient times, and was probably the most commonly used route from Egypt to Asia.

An attempted escape through northern Sinai would
have placed the Hebrews in harm's way because the
primary roads in that region were guarded by a series of
Egyptian forts.[2] God was well aware of the character of the
Israelites, that they would flee at the first sign of danger
and war. They would simply prefer to return to Egypt and
its oppression rather than face the hazards of battle
(consider Num. 14:1-4 where God's assessment is shown
to be correct).

A play on words is evident in two of the major verbs of
the verse. The verb for God's 'leading' them is *nāhām*. The
verb used for the Hebrews' changing their minds is *yĭnnā-
hēm*. Although the two verbs derive from different roots,
here they look and sound alike. The reason for it is perhaps to underscore the contrast between God's leading
and Israel's desire to go elsewhere — i.e., back to Egypt.

13:18. **So God led the people by the way of the wilderness to
the Red Sea, and by divisions the children of Israel went up
from the land of Egypt.**

God guides the people in a more south-easterly direction
by a desert road towards the Red Sea (Hebrew, *yām sûph*).
The identification of the latter body of water has been
much disputed. Since I have dealt with the issue elsewhere at length, I will quote from that study:

> Throughout the parallel accounts of the
> crossing, the water is often referred to as the *yām
> sûph* (Exod. 15:4; Deut. 11:4; Josh. 2:10; 4:23;
> 24:6; Ps. 106:7, 9, 22; 136:13,15). Many modern
> scholars translate *yām sûph* as 'Sea of
> Reeds/Papyrus' because the term *sûph* is used in
> the Old Testament to refer to the reeds growing
> along the side of the Nile River (see Exod. 2:3).

Furthermore, we are told that *sûph* may in fact be related to the Egyptian word *ṭwf(y)*, 'marsh plant'.[3] Since papyrus does not grow along the Red Sea/Gulf of Suez, scholars conclude that the *yām sûph* is one of the marshy lakes in the eastern delta region north of the Red Sea.[4]

Recent studies by Bernard Batto have demonstrated, however, that this common view cannot be sustained by the evidence, but in fact *yām sûph* does refer to the Red Sea/Gulf of Suez.[5] In the first place, every certain reference to *yām sûph* in the Bible refers to the Red Sea or its northern extensions in the Gulfs of Aqaba and Suez (e.g., 1 Kings 9:26; Jer. 49:21). Second, the parallel drawn between Egyptian *p3-ṭwfy* and *yām sûph* is not without its problems. Whereas *yām sûph* refers to a body of water, that is not true of *p3-ṭwfy*. Egyptian *p3* is a demonstrative pronoun meaning 'the'. The term *ṭwfy* is properly translated 'papyrus, papyrus thicket', and sometimes designated a region or district where papyrus grows. Nowhere in Egyptian texts does *p3-ṭwfy* refer to a body of water; it means 'the land/area of papyrus'.

Batto has also demonstrated that the word *sûph* in Hebrew is not related to the Egyptian *ṭwfy*, but derives instead from the Semitic root *sôph*, which means 'end'. Therefore the Hebrew place-name *yām sûph*, literally meaning 'the sea of the end', refers to the waters to the far south, the waters at the end of the land. And that, of course, would be the Red Sea.[6]

Numerous ancient and modern translations (such as the Targums and the Vulgate) say that the Hebrews left Egypt 'armed' or 'equipped for battle'. The meaning of the Hebrew term is uncertain, however. The Septuagint translators render it 'the fifth generation'. It seems to be a derivative of the number five, and it may possibly refer to an army in five parts/divisions. Thus the word may indicate that the Hebrews were leaving Egypt not necessarily in a military posture, but rather in an orderly, military-like fashion. They were well organized in their departure from Egypt.

13:19. And Moses took the bones of Joseph with him because he made the children of Israel truly swear, saying, 'God will certainly visit you, and you will bring up my bones from this [place] with you.'

Moses performs a curious act. He retrieves and takes the embalmed body of Joseph to go up with the Hebrews to the promised land. This incident is in fulfilment of a promise the Hebrews of earlier generations had made to the patriarch Joseph — in fact, the author of Exodus quotes Genesis 50:25 word for word. It is related later that the body of Joseph was eventually buried in Shechem in Palestine (see Josh. 24:32).

13:20. And they journeyed from Succoth, and they camped at Etham on the edge of the wilderness.

An Egyptian text, called *Papyrus Anastasi V*, from the thirteenth century B.C., may be helpful in determining the route out of Egypt taken by the Hebrews. The text is in the form of a letter written by a soldier from a place called Tjeku. He tells of his pursuit of two slaves fleeing from Egypt to the wilderness. The soldier mentions three place-names: 'I reached the enclosure wall of Tjeku on the third month of the third season ... to the south... When I reached *htm*, they told me that the scout had come from the desert [saying that] they had passed the walled place north of Migdol.'[7] Tjeku has already been identified as Succoth (see 12:37). The slaves headed south from Succoth to *htm*, which perhaps corresponds to the biblical

Etham (it is phonetically possible). They then fled to Migdol, which appears to be on the fringe of the desert. Migdol is mentioned in Exodus 14:2 as a location near which Israel camped. The order of this escape — Succoth-Etham-Migdol — is similar to the account of the Israelites' departure recorded in Numbers 33:6-7: 'And they journeyed from Succoth, and camped in Etham, which is on the edge of the wilderness. And they journeyed from Etham, and turned back to Pi-hahiroth, which faces Baal-zephon; and they camped before Migdol.' The Egyptian papyrus raises the possibility that the Israelites fled from Egypt on a common escape route into the wilderness.

In any event, the Hebrews are now at the gate of freedom, arriving at the final town or outpost before escape into the wilderness. Nothing appears to be standing in the way of their deliverance.

13:21. And Yahweh was going before them by day as a pillar of cloud to lead them on the way, and by night as a pillar of fire to give light to them, in order to travel by day and by night.

Moses now presents Yahweh in theophany. In the Old Testament, the appearance of Yahweh arrives in many forms: at times he appears as a man (e.g., Gen. 18:1-33) or in a bush (Exod. 3:1-6).[8] Often he would appear as a glory cloud, called the Shekinah glory by some writers.[9] The glory cloud was a visible symbol of God's presence among his people.

In the present story we see Yahweh in a double theophany. It is, as Kline remarks, a 'double-columned cloud-and-fire revelation of the Glory-Spirit at the exodus'.[10] The reason for the two theophanies is clear: it is so that Yahweh would be with his people and lead them **'by day'** and **'by night'**. The use of the two opposites underscores the all-inclusive nature of God's presence with Israel.

Both occurrences of the word **'pillar'** are introduced by a form of the preposition *beth*. Here it is probably used as a *beth essentiae*, meaning 'as' rather than 'in'.[11] This grammatical point accentuates the fact that both the cloud and the fire are no more nor less than theophanies.

For the Hebrews these manifestations of God were no small thing. Although they were traversing unknown territory they had no reason to fear. Yahweh **'was going before them'**, guiding, directing and leading them.

13:22. He did not take away the pillar of cloud by day nor the pillar of fire by night from before the people.

Opening the verse are the words, **'He did not re-move/take away...'** The subject is clearly Yahweh from verse 21. The verb is in the third person masculine singular, a Hiphil causative stem. The point is that Yahweh is the one who appeared as the cloud and fire, and he is the one who controlled and decided the length of time that these manifestations were to appear. Obviously they were constantly before the people because God had not removed them.

Application

How often God does not lead his people by what they perceive to be the easiest and shortest way! He knows our hearts, that they would falter in times of danger. Oh, how like the Israelites we are! Thus God will frequently take us by the long road in many things. In that way, he protects us from danger and destruction. His leading also has a didactic purpose, to teach us to rely upon him and his timing. We think we know best: 'There is a way which seems right to a man, but its end is the way of death' (Prov. 14:12).

But, even today, God is always with his people. In the barren wilderness, God travelled with the Hebrews by day and by night as a pillar of fire and a pillar of cloud. He is also with us even in times of distress, turmoil and suffering. Many are the saints who had a clear perception of the presence of the Almighty during such periods of danger.

Pharaoh as pursuer (Exodus 14:1-12)

At the close of chapter 13 we see the Israelites quickly fleeing from Egypt. They have reached the very edge of the wilderness and are about to enter it for their final escape from the land of death to go to the land of promise. They are carrying Joseph's bones with them as a reminder that the promise of the exodus event in Genesis 50 has now been fulfilled. In addition, God is leading them in a pillar of cloud by day and a pillar of fire by night. The Hebrews have all the evidence they need to believe that God is protecting them and that they will succeed in their escape from Egypt. How soon that assurance is shattered! God is about to place Israel back into the fiery furnace, into the raging crucible!

14:1-2. And Yahweh spoke to Moses, saying, 'Speak to the children of Israel that they turn back and camp in front of Pi Hahiroth, between Migdol and the sea. You shall camp in front of Baal Zephon, opposite it, near the sea.'

Israel is on the brink of escape into the wilderness.[12] But God orders the people to **'turn back'**. Instead of breaking out of the land of death, God causes the Hebrews to reverse their course. He then commands them to encamp with their backs to the sea, and so it appears that they have no escape route out of Egypt. They are sitting ducks.

Locations of the three sites mentioned are uncertain. Migdol is a term of Semitic origin meaning 'tower/fortress'.[13] It was borrowed by the Egyptians during the New Kingdom period and used as a place name for various sites.[14] A network of Egyptian outposts lined the eastern border of Egypt during the New Kingdom, and any one of them could have gone by the name of Migdol.

Three major proposals have been proffered regarding the location of Baal-zephon. It has been placed at Tell Daphneh, about ten miles west of el-Qantara;[15] in the vicinity of the Bitter Lakes, about twelve miles south-east of Tell el-Maskhuta;[16] and at the head of the Gulf of Suez on the Red Sea.[17] Its location cannot be identified with any certainty.

A clue to the location of Pi-hahiroth is the meaning of its name. It appears to be a Hebraized form of the original Akkadian *Pi-hiriti*, which literally means 'the mouth or opening of the canal'.[18] The eastern delta has a defensive canal from the Mediterranean Sea to at least the area of the Bitter Lakes and this may have extended further south during the period of the New Kingdom.[19] Pi-hahiroth may therefore have been an opening or break in the canal system that allowed entrance into the wilderness of the Sinai Peninsula.[20]

14:3. 'And Pharaoh will say of the children of Israel, "They are wandering in confusion in the land; the wilderness has closed them in."'

The position of the Hebrews is so poor strategically that when Pharaoh is told where they are camping he will think their situation to be utterly hopeless. In fact, he will be vocal about the matter: the verse begins, **'And Pharaoh will say...'** The monarch of Egypt will thus conclude that he has the utmost advantage and he will desire to crush Israel.

The Hebrew verb for **'wandering in confusion'**, or 'aimlessly', is used elsewhere in the Old Testament of cattle that roam to and fro not knowing where they are headed (see Joel 1:18).

The first words of Pharaoh begin with a *lamed* preposition, which literally means, **'of the children of Israel'**. However, it is probably an emphatic use of *lamed* that can be translated 'indeed',[21] so that the sentence reads, 'Indeed the children of Israel are wandering aimlessly!' The emphasis demonstrates Pharaoh's excitement over the prospects he now has of crushing Israel.

14:4. 'And I will harden Pharaoh's heart that he will pursue after them. And I will be glorified in Pharaoh and in all his army. And the Egyptians will know that I am Yahweh.' And they did so.

To add fuel to the fire, God says he will then harden Pharaoh's heart so that the King of Egypt will chase after the Hebrews. The verb **'pursue'** in Hebrew is normally used in the Old Testament of a man or a group pursuing others for revenge. And, thus, it sometimes bears the connotation of 'persecution'.[22]

Why did God place the chosen people in such treacherous and trying circumstances? Certainly Yahweh could have conducted Israel far beyond the reach of Pharaoh and his army, even before the latter had set out from Egypt. Why did he not do that? The answer is not cryptic but crystal clear: God desired to display his power in the salvation of his people so that he would be greatly glorified.

Ironically, the word for God's glory in this verse is *kābēd*, which, as we have seen earlier, literally means 'heavy/weighty'. The same word is employed throughout the Exodus account to describe the state of Pharaoh's heart (see 7:14). Pharaoh's heart is 'heavy' so that 'heaviness' would be given to Yahweh!

In any event, the plight of Israel appears, in human terms, to be grave. The Egyptians have them trapped with their backs to the sea. Escape seems to be out of the question. Pharaoh's evil object is at the very point of attainment. On a higher level, however, God is controlling this event to his own end and glory. Yes, Israel is placed in the fiery furnace, but man's extremity is God's opportunity. The sovereignty of God is the point of this lesson: it is he who puts Israel in a dire situation, and it is he who hardens Pharaoh's heart. He is directing the scene. We are witnessing a great maestro conducting a grand symphony!

14:5. When it was reported to the King of Egypt that the people had fled, the heart of Pharaoh and his servants turned against the people, and they said, 'What is this we have done, that we have sent forth Israel from our service?'

The setting of the story now changes, reverting to the scene of the Egyptian palace. Pharaoh is told by his counsellors that the Hebrews are trying to flee Egypt, and that they are curiously entrapped by the sea. The first response of the king (and his courtiers) is, literally, that his **'heart changed/turned back'** (the verb is a Niphal passive). This is the same verb, in the same form, that was employed in the story of the rod changing to a serpent (7:15). Pharaoh's heart, which had been softened to allow Israel to leave Egypt, now returns to its hardened state.

The Egyptian leaders realize that they have lost a major source of cheap labour. With all the colossal building programmes in Egypt during the New Kingdom period, this loss was no small thing. The Ramesside pharaohs constructed buildings and monuments in the delta by employing much foreign labour, most of which consisted of slaves. The Egyptian document *Papyrus Leiden 348* informs us that a group called the *'apiru* were engaged in 'hauling stones to the great pylon' of one of Pi-Rameses' temples.[23] The *'apiru* are not to be equated with the Hebrews, although the Israelites may have constituted a segment of that social group. In any event, Egypt could not afford to forfeit such a large workforce.

14:6. So he made ready his chariot, and he took his people with him.

A literal translation of the verse is: '**And he harnessed** [or "hitched"] **his chariot and his people he took with him.**' The verb *'āsār* ('to harness') is a common Old Testament term meaning to prepare a chariot for action (see Gen. 46:29; 2 Kings 9:21). The word for **'chariot'** is often used collectively in the Bible signifying 'chariotry', or 'force of war chariots'.[24] It is likely that Pharaoh was responding to Israel's attempted escape by amassing his chariot force to recapture the Hebrews.

'People' in Hebrew sometimes refers to a group bearing arms, that is, an army (1 Sam. 11:11; 1 Kings 20:10). This term perhaps relates to groups of foot-soldiers gathered to pursue Israel (see 14:9). Thus Pharaoh answers Israel's flight by mustering a significant and substantial military force — made up of cavalry and foot troops — in order to hunt down the people of God.

14:7. And he took six hundred chosen chariots, and all the chariots of Egypt, and officers over all of it.

A description of the make-up of the chariot force is now provided. Pharaoh, apparently at the head of one grouping, assembles **'six hundred chosen chariots'**. According to the Old Testament, six hundred was a standard military unit (Judg. 18:11,16,17; 1 Sam. 13:15; 14:2).

The king also gathered all the remaining chariots of Egypt, and he placed **'officers over all of it'**. The word for 'officer' is related to the term for the number three. Based upon that relationship, some scholars have suggested that the 'officer' is 'best explained as *third* man [in the chariot]'.[25] Thus in each chariot there would be three men, one of whom served as officer in command of the chariot. This is unlikely, however. The 'officer' was probably an adjutant to Pharaoh, one who was 'of the third rank'.[26] Consequently, officers of the third rank supervised the chariots of Egypt, but they were not in each and every chariot.

The reason why these details of the Egyptian chariots are given is to underscore the hopeless situation of the Israelites. Probably the greatest fighting force in the world was preparing to pursue them. Many of their attackers would come speedily in chariots. The Hebrews were on foot and locked in by the Red Sea. What chance did they have?

14:8. And Yahweh hardened the heart of Pharaoh, the King of Egypt, so that he would pursue after the children of Israel, who were going out boldly.

God further providentially sets the scene by hardening the heart of the Egyptian king so that he would pursue the Hebrews. This action is in fulfilment of the prophecy that Yahweh had spoken in verse 4. For commentary on the use of the word **'hardened'**, see 4:21.

The end of the verse is normally understood to describe the Israelites' demeanour as they left Egypt as being, literally, **'with a high hand'**. This is a Hebrew idiom that many believe means 'in defiance' (see Num. 15:30) or 'in triumph' (see Deut. 32:27). It is a metaphor 'drawn from the depiction of ancient Near-Eastern gods menacingly brandishing a weapon in the upraised right hand'.[27] Thus, many commentators argue that Israel was leaving Egypt in great and complete confidence.

I would suggest, on the other hand, that perhaps the final clause is not speaking of the attitude of the Hebrews at all. Rather, the phrase may be expressing the *means by which* Israel was departing from Egypt. If the preposition is understood to be a *beth* of instrumentation, then the clause reads, **'who were going out *by* a high/mighty hand'**. In other words, the verse is speaking of Yahweh's power and not Israel's defiance. In support of this idea is the fact that the idiom 'high hand' is used in the Old Testament of God's power (see Isa. 26:11; Ps. 89:13).

14:9. So the Egyptians pursued after them, and they overtook them camping near the sea — all the horses and
chariots of Pharaoh, his cavalry and his army — near Pi
Hahiroth in front of Baal Zephon.

The Israelites were encamped by the sea. The Hebrew verb
for 'to camp' bears the basic meaning of 'to bend', or
'curve', and when it is applied to settlement areas, it may
perhaps reflect the circular configuration of an encampment. Recent studies by Israel Finkelstein have demonstrated that the Hebrews probably camped in an elliptical
pattern at the sea and during the wilderness wanderings.[28]
Later, the Israelites designed their first settlements in
Canaan in an ovate form.

Some scholars have been suspicious of references to
horsemanship and chariots in the story, many believing
that those arts were late in coming to Egypt. In reality,
Egypt is well known for its mastery of equestrian practices
as early as the beginning of the Eighteenth Dynasty (c.
1550 B.C.).[29] Any doubt regarding the accuracy of the
biblical text on this point is unwarranted.

Pharaoh's cavalry, chariots and foot troops **'overtook'**
the Hebrews by the sea. This verb does not mean there
was any direct physical contact, but it signifies that the
Egyptians 'reached/caught up with' the Hebrews.[30]

14:10. As Pharaoh drew near, the children of Israel lifted
their eyes, and behold the Egyptians were marching after
them. And they were very afraid, and the children of Israel
cried out to Yahweh.

The Israelites, on foot, encamped by the sea with no
means of escape, saw Pharaoh approaching from a distance. The Egyptians were drawing near with evil intent.
What was perhaps the most powerful military force of the
time was nipping at the heels of God's people. In front of
them lay the sea, and behind them the army of darkness

was closing in. From a human perspective, the situation appeared bleak and grim — no human power could save them. What chance did they have? What were they to do?

This entire scene is dominated by Pharaoh — only he is mentioned as drawing near to the Hebrews. Pharaoh is commonly depicted as the central figure of battle scenes in Egyptian representations and designs. The Egyptians believed that in war the 'acts of the king alone count; he is invincible, nay, unassailable'; '[No] man can hope to resist the divine ruler and survive,' and 'It is no mere assertion that so many are powerless against the single figure of Pharaoh.'[31]

Israel's response was swift and spontaneous: **'They were very afraid.'** And then they reacted properly by **'[crying] out to Yahweh'**. Earlier they had cried out to Elohim (2:23), and some of them had even cried out to Pharaoh because of oppression (5:15). But now they pleaded for Yahweh, the God of their salvation, to intervene.

14:11. And they said to Moses, 'Were there no graves in Egypt that you brought us to die in the wilderness? What is this you have done to us, to bring us out of Egypt?'

Note the irony of this verse. The phrase **'no graves in Egypt'** borders on the humorous because Egypt was the land known for its graves, death and preoccupation with the afterlife.

With their sarcastic remarks the Israelites display panic and urgency. Their opening question begins with a double negative: the two negatives are *'en* and *b'lî*. Gesenius comments that 'Two negatives in the same sentence do not neutralize each other but make the negation the more emphatic... This especially applies to the compounds formed by the union of *'en* or *b'lî.*'[32]

Murmuring becomes a dominant negative theme in the wilderness wanderings (Exod. 15:23-26; 16:2-3; 17:2-3;

etc.).[33] Moses, the author of the Torah, sees it as the antithesis of Yahweh's grace and favour to the people; the alternation of Yahweh's long-suffering patience with Israel's complaints and demands is all too obvious.[34]

14:12. 'Was this not what we told you in Egypt, saying, "Leave us alone so that we might serve the Egyptians"? Because it would have been better for us to serve the Egyptians than for us to die in the wilderness.'

The Hebrews now recount what they supposedly said to Moses while they were still in Egypt. No record exists in the earlier parts of Exodus that would confirm such a conversation. However, there is little doubt that the people of God were reluctant to leave Egypt: 'So Moses spoke thus to the sons of Israel, but they did not listen to Moses on account of their despondency and cruel bondage' (6:9).

Verse 12 constitutes treasonable words. The Israelites desire to deny Yahweh's deliverance and salvation! And, more to the point, they announce that they would rather serve the Egyptians than Yahweh (see commentary on 8:1).

Application

We may well feel disposed to judge Israel at the sea, and not be able to account for her lack of faith in the trial. However, the more we know of our own lack of resolve and our own cowardice, the more we shall see how like the Israelites we are!

We must be aware of the sovereignty of God in all things. We too frequently lose sight of this great truth, and the consequence is that our hearts give way in time of trial. If we could only look upon each of our trials and persecutions as an occasion for God to be more greatly honoured and glorified, it would certainly enable us to endure any crisis. Thus, when we are put in the fiery furnace it is God who wills us there, and we can persevere because of him: 'Who shall separate from the love of Christ? Shall tribulation, or distress, or persecution, or famine, or nakedness, or peril, or sword? Just as it is written, "For your sake we are being put to death all day long, we were considered as sheep to be slaughtered." But in all these things we are more than conquerors through him who loved us' (Rom. 8:35-37).

Separation of the sea (Exodus 14:13-31)

This next paragraph relates the actual event of the dividing of the Red Sea. It tells of the destruction of the Egyptian army, one that was so significant that Egypt was not again a force to be reckoned with by Israel until after the death of Solomon (the reign of Pharaoh Shishak in Egypt). It also gleefully describes the salvation of the people of God, and how they finally became free of the Egyptian oppression.

The Red Sea crossing is the salient incident in the history of Israel. It left a striking and lasting impression upon the later writers of the Old Testament (see, for example, Ps. 78:13; 106:9-10; Isa. 50:2; 51:10; 63:12). Deliverance at the sea was so important that it came to be viewed as a paradigm for later salvation events in the life of Israel, such as the return from Babylonian captivity (see Zech. 10:10-11).

14:13. And Moses said to the people, 'Do not be afraid! Take a stand! And watch the salvation of Yahweh which he does for you today. For the Egyptians whom you see today, you will not see them again — not ever.'

Moses' reply to the people's complaints is somewhat harsh. He begins with a volitional statement: **'Do not fear!'** The negative followed by an imperfect verb 'constitutes the negative imperative' in Hebrew. True imperatives cannot be preceded by a negative particle.[35] Therefore, what we have here is the strongest possible form of expressing negation in the Hebrew language. It is followed by two imperatives: **'Stand!'** and **'See!'** Moses is ignoring, and refusing to sanction, the murmurings of Israel.

The prophet is calling the Israelites to 'take a stand'. The verb 'to stand' is in the Hithpael pattern, indicating its reflexive nature. It is best understood as signifying, 'taking one's stand/holding one's ground/stationing oneself'.[36] Moses is probably telling the people to choose with whom they stand — Yahweh or Pharaoh? How long will they limp between two opinions?

It is enlightening that the Hebrews are called merely to 'see' the salvation of Yahweh. They have nothing to contribute. They are spectators. Salvation is by God's power, by his grace alone.

14:14. 'Yahweh will wage war for you, and you shall be quiet.'

This short and simple statement goes to the very heart of the Red Sea event. First, it says, **'Yahweh will wage war for you.'** God is the one who is going forth to battle, and to face Pharaoh of Egypt, with his claims to divine status. As Pharaoh dominates the military might of Egypt (14:8), so Yahweh is the sole character representing Israel's military prowess. When Moses praises God for his work at the Red Sea in the next chapter, he declares, 'Yahweh is a man of war!'[37]

In contrast, Moses commands the Israelites, literally, **'... but you, you shall be quiet.'** This declaration is accentuated by the inclusion of the second person masculine plural independent personal pronoun, **'you'**. Again, the inability of the people to help in their deliverance is underscored. Yahweh will act; Israel will watch and remain silent.

14:15. And Yahweh said to Moses, 'Why do you cry out to me? Speak to the children of Israel that they should go forward.'

The Syriac Old Testament adds, by way of introduction to the verse, the clause, 'And Moses cried out to Yahweh.' Its translators were trying to solve the problem of God's confronting Moses about crying out, although he apparently had nothing to do with it (see 14:10). The proper solution is to understand that Moses is being addressed by God as the mediator of the covenant, the representative of the people.

This interrogative normally means 'What?' But in a few instances, such as the present, it means 'Why?' (see, for example, 2 Kings 7:3).

The time for pleading and prayer is over. The time for action has arrived. Moses is to command (**'Speak'** is a Piel imperative) the Hebrews to **'set out'**.

14:16. 'Lift up your staff and stretch your hand over the sea and divide it. And the children of Israel shall go in the midst of the sea on dry ground.'

In spite of Israel's unbelief, God orders Moses to stretch out his hand (apparently with the rod of God in it) over the Red Sea in order to divide it. It is essentially the same command God had given in the opening plague (see comment on 7:19). On that earlier occasion, the miracle had worked primarily as a curse upon Egypt. Here, as we shall see throughout the passage, it serves as both blessing and curse.

The term for **'dry ground'** refers to something which is 'dry, withered, without moisture, drained'.[38] In Scripture, it is the exact opposite of, or contrast to, to the sea. In the creation account, for instance, the separation of the **'dry ground'** on the third day (Gen. 1:9) is in antithesis to the waters that are gathered into one place.

Yahweh's power as the source of this miracle is confirmed by the later prophets, such as Isaiah, who says:

Was it not you who dried up the sea
the waters of the great deep;
who made the depths of the sea a pathway
for the redeemed to cross over?

                                   (Isa. 51:10; cf. 63:12).

14:17. 'And, behold, I am hardening the heart of the Egyptians that they might go in after them. And I will be glorified in Pharaoh and in all his army, in his chariots and in his cavalry.'

God's role as the source and engineer of the scene at the Red Sea is emphasized at the outset of this verse. It begins with an independent personal pronoun followed by a demonstrative particle with a first person singular suffix: **'And I, behold I'**. God is the subject and main character of the Red Sea episode!

The verb **'I am hardening'** is actually a Piel participle being used predicatively. In that form it reflects a continuous exercise of action.[39] The construction signifies an action in process: **'And I, behold I, am hardening the hearts of the Egyptians.'** The verb is the same word used in verses 4 and 8 (and elsewhere) of God hardening Pharaoh's heart. Now Yahweh stiffens the resolve of the entire Egyptian army to chase the Hebrews into the sea.

The second half of the verse is dominated by four instances of the preposition *beth* being used to convey instrumentality. It literally reads, **'I will be glorified** *[kābēd]* **by Pharaoh, by his army, by his chariots and by his cavalry.'** This is a statement of the ultimate purpose and significance of the Red Sea incident.

14:18. 'And the Egyptians will know that I am Yahweh when I am glorified in Pharaoh, in his chariots, and in his cavalry.'

What ended verse 17 is now repeated in verse 18. The principal aim of the event at the Red Sea is the glorification of Yahweh and the recognition of his sovereignty over all. This has been the theme of the book of Exodus (see 7:5,17; 8:19,22; 10:2; 14:4,18,25).

14:19-20. Then the angel of God who had been going before the camp of Israel travelled and went behind them; and the pillar of cloud travelling in front of them stood behind them. And it came between the camp of Egypt and the camp of Israel. And there was the cloud with the darkness and it gave light to the night. And one did not come near the other all night.

Yahweh now acts to protect his people. First, the angel of God, who had been leading the Israelites in their escape, moves between God's people and the Egyptians. It may be that the angel of God poses in a military stance, as he does in Numbers 22:22-23,31-32. This is the same figure who appeared in the burning bush in Exodus 3:2. There he spoke and acted as if he was God. (The suggestion has already been made that perhaps this person is a pre-incarnate appearance of the Messiah — see commentary on 3:2).

The second event is that the pillar of cloud also moves to stand between Israel and Egypt. This is the theophany of Yahweh that leads Israel out of Egypt into the wilderness (13:21-22). It is the Shekinah glory by which God often makes his presence known to his people (19:9; 33:9-10).

Verse 20 expresses the work of the cloud that night to bring both blessing and curse. One side of the cloud brought light; the other side gave darkness.[40] The Egyptians were clothed in darkness, as they had been during the ninth plague; Pharaoh, the incarnation of the sun-god Ra, could not bring light to his people. But the Hebrews were bathed in the light of the pillar. Symbolically, one represents the children of darkness, and the other the children of light.[41]

14:21. Then Moses stretched out his hand over the sea, and Yahweh caused the sea to go back all night with a strong east wind. And he turned the sea into dry land. And the waters were divided.

Moses obeyed God's command of verse 16 and stretched his hand out over the sea. Then, Yahweh, literally, **'caused the sea to retire/go back'** (Hiphil causative).[42] And the Lord accomplished this feat by using **'a strong east wind'** (note the *beth* used here to convey instrumentality, i.e. 'by'). The miracle is not instantaneous, however; it takes **'all night'**.

The consequence of God's activity is that **'He turned the sea into dry land.'** The verb here is *śîm*, which normally means to 'set/put/place'. But when it is followed by a *lamed* preposition, as in this verse, it conveys the concept of making or fashioning (see 4:11).[43]

For an excellent study of the changing of the waters into dry land, see the work of M. Barlian.[44]

The direction of the mighty wind that divides the sea is from the east (cf. 10:13). That means that the wind was coming from the opposite side of the sea from where the Hebrews were standing. Obviously the waters would first open on the eastern shore of the Red Sea. The Hebrews would thus have to wait until the entire sea was divided before they could put one foot into it. In other words, the people of God had to be patient all night, watching the sea separate *from the far side.*

Many scholars attempt to explain the event in wholly naturalistic and rationalistic terms.[45] Nothing in the text supports that position.

The dividing of the Red Sea may be an ironic, belligerent critique of Egyptian magic and its spells.[46] The Egyptians themselves had an account of a priest separating a large body of water. The Westcar Papyrus tells the story of the bored King Snofru who summons his chief priest Djadjaemonkh to give him advice on how to find some pleasure.[47] The priest suggests that the pharaoh travel on a lake in a boat rowed by many beautiful naked women. His heart is happy until one of the rowers drops her fish-shaped charm into the water. She will accept no substitute, so Snofru calls for Djadjaemonkh to solve the problem with his secret arts. Through his magic sayings Djadjaemonkh places one side of the lake upon the other and finds the fish-shaped charm lying on a potsherd. Having returned it to its owner, Djadjaemonkh utters some more magic sayings that bring the water of the lake back to its original position.[48]

The Egyptian tale is reminiscent of the biblical account of the crossing of the Red Sea. One wonders whether the Hebrew writer may have regarded this event as a polemical parallel. The chief lector priest of Egypt may have divided a lake in search of a valuable charm, but the God of the Hebrews parts the entire Red Sea and causes a nation to pass through on dry ground. Who has the greater power?

14:22. **And the children of Israel went into the midst of the sea on dry ground, and the waters were a wall for them on their right and on their left.**

The Hebrews, literally, **'entered into the midst of the sea'** and they walked through on **'dry ground'** (see discussion of verse 16). The latter term is used in the Bible to describe land that is exceedingly dry, with no moisture. It appears in Genesis 1:9 as the 'dry ground' which becomes visible at creation (in antithesis to the waters). The earth's surface is called 'dry ground' after the flood of the day of Noah (Gen. 8:7,14). In all three events, God causes water to be removed so that dry land might appear. This truth underscores the sovereignty and omnipotence of Yahweh!

The divided waters are described as 'walls'. **'Wall'** is an architectural term in Hebrew often employed for the fortifications surrounding a city — walls which are high and strong for protection and security.[49]

14:23. And the Egyptians pursued and they went in after them — all the horses of Pharaoh and his chariots, and his cavalry into the midst of the sea.

Some time after Israel entered the Red Sea, the angel of God and the pillar of cloud must have stood aside. The Egyptian army was thus allowed free viewing of what was happening and access to the sea.

Pharaoh's troops see Israel traversing the sea, and in their hardness and obstinacy they believe they also can go through protected. So they take up the evil pursuit. Note, however, that it is only the mobile forces, the chariots and cavalry, who take up the chase. Certainly they would have thought that they would overtake Israel very quickly.

14:24. And it came to pass in the morning watch that Yahweh looked down upon the Egyptian camp in the fire and in the cloud, and he threw the camp of Egypt into confusion.

The verse opens with the clause, **'And it came to pass in the morning watch'** (see 1 Sam. 11:11 for the identical expression). The term **'watch'** signifies a division of time. In the Old Testament, the night is comprised of three watches: 6:00-10:00 p.m., 10:00-2:00 a.m. and 2:00-6:00 a.m. (Ps. 63:6; 119:148; Lam. 2:19; and cf. Judg. 7:19 that speaks of a middle watch). The morning watch is the latest of the three divisions of time, that is, 2:00-6:00 am.

During these early morning hours, Yahweh **'leant over and looked down'** upon the Egyptian forces. He then acted by, literally, **'throwing the army of Egypt into confusion by noise'**.[50] This latter verb is used in 1 Samuel 7:10 when God thunders with a great thunder against the Philistines, and they become confused. Back in Exodus 14:3, Israel was the one in apparent confusion, but now we see it is Egypt who is truly in a panic.

14:25. He removed the wheels of their chariots so that they drove with difficulty. And the Egyptians said, 'Let us flee from Israel because Yahweh fights for them against Egypt.'

As the Egyptian chariot force moved through the Red Sea, God **'removed'** (a Hiphil form) the wheels from their chariots. The Septuagint, Syriac, Samaritan Hebrew Pentateuch and some modern commentators prefer to understand the root of this verb to be 'to tie/bind'.[51] So, in some manner, God locked up the wheels of the chariots in order that they could not easily move. In reality, however, there is no compelling reason to accept this proposal in place of the direct, straight reading of the Masoretic Text.

The second verb of the passage literally says, **'He caused them to drive in heaviness.'**[52] The subject of the clause is Yahweh, and he is causing the situation to occur, or effecting it (the verb is a Piel form reflecting 'the bringing about of a state').[53]

'Heaviness' is a derivative of the noun *kābēd*, which, as we have seen, is often used in Exodus of what God does to Pharaoh's heart. Here we see that not only is Pharaoh subject to the hardening activity of Yahweh, but so too are the chariots of Egypt!

14:26. And Yahweh said to Moses, 'Stretch forth your hand over the sea and return the waters over the Egyptians, over their chariots and over their cavalry.'

As the Egyptian forces are bogged down inside the sea, God orders (with an imperative form) Moses to put forth his hand and cause the waters to close over the army. Here, then, is 'the final retribution, measure for measure, for the casting of the infant sons of the Israelites into the waters of the Nile (1:22)'.[54]

14:27. And Moses stretched out his hand over the sea and he returned the sea at daybreak to its place. And the

Egyptians were fleeing to meet it. And Yahweh shook off the Egyptians in the midst of the sea.

We are told that the destruction of Egypt's army occurred **'at daybreak'**. As the sun-god Ra rose in the east, the Egyptian forces were destroyed. The sun-god could do nothing for his worshippers; he was impotent to stop the decimation of his people. Who is sovereign? Who is God? Is it Ra, Pharaoh, or Yahweh?

On this day, the triumph of the God of Israel is trumpeted forth throughout creation. The fears of the Hebrews and the boastings of the Egyptians are dashed by the overwhelming power of Yahweh!

The same waters that formed a wall of protection for God's people served as a tumbling wall of death for the Egyptians. The water thus signifies both blessing and curse. That curse finds its import in the verb that means 'to shake off' (in Piel pattern; cf. Ps. 136:15). God shakes off wicked men from the face of the earth (Neh. 5:13; Job 38:12-13).

After the destruction the water returns **'to its place'**. A more literal translation would be, 'to its steady flow' — that is, to its permanent and previous position.

14:28. And the water returned and it covered the chariots and the cavalry of all the army of Pharaoh which was going after them into the sea. Not one remained from them.

Attached to the phrase **'the entire army of Pharaoh'** is a *lamed* preposition. Many understand it to be in apposition, and to mean 'that is'. Thus an equation is made between 'the chariots and horsemen' and 'the entire army of Egypt'. This is probably not correct. Rather, the particle may be used to indicate possession, so that the phrase means, **'the chariots and horsemen *which belonged to* the entire army of Pharaoh'**.[55] It is not the whole army of Pharaoh that was destroyed in the Red Sea, but only the chariots and cavalry of Egypt (this fits with commentary on 14:23).

14:29. **But the children of Israel went on dry ground in the midst of the sea. And the water was a wall for them on their right and on their left.**

This verse is a repeat of verse 22 in order to contrast the fate of the Egyptians and that of the Hebrews.

It is worth noting that the Genesis creation account serves as a paradigm for Israel's deliverance at the sea. That is to say, 'The redemptive creation of Israel at the sea is cast in the same narrative style of original creation as the pillar of divine presence brings light into darkness (Exodus 13:21, cf. the first creative day), the waters are divided (Exodus 14:21; cf. the second creative day), and the dry land emerges (Exodus 14:29, cf. the third creative day).'[56] In other words, the account of the deliverance of Israel out of the oppression of Egypt through the crossing of the Red Sea reflects the narrative of the original creation. The sea crossing is so structured 'as to be a redemptive re-enactment of creation.'[57] (For a fully developed presentation of this theme, see my book on ancient Egypt.)[58]

14:30-31. **On that day Yahweh saved Israel from the hand of the Egyptians. And Israel saw the Egyptians dead on the shore of the sea. And Israel saw the great hand that Yahweh used against Egypt. And the people feared Yahweh, and they believed in Yahweh and in Moses his servant.**

These two verses set out an important contrast. In verse 30, the writer says that Yahweh saved Israel **'from the hand** [sing.] **of the Egyptians'**. Verse 31 literally says that **'Israel saw the great hand that Yahweh used'** against the Egyptians. Here is the antithesis! Whose hand is more powerful? Yahweh's hand is omnipotent, and his alone.

The reference to the 'hand' of Yahweh is also a fulfilment of his promise back in 6:1, in which he said, 'Because by a mighty hand he will send them out, and by a mighty hand he will drive them from his land.'

In verse 13 of this chapter Moses had proclaimed that the Hebrews would not *see* the Egyptians ever again. The Israelites did *see* them in verse 30, but not as they had the day before. Now they were dead, and simply powerless adversaries.

Application

Donald Bridge tells the story of 'an American congregation which included some negroes accustomed to answering the preacher as he went along. On one occasion they were addressed by someone with "liberal" leanings, tending to dismiss the miracles of the Bible. He referred in his sermon to the Israelites crossing the Red Sea. "Praise de Lord," shouted a negro. "Takin' all dem children through de deep waters. What a mighty miracle!" The preacher frowned. "It was not a miracle," he explained condescendingly. "They were doubtless in marsh-land, the tide was ebbing, and the children of Israel picked their way across in six inches of water." "Praise de Lord!", shouted the negro unabashed. "Drownin' all dem Egyptians in six inches of water. What a mighty miracle!"'[59]

How like Israel we are! Unbelief is the same in all ages. David, in an evil hour, said, 'I shall one day perish by the hand of Saul' (1 Sam. 27:1). Unbelief led Elijah to flee from the evil rantings of Jezebel, that evil queen who was the power behind the throne of Israel. It caused Peter to disown his Lord and flee from the place of trial. How many of us facing suffering or tragedy or persecution have not cowered, having moments of unbelief and doubt?

Yet, truly, there is no difficulty too great for the Lord. In fact, the greater the trouble, the greater the opportunity for God to display his power and grace. Man's weakness is God's opportunity.

It is Yahweh who does battle for us — if he is for us, who can be against us? Dare we think that the God who divided the Red Sea is powerless to intervene in our lives, that he is unable to care for us? Do we think that he is somehow shackled?

Paul in 1 Corinthians 10:1-6 tells us that the exodus event speaks to the church today. He basically argues that the Hebrews were specially chosen people and they received the great blessing of being delivered by God's work at the Red Sea. Yet, though they had been set apart by God, they 'were strewn in the wilderness' because of their disobedience. And Paul warns the Corinthian church and the church today that we ought to beware of, and take warning from, this incident. John Calvin comments: 'If God did not spare them, he will not spare us, for our situation is the same as theirs.'

The Song of the Sea (Exodus 15:1-21)

The Song of the Sea is the first recorded psalm or hymn of the Hebrew nation. It sings praises to God because of his redemptive work of bringing Israel out of the land of death and darkness into freedom. It is a symphony of adoration!

The Song of the Sea is the first of many psalms or songs that extol God's majesty at the exodus event.[60] For example, the psalmist proclaims that:

> He saved them for the sake of his name,
> That he might make his power known.
> Thus he rebuked the Red Sea and it dried up;
> And he led them through the deeps,
> As through the wilderness.
> So he saved them from the hand of the one who
>   hated them,
> And redeemed them from the hand of the enemy.
> And the waters covered their adversaries;
> Not one of them was left.
> Then they believed his words;
> They sang his praise
>
> (Ps. 106:8-12).

The reader should also see, in particular, Psalms 78 and 136. The fact is that the Red Sea crossing was for the Hebrew the most important physical redemption in the history of the Old Testament.

The strophic structure of the hymn is straightforward.[61] It is divided into three stanzas: verses 1-6, verses 7-11, and verses 12-16. At the end of each stanza appears the vocative, **'O Yahweh!'** to mark the stanza's conclusion. In addition, it should be observed that near the end of each of the three strophes appears a related simile: **'like a stone'** (end of v. 5); **'like lead'** (end of v. 10); and **'like stone'** (end of v. 16).[62] These three stanzas are followed by an epilogue (vv. 17-18) and a responsive refrain (vv. 19-21).

The great antiquity of this song has long been recognized.[63] Various grammatical points in the text will confirm that age.

15:1. Then Moses and the sons of Israel sang this song to Yahweh, and they spoke saying:

'I will sing to Yahweh,
for he is surely exalted;
the horse and its rider,
he has hurled into the sea.'

The opening verses of the stanza set forth the theme of the song: it is a doxology, a hymn of praise and honour to Yahweh. Hymns of the ancient Near East commonly open with such adoration, but usually they are in praise of an earthly king.[64] But here only God is so honoured.

A grammatical construction that begins with **'then'** and is followed by an imperfect verb (**'sang'**) indicates that the singing occurred at 'approximately the time when' God destroyed the Egyptian army and they lay strewn on the seashore.[65] In other words, the joyful singing of the Hebrews was spontaneous and an immediate reaction to God's wondrous work. It is as if the people could not help but break forth into song!

'I will sing' is a first person singular verb. But it does not merely refer to Moses; it includes all the men of Israel (**'the sons of Israel'**) in covenant oneness, singing forth the praises of God.

When the Hebrew men sing that Yahweh **'is surely exalted'**, they are using the same verb twice. It is an infinitive absolute form followed by a perfective form of the verb. Repetition in this type of construction has an intensifying effect — that is, there is no doubt or question regarding the statement made.

15:2.
'And Yahweh is my strength and song,
and he is my salvation.
This is my God and I will praise him,
The God of my father and I will exalt him.'

This verse is classic Hebrew poetry because it contains parallelism and a chiasm. The original word order displays its deliberative construction:

a	b	c
My strength	and song [is]	Yahweh
c¹		a¹
And he has become to me		for salvation.
a		b
This is my God		and I will praise him,
a¹		b¹
The God of my father		and I will exalt him.

The name given to the LORD is an abbreviated form of Yahweh, literally, **'Yāh'**. It only appears in poetry when standing alone. However, often Hebrew names end with *-yāh* as a suffix: for example, Jeremiah, Hezekiah and Josiah.

The meaning of the word translated **'my song'** is unclear. Some scholars argue that it means 'protection/defence' and, therefore, it is in parallel with **'my strength'**.[66] Others contend that the word does in fact refer to 'the praise of God in cultic music'. [67] Sarna reasons, unconvincingly, that the word is a *double* *entendre*, so that it deliberately means both strength and song.[68]

Attached to the last verb, **'I will exalt him'**, is a *nun energicum*, a special connecting syllable linking the verb and the pronominal suffix. Older grammars believed this ending provided intentional emphasis to the action of the verb.[69] That conclusion is probably incorrect; it seems that the form simply reflects an early stage of the Hebrew language.[70] It does, however, confirm the great antiquity of the poem.

See the commentary on 3:6 regarding the phrase, **'God of my father'**.

This verse is quoted in Psalm 118:14 and Isaiah 12:2. It may have attained the status of a confessional statement in later Hebrew religion.

15:3.
'Yahweh is a man of war,
Yahweh is his name.'

Yahweh as a warrior, or **'a man of war'**, becomes a central biblical motif. Regarding Exodus 15, Longman and Reid comment: 'This poem represents the first explicit statement of the warlike nature of God ... this theme of God as a warrior became a recurrent refrain in the Old Testament. The Exodus event itself became an important archetype in the biblical tradition, a means of telling and retelling God's acts of deliverance. God often dramatically revealed himself to the Israelites as the one who saved them from physical harm. He fought against their enemies.'[71]

The **'name'** of this warrior is **'Yahweh'**. The basis of this declaration is the recognition by Israel of who it is that fights for them. They have seen his power and his majesty with their own eyes, and they are convinced and convicted — at least for now.

15:4.
'The chariots of Pharaoh and his army
he has cast into the sea;
and his chosen officers
have drowned in the Red Sea.'

The structure of this verse of poetry is a complete synonymous parallelism:

a	b	c
The chariots of Pharaoh and his army	he has thrown	in the sea.
a	b	c
His chosen officers	have sunk	in the Red Sea.

Parallelism, or repetition of lines (technically known as
cola), is principally for the purpose of emphasis in poetry.
The fate or end of the Egyptian army is here being
accentuated.

For commentary on the identity of the **'officers'**, see
14:7.[72]

15:5.
'Deeps cover them,
they went down into the depths like a stone.'

'Deeps' is the same word as in Genesis 1:2: '... and
darkness was over the surface of the *deep*.' Some scholars
have attempted to find a parallel with Mesopotamian
creation accounts.[73] In those myths a goddess appears
whose name is Tiamat, a term that some say is related to
the Hebrew *tᵉhôm*, 'deep'. Tiamat was a mighty foe of the
Mesopotamian creator-god Marduk, and she had to be
vanquished before creation could occur. According to this

theory, at creation and at the Red Sea, Yahweh is the Creator God who is conquering the chaos deity Tiamat. What lies behind the biblical account is a pagan world-order. In reality, the equation of Mesopotamian Tiamat and Hebrew *t'hom* is at best dubious.[74] Unfortunately, it has come to be regarded as fact in much recent literature.[75]

Rare endings appear on the verb **'covered'** and on the preposition **'like'**. They are old forms that reflect the antiquity of the hymn of the sea.[76]

15:6.
'Your right hand, O Yahweh, was majestic in power,
your right hand, O Yahweh, shattered the enemy.'

The poetical symmetry of this verse is obvious. It is, however, a complete synthetic parallelism: that is, each line, or colon, contains the same number of components but a new or more detailed idea is added to the second line.

a	b	c
Your right hand	O Yahweh	was glorious in power.
a¹	b¹	c¹
Your right hand	O Yahweh	shattered the enemy.

The second line helps to define the first line and, therefore, God's destruction of the Egyptian army explains what is meant by his right hand being **'majestic/glorious in power'**.

Hebrew culture places great importance on the right hand. It symbolizes power, pre-eminence and strength. Here it signifies the power of God as an instrument to deliver his people:

O sing to Yahweh a new song,
for he has done wonderful things,

> his right hand and his holy arm
> have gained the victory for him
>
> (Ps. 98:1).

Connected to the word **'majestic'** is a remnant of an early case-ending known as a *hireq compaginis.*[77] This also points to the antiquity of the Song of the Sea.

15:7.
'In the greatness of your majesty,
you overthrew those who rose up against you.
You sent forth your burning anger,
it consumed them like stubble.'

The second stanza of the hymn begins in much the same way as the first. In fact, the term **'majesty'** is a noun derivative of the verb 'to rise up'. The latter verb occurs twice in the first stanza as 'highly exalted'.

The **'burning anger'** of God is used exclusively of divine anger and fury in the Old Testament.[78]

The simile, **'It consumed them like stubble,'** is a prominent figure in the Bible describing the end of the wicked (Isa. 40:24; 41:2; Jer. 13:24; Ps. 83:13). What makes the figure so potent in the present context is the fact that **'stubble'** was what the Hebrews had to gather to make bricks in Egypt (see 5:12). Now the Egyptian army is consumed like stubble!

15:8.
'And at the blast of your nostrils,
the waters were piled up;
the floods stood firm like a heap;
the deep waters congealed in the heart of the sea.'

'Blast' is actually the common Hebrew word for 'wind'. It certainly refers to the east wind from 14:21. The great dividing blow is not of natural origin, but comes from the very nostrils of God.[79]

The resulting action is narrated by three lines of synonymous parallelism (following in the word order of the Masoretic Text):

a	b	
They piled up	the waters;	
a[1]	c	b[1]
They stood firm	like a heap	the floods;
a[2]	b[2]	d
They congealed	the deep waters	in the heart of the sea.

The first verb appears only here in the Old Testament. It is in the Niphal pattern (i.e. it is passive), and it means 'to be heaped up'. Its noun derivative describes a heap of grain or of rubbish (Ruth 3:7; Neh. 4:2).

The second verb (also in Niphal) means 'to take an upright position/to stand firm'. In cognate languages, a related word is used of statues and monuments that do not move. The line is sometimes translated to say the waters 'stood firm like a wall', but the noun is better rendered as a 'heap' (see Josh. 3:13,16; Ps. 78:13). In Isaiah 17:11, the term denotes a heap of grain. That translation aligns well with the parallel of the first line.

The third verb conveys the idea of something thickening/condensing/congealing. Job 10:10 describes the curdling of cheese by using this verb. Cross and Freedman contend that the verbal form actually means 'to churn', which would be the exact opposite of the traditional translation.[80] Their definition destroys the sense and symmetry of the threefold parallelism and is, therefore, unnecessary.

15:9.
'The enemy said:
    "I will pursue, I will overtake,

I will divide the spoil;
my life will be filled with them;
I will draw out my sword,
my hand will destroy them."'

In these boastings of the Egyptians, five verbs appear in relative succession. They are not connected by conjunctions. This is vigorous poetic imagery that Gesenius calls *constructio asyndetos*. Its purpose is as 'a rhetorical expedient to produce a hurried and so an impassioned description'.[81] An exalted poetic style is the result of the verse's construction.

Poetic form is further accentuated by alliteration. The first five words of the verse begin with the Hebrew letter *aleph*.[82]

The verbs for 'gorge/fill' and 'destroy' each end with an enclitic *mem*.[83] This form was common in the early stages of the Hebrew language, but its usage died out over time. Remnants still can be seen in poetry.[84] The meaning of the construction is uncertain, although it may have an emphatic force. In any event, its repeated appearance points to the antiquity of the poem.

15:10.
'But you blew with your breath,
the sea covered them;
they sank like lead
in the mighty waters.'

A conceptual parallel exists between this verse and verse 5 of the opening stanza. In both cases, the waters of the Red Sea envelop (the same verb in Hebrew, 'to cover') the Egyptians, and the army subsequently sinks into the watery depths. Pleonasm and parallelism serve to emphasize the point.

The verb 'to sink' is a hapax legomenon. Perhaps it is related to the verb with the same root that means 'to be or grow dark'. Darkness in the Old Testament can symbolize being near to death (Ps. 102:11; 109:23). Thus, the verb may be translated, **'They sank into the darkness/abyss.'**

'Breath' is a word meaning 'wind'. It is a reference to verse 8 of this chapter, and to the east wind of chapter 14.

The description of the waters is that they are **'mighty'**. That word really means 'majestic/magnificent'. The waters are reflecting the character of the Creator (Ps. 18:1; and especially Ps. 93:3-4).

15:11.
'Who is like you among the gods, O Yahweh?
Who is like you?
Majestic in holiness,
awesome in praises,
performing wonders.'

This second stanza concludes in the same manner as the final verse of the opening one: with glowing praise and adoration of Yahweh. The parallel nature of the two verses is confirmed by the fact that the word **'majestic'** is a focus of both.

Two rhetorical questions are asked in the verse. No answer is expected. The response is obvious: no one is like Yahweh! Truly, who can be compared to Yahweh from among the pagan deities? Can the gods of Egypt, who failed to deliver their worshippers?[85]

Some translators want to render **'holiness'** as a plural noun, 'holy ones'.[86] That rendering is in agreement with the Septuagint. However, the Masoretic Text makes perfect sense as it stands and thus is in no need of emendation. 'Holiness' in Hebrew culture means 'to be set apart/distinct/unique', and indeed Yahweh is majestic in his wholly otherness. He is like nothing else.

15:12.
'You stretched out your right hand,
the earth swallowed them.'

This final stanza describes the results of the Red Sea
crossing. First, what God has done is relayed in terms
similar to what Moses had been commanded to do — in
14:16, Yahweh told Moses to *stretch out his hand* over the
sea. That terminology is now being used in relation to God
because he is the one who truly had the power to open
and close the waters.

The consequence of God's work is that the earth **'swallowed'** the Egyptian army. In Exodus 7:12, that same verb
is used of Aaron's staff swallowing the rods of the Egyptian
magicians. Ancient Near-Eastern literature often employs
the act of swallowing to signify desolation and death. In
Egyptian magic, 'The act can serve a principally hostile
function, whereby "devour" signifies "to destroy."'[87]

The verb 'swallowed' is an imperfective form. According
to Driver, the imperfect expresses progressive duration.[88]
Gesenius assumes that the use of that form in the present
verse 'represents the Egyptians, in a vivid, poetic description, as being swallowed up one after another'.[89]

The word **'earth'** sometimes means 'Sheol', or 'the place
of the dead' (Isa. 14:9; 29:4; Jonah 2:6). Other ancient
Near-Eastern literature draws the same conclusion.[90]

15:13.
'You lead by your loving-kindness
the people that you have redeemed;
you guide by your power
to your holy dwelling.'

Another synthetic parallelism arises in this verse. In the
order of the Masoretic Text it looks like this:

a	b	c
You lead	by your loving-kindness	the people that you have re-deemed.
a¹	b¹	d
You guide	by your power	to your holy dwelling.

The Hebrew word translated **'that'** is a demonstrative pronoun being used as a relative pronoun.[91] This form appears exclusively in Hebrew poetry.

The Hebrew word for **'loving-kindness'** denotes 'covenant loyalty', that is, God's keeping of the covenant promises he made to his people. Indeed, this fidelity to his covenant refers back to the time of Abraham, Isaac and Jacob, and it continues to the present.

The identity of the **'holy dwelling/habitation'** is ambiguous. Some commentators believe it may refer to the promised land, on the basis of passages such as Jeremiah 10:25; 23:3 and Psalm 79:7. Others argue it is specifically alluding to the temple mount on Mount Zion (2 Sam. 15:25; Isa. 27:10). Verse 17 of the present chapter lends great support to this position. On the other hand, the reference may simply be to Mount Sinai (see commentary on 3:12).

15:14-15.
'Peoples have heard, they tremble;
writhing seizes the dwellers of Philistia;
the chiefs of Edom are terrified;
trembling seizes the leaders of Moab;
the dwellers of Canaan melt away.'

A further consequence of the incident at the Red Sea is that pagan peoples will be told what has happened and they will be afraid. Four countries are specifically mentioned, and they are listed in a poetic parallel structure (based upon the Masoretic Text):

Line 1	a	b	c
	Writhing	seizes	the dwellers of Philistia;
Line 2		b^1	c^1
		are terrified	the chiefs of Edom.
Line 3	c^2	a^1	b^2
	The leaders of Moab	trembling	seizes them.
Line 4		b^3	c^3
		They melt away	the dwellers of Canaan.

The order in which the nations are listed follows the geographical sequence of the route the Hebrews will use to travel to the promised land: Philistia – Edom – Moab – Canaan.

All four nations were to become notorious enemies of Israel. Philistia was located in the coastal plain of Palestine, and the Philistines often fought with Israel during the early centuries of her existence (e.g., Judg. 13-15; 1 Sam. 4-7). The Edomites were descended from Esau, and they populated the area of southern Transjordan. They struggled with Israel in order not to let her pass through their territory (Num. 20). Moab, in central Transjordan, was the home of the descendants of Lot. Balak was one of the kings of Moab during the conquest period, and he strongly resisted Israel (Num. 22). The Canaanites, of course, inhabited the land of promise, and many of them were destroyed by the Hebrew invasion of Palestine.

Attached to the end of the verb 'tremble' is a *nun paragogicum* (or a 'flying nun'). The purpose of the ending in poetic text is uncertain.[92] It is true, however, that it is more common in earlier texts than later ones.

The same word is used for the **'people'** of Philistia and the **'people'** of Canaan: literally, 'the dwellers/sitters of'. It may, in fact, refer to those sitting on thrones, or the leaders of those peoples (see Exod. 11:5; 12:29). That rendering would fit better with the four-part parallelism of the verse.

15:16.
'Terror and dread will fall upon them;
by the strength of your arm,
they will be as still as a stone;
until your people pass by, O Yahweh;
until the people whom you have purchased pass by.'

A few minor grammatical points help to show the emphatic force of this final verse of the third stanza. First, the word **'terror'** has an early accusative ending (called the accusative of intention) which serves the goal of poetical emphasis.[93] Second, **'strength'** translates an adjectival construction which usually conveys a superlative force.[94] Gesenius comments that 'The adjective which is made into a *regens* is strongly emphatic, and is frequently equivalent to a superlative.'[95]

The translation, **'They will be still'**, has been challenged. Some scholars want to repoint the verb and make it into a Niphal (passive) reading, 'They will be struck dumb as a stone.'[96] Dahood suggests it comes from a different word altogether that means 'to throw/hurl'. And, thus, he sees an echo here of verse 5.[97] However, the reasons advanced for altering the Masoretic Text from its present state are noticeably weak.

The power of Yahweh's arm should be seen in the light of Egyptian texts that characteristically describe Pharaoh's might in the same way (see commentary on 3:19-20).

The verb 'to purchase' sometimes bears the sense of originating/creating (see Gen. 4:1; 14:19,22; Deut. 32:6). This meaning supports the idea that the crossing of the Red Sea is a re-creation event. See analysis of 14:29.

15:17.
'You will bring them in and plant them
on the mountain of your inheritance;
the place that you have made for your dwelling, O Yahweh;
the sanctuary, O Lord, established by your hands.'

This epilogue looks even further into the future when God
will establish Israel in the land of promise. The Hebrews
will build a sanctuary there to worship Yahweh. The
designation of a mountain obviously refers to Mount Zion
where the temple will ultimately reside.

It is unnecessary to suppose that this reference to the
mountain means that the song must have been written
after the Israelites had settled in the land. It may simply
indicate intention rather than accomplishment (see 23:20;
32:34).

The parallel designations

a	b
on the mountain of	your inheritance,
a^1	b^1
the place of	your dwelling,

are well-attested in Ugaritic literature of the fourteenth
century B.C.[98] This formula refers in those instances to the
sanctuary of the Canaanite god Baal. The use of this
expression, however, does not indicate borrowing on the
part of the Hebrew writer. It is more likely that it has a
polemical thrust. In any event, because of these early
attestations, some scholars leave the door open for an
early dating of verse 17 and for the entire poem.[99]

15:18.
'Yahweh will reign for ever and ever.'

The song ends as it began — with the glorification of Yahweh. He is the subject of the hymn. As all begins with him, all ends with him. Yahweh is the eternal King![100]

15:19. When the horses of Pharaoh and his chariots and his cavalry went into the sea, Yahweh returned the waters of the sea upon them. And the children of Israel went on the dry ground in the midst of the sea.

Although this verse is not part of the song — it is narrative prose — it is the writer's summing up of the Red Sea crossing. It simply and concisely gives a synopsis of the grand event of Israel's history.

15:20. Then Miriam, the prophetess, the sister of Aaron, took the tambourine in her hand, and all the women went out after her with tambourines and with dancing.

The Song of Miriam in the next verse is introduced by this prose passage. This is the first time that Miriam is mentioned by name in the Bible. She is probably the sister anonymously designated in 2:4-9, although that is not completely certain.

Miriam is identified by two titles. She is, firstly, called a **'prophetess'** (feminine ending). Only four other women in the Old Testament bear that epithet: Deborah (Judg. 4:4), Huldah (2 Kings 22:14), Noadiah (Neh. 6:14) and the unnamed wife of Isaiah (Isa. 8:3). The position and duty of a prophetess are the same as those of a prophet — that is, as one who is authorized to speak for another (see Micah 6:4). Thus Miriam had a favoured status in the nation of Israel.[101] Her prophetic function (along with Aaron's) was later to lead to great problems (Num. 12:1-2).

Secondly, Miriam is recognized as **'Aaron's sister'**. This is a biblical example of fratriarchy, in which authority in the family is invested in the eldest brother.[102]

The word translated **'tambourine'** is actually a frame-drum.[103] Whenever that instrument is used in connection with dancing in the Old Testament it appears to reflect a genre known as the 'Victory Song'.[104]

15:21. And Miriam answered them:

> 'Sing to Yahweh,
> for he is surely exalted;
> the horse and its rider,
> he has hurled into the sea.'

A direct translation of the opening clause is: **'And Miriam answered them...'** The pronominal suffix **'them'** is a masculine plural, and thus refers to Moses and the men of Israel.[105] Because the song is an answer/response to the men, then the women were singing antiphonally with the men.[106] The content of the song is exactly the same as verse 1 of the chapter, the opening of the first stanza of the Song of Moses. Apparently this passage served as a refrain to the larger hymn.[107]

Application

After crossing the waters, the victorious people of Israel stood by the sea and sang a song of deliverance and triumph. This event was a foreshadowing of the victory of God's redeemed at the end of time. In Revelation 15:1-4, the apostle John has the following vision: 'I saw in heaven another great and marvellous sign: seven angels with the seven last plagues — last, because with them God's wrath is completed. And I saw what looked like a sea of glass mixed with fire and, standing beside the sea, those who had been victorious over the beast and his image and over the number of his name. They held harps given them by God and sang the song of Moses the servant of God and the song of the Lamb:

"Great and marvellous are your deeds,
Lord God Almighty.
Just and true are your ways,
King of the ages.
Who will not fear you, O Lord,
and bring glory to your name?
For you alone are holy.
All nations will come
and worship before you,
for your righteous acts have been revealed."'

Thus John sees a sea, and on the seashore stands a victorious multitude. They are playing harps and singing the Song of Moses. Hendriksen comments, 'Clearly, this vision is based on the story of the drowning of Pharaoh's host in the Red Sea.'[108]

So the church in covenant will at the end times sing hymns of adoration before the throne of God. One of those hymns will be the Song of the Sea from Exodus 15. And note that the subject matter is the same in Exodus and in Revelation: the glorification of God. He is worthy of the church's honour and praise because of who he is, and because of his great redemptive work. Amen and amen.

Parallels between Israel at the sea and the church at the sea are striking. The general theological thrust of the two episodes is similar as well: as Israel moves from a scene of redemption to communion at the sea and on to inheritance of the land of promise, so does the church. The church has been redeemed by the blood of Christ; it communes at the sea in Revelation 15 and, finally, it receives an eternal inheritance that is imperishable and will never fade away (1 Peter 1:4).

7. Grumblings in the desert

Exodus 15:22 - 17:7

The incident at Marah (Exodus 15:22-27)

We mentioned earlier that the grumbling of the Israelites becomes a dominant negative motif of the wilderness wanderings (see comment on 14:11). Instances of it occur repeatedly throughout the books of Exodus and Numbers (see, e.g., Exod. 14:11; 15:23-26; 16:2-3; 17:2-3; Num. 11:4-6; 14:1-4; 16:11-14; 20:2-5). George Coats remarks: 'A form-critical study of the relevant texts reveals that the murmuring motif is not designed to express a disgruntled complaint. Quite the contrary, it describes an open rebellion... In the wilderness theme the murmuring motif characterizes a basic tradition about the rebellion of Israel.'[1] The biblical author sees this rebellion in direct contrast to the grace and favour that Yahweh has bestowed upon the people. This episode is also to be seen by way of antithesis to the preceding scene of joyful singing. And what a contrast it is!

This section is carefully written and crafted. It employs elaborate word-plays that anchor the entire section to the main idea, which is that the Israelites are living by sight and not by faith.[2] The Hebrews are required to depend totally upon God for their sustenance and means.

15:22. Then Moses led Israel from the Red Sea, and they went out to the wilderness of Shur. And they went three days in the wilderness, and they did not find water.

The style of the initial phrase of this verse is unusual. It employs a Hiphil verb (causative), meaning, literally, **'Moses caused Israel to set out.'** It may be that the Hebrews were lax, or slow, in departing from the Red Sea region — perhaps they were merely basking in the glory of victory over the Egyptians. In any event, the prophet is described as having been the catalyst, or prime mover, in Israel's decampment and setting out.

Israel entered the wilderness of Shur. The term *šûr* means 'wall' in Hebrew. For years scholars have supposed that it denotes a wall of fortresses built by pharaohs to the east of Egypt, the purpose of which was to deny access to Egypt by Asiatics.[3] The wilderness of Shur is mentioned elsewhere in the Torah (see, for instance, Gen. 16:7; 20:1; 25:18). It appears to have been one of the principal caravan routes to Palestine, in particular, through the Negev to the town of Beersheba.

Three days of travel in the wilderness yielded no sources of water.

15:23. And they came to Marah. And they were not able to drink from the waters at Marah because they were bitter. (Therefore its name was called Marah.)

When the people of God finally discover water they cannot drink it because of its unsavoury taste — a possible indicator of poisoning. Thus begins a testing of the Hebrews, and the reader is anxious to see how they will respond.

This is a good example of the writer of Exodus' penchant for using plays on words.[4] The name of the location, **'Marah'**, is the Hebrew word for **'bitter'**. So the name of the site reflects the noteworthy event now taking place there. No wonder the location of Marah is uncertain.[5]

15:24. So the people grumbled against Moses, saying, 'What shall we drink?'

The Hebrews react unfaithfully. This is the first time the verb 'grumble/murmur' appears in the Old Testament. It is used only in the following chapters of the Hebrew Bible: Exodus 15, 16, 17; Numbers 14, 16, 17; and Joshua 9 (v. 18). In every instance it reflects the rebellious attitude of the Israelites against their leaders and authority structures.

15:25. And he cried out to Yahweh, and Yahweh showed him a tree. And he threw it into the waters, and the waters became sweet. There he set a decree and a law for them, and he tested them there.

In response to Israel's distress, God causes the water to become sweet. He performs that miracle by first **'show[ing]'** Moses **'a tree'**. That verbal form is from a root which in the Hiphil pattern means 'to teach/instruct'. The noun Torah, or law, is a derivative of that verb. Thus God is directing Moses how to change the nature of the water.

Some commentators explain the water's transfiguration in naturalistic terms. Purportedly wood absorbs salt and, thus, it filters impurities from the water.[6] But in reality there is nothing in the text to support this anti-supernatural understanding of events.

The last part of the verse is a parenthesis or an editorial. We are not told of what the pre-Sinaitic law consisted. However, Yahweh apparently tested Israel by that law through the episode of the bitter water. Israel obviously failed the test. The lesson seems to have been that the Hebrews were totally dependent upon God for their survival. They needed divine guidance and aid, apart from which they would surely perish.

15:26. And he said, 'If you will certainly listen to the voice of Yahweh your God, and you do the right thing in his eyes, and you listen to his commandments, and you keep all his decrees, then I will not set upon you any of the diseases which I put on Egypt. Because I am Yahweh, the one who heals you.'

Perhaps this verse constitutes the 'law' referred to in verse 25. Moses records it in a series of three parallel couplets: first, a complete synonymous, chiastic one; secondly, a complete synonymous one; and, finally, an incomplete synonymous one. The following is a translation according to the order of the elements in the Masoretic Text:

a		b	
If you certainly listen		to the voice of Yahweh	A
b¹		a¹	
And the right thing in his eyes		you do,	B
a		b	
And you listen		to his commands	A
a¹		b¹	
And you keep		all his statutes,	B
a	b	c	
Every disease	I set	on the Egyptians	A
b¹		c¹	
I will not set		on you.	B

The directive to **'listen carefully'** is actually two forms of the same verb. It is an infinitive absolute followed by an imperfective form. In Hebrew the verbal idea is strengthened and made more forcible by this construction.

Yahweh is called **'your healer/physician'**. This is a common title for the Lord in Scripture (see Isa. 19:22; Hosea 6:1; 11:3). The episode of changing the waters at Marah from bitter to sweet is a physical symbol of this spiritual reality that Yahweh is the healer of his people.

The **'diseases'** or 'sicknesses' that God had sent upon Egypt obviously refer to the plagues of Exodus 7-12 (see the references in Deut. 7:15; 28:27-29).[7]

The healing of the waters at Marah serves as a paradigm for a similar event in 2 Kings 2:19-22. In that incident, Elisha purifies bad water by throwing salt into it. Even some of the vocabulary of the two episodes is alike. For example, God proclaims in the later episode in that 'I have healed these waters' (2 Kings 2:21).

15:27. Then they came to Elim, and there were twelve springs of water and seventy date palms. And they camped there near the waters.

Soon the people travelled to Elim, where they found plenty of food and water for their sustenance (in contrast to Marah). The location of Elim is much disputed, although a good case for it is made by Simons: 'From Marah the Israelites came to Elim (Exod. 15:27; Num. 33:9), whose well-watered and wooded oasis is usually recognized in Wadi Gharandel. Though the stopping-place by the Sea of Reeds, mentioned only in Numbers 33:10, is not further specified, we may think of the plain of El-marhah providing a comfortable camping-ground, where the travellers could prepare for the march inland.'[8]

Application

The Israelites move from a period of ecstatic joy (at the Red Sea) to a phase of unbelief, grumbling and murmuring (at Marah).

What was it that brought the Hebrews to so great a depression in so little time? They were living by sight, and not by faith. At Marah they ran into a material problem, and they responded unfaithfully. But, again, let us not judge them too harshly, because — oh, how like the Israelites we are!

Sin in the wilderness of Sin (Exodus 16:1-7)

We have seen that near the end of chapter 15 God had supplied abundantly for the needs of the Hebrew people. They had grumbled because of bitter water, but God made the water sweet. In the final verse of that chapter we viewed a people who must have been quite content at the site of Elim, where there were twelve springs and seventy date palms. All was well with Israel — or was it? Unfortunately, the writer brings us back to the refrain of the wanderings — the faithlessness of Israel.[9]

16:1. And they journeyed from Elim and all the congregation of the children of Israel came to the Wilderness of Sin, which is between Elim and Sinai, on the fifteenth day of the second month after they came out from the land of Egypt.

According to Numbers 33:10, after the Hebrews left Elim they then returned to camp by the *yām sûph* (Red Sea). In other words, the people had passed through the Red Sea, had encamped at Marah and Elim, and now they set up camp at a more southerly place next to the Red Sea. This southern route was one of the principal roads for Egyptian mining expeditions during the Middle and New Kingdoms (*c.* the twentieth to twelfth centuries B.C.).[10] We know that Semites participated in these expeditions. The Hebrews who had been in Egypt for four centuries would most certainly have known of this route.

A clash between the escaping Israelites and Egyptian mining expeditions was not inevitable. Egyptian activity at the mines occurred primarily during the months of

January to March,[11] while the Hebrews were traversing the
territory after April.[12] According to Exodus 13:4, Israel left
Egypt during the month of Abib (around March), and
according to the present verse they reached the mining
area a month and a half later.

**16:2. All the congregation of the children of Israel grumbled
against Moses and against Aaron in the wilderness.**

This complaint is more severe and more widespread than
the grumbling of which we read in 15:22-26. First, the
outcry of the people is not now merely directed at Moses
(as on the earlier occasion), but against his brother as well.
Secondly, in 15:24 it was the generic 'the people' who
lodged a complaint. Here **'the entire congregation of the
children of Israel'** deplore and protest against the present
conditions. Finally, whereas the incident in chapter 15
begins with a description of a need followed by murmuring
on the part of the people, this passage does the opposite.
The author 'begins with the grumbling and thus casts the
complaint immediately in a negative light'.[13] Unbelief and
sedition are becoming habitual for the Israelites.

**16:3. And the children of Israel said to them, 'Would that we
had died by the hand of Yahweh in the land of Egypt when
we sat by the pots of meat, when we ate bread to the full —
because you have brought us forth to this wilderness to kill
all this assembly with hunger.'**

Although the assault is directed at Moses and Aaron, in
the final analysis the Hebrews are grumbling against
Yahweh. They doubt God's care for them and thus cast
aspersions on his power. These facts result in hostile
opposition to his leaders in whom he has invested authority. This is a very serious act of open rebellion. In fact,
verse 3 narrates treasonable words: **'Would that we had
died by Yahweh's hand!'** The very *hand* that had

destroyed the Egyptians (15:6) and that had delivered Israel is now blamed because it did not destroy Israel!

Their complaint is spelled out. The Hebrews crave two things: meat and bread.[14] They argue that Egypt was better than what they have now. There they ate meat and bread **'to the full'**, a term that reflects the idea of satisfaction. Really? How well do they remember Egypt? Is this honestly how Pharaoh treated them? This point goes to the very heart of the exodus story: was Pharaoh's servitude easier to bear and more comforting than that of Yahweh? (Ironically, the Israelites are now groaning under Yahweh's service as they did under Pharaoh's.)

The discourse of the Israelites actually begins with the interrogative 'Who?' However, when that particle is followed by an imperfective verb it expresses a wish. Thus it is correctly translated, 'Would that…' (cf. Num. 11:29).[15]

16:4. And Yahweh said to Moses, 'Behold, I will rain bread from heaven for you. And the people shall go out and gather a day's portion in its day — in order that I may test them, whether they will walk in my law or not.'

When the Hebrews groaned under the slavery of Egypt, Pharaoh took straw from them to make their lives harder. Yahweh responds to the complaining by abundantly providing for them. He promises to **'rain bread from heaven'**. This is another miraculous sign that God is with his people; it is a concession to a people who live by sight.

However, it is not a gift that arrives with no strings attached. God is going to test the Hebrews in order to refine their characters into obedience. Deuteronomy 8:16 declares, 'In the wilderness he fed you manna which your fathers did not know, that he might humble you and that he might test you, to do good for you in the end.' It is to teach God's people to depend upon him.

The test for Israel is stated in general terms at the close of the verse. The question is, will Israel **'walk in my law'** (literally, 'go in my Torah') or not? One of the specific laws is also revealed: the Israelites are to go out to the fields daily and bring in enough bread for daily consumption.

16:5. 'It shall be on the sixth day that they shall prepare what they bring in, and it shall be twice what they gather daily.'

The second specification of the law is that five days a week the Hebrews are to gather bread for each day, but the sixth and seventh days are to be different. On the sixth day they are to collect a double portion of bread, so that they will have enough for the next day as well. Work on the seventh day is not allowed.[16]

Sabbath laws predate the giving of the Sinaitic legal code. That is not a problem because they reflect the creation account of Genesis 2:1-3. Sabbath is a creation ordinance.

No concept of Sabbath rest has been found in ancient Egypt.[17] That fact underscores the differences between Yahweh and Pharaoh: the God of the Old Testament is compassionate and caring towards his people. Pharaoh was merely a burdensome taskmaster. That is why the recitation of the Sabbath law in the version of the decalogue recorded in Deuteronomy stresses its purpose as commemorating Israel's deliverance from slavery (Deut. 5:15).

16:6-7. And Moses and Aaron said to all the children of Israel, 'At evening you will know that Yahweh brought you forth from the land of Egypt; and at morning you will see the glory of Yahweh, because he has heard your grumblings against Yahweh. And what are we, that you grumble against us?'

Two physical signs will be given to Israel so that the people will cease their grumbling and see the foolishness of their ways. The first sign is that the Hebrews will receive food that very evening — probably the meat mentioned in verse

8 (cf. the use of **'evening'** in both verses). A second sign will occur in the morning: **'the glory of Yahweh'**, the Shekinah glory, will make an appearance before the people. In verses 9-10 the presence of Yahweh manifests itself in the cloud that had been leading the Hebrews through the wilderness. It is also in the morning that bread is miraculously given to the people (16:13).

Moses and Aaron rightfully discern the hearts of the people. The Israelites' fight is with Yahweh because it is he who is leading them out of Egypt. They are venting their anger at the two prophets unjustifiably, and thus they are hiding their unbelief in, and unfaithfulness to, Yahweh.

Application

The Hebrews were worrying about not having any food and wishing that they had died in Egypt. They remembered, perhaps falsely, that in slavery they had food in abundance. Now they had nothing. They were very anxious about their lives.[18] These were people who could have benefited from Jesus' teachings in the Sermon on the Mount, when he said, 'For this reason I say to you, do not be anxious for your life, as to what you shall eat, or what you shall drink; nor for your body, as to what you shall put on. Is not life more than food, and the body than clothing? ... Therefore do not be anxious for tomorrow; for tomorrow will care for itself. Each day has enough trouble of its own' (Matt. 6:25,34).

Are we not like the Hebrews? We often find ourselves in difficult situations, and we grow anxious and we look back, full of regrets and wishing things had turned out differently. In reality, such attitudes display a keen lack of trust in the sovereignty of God and in the idea that his plan is being worked out in heaven and upon earth. Certainly we should regret our sin and repent of it, but we should also realize that God's will is coming to pass and it can happen in no other way.

In addition, we need to understand that God will test us as he tested Israel. And such trials may have great benefits for us as

Christians, such as increasing our trust and dependence upon God, or bringing us back to the godly way of living and thinking, or they may be for a myriad of other reasons. So let us not rebel when things become difficult, but let us rather go to God in prayer and serve him with all our hearts, souls and minds.

Yahweh's provision (Exodus 16:8-20)

The Lord again responds to Israel's unfaithfulness by abundantly providing for them. At issue is not a lack of water but an acute desire for food. In this section, God answers the people's grumbling by appearing to them in the cloud, and then miraculously giving them bread and meat. The scene demonstrates God's wonderful care for his people, in spite of their wicked ways.

16:8. And Moses said, '[It will happen] when Yahweh gives you in the evening meat to eat, and in the morning bread to satisfy you, because Yahweh has heard your grumblings which you are grumbling against him. And what are we? Your grumblings are not against us but against Yahweh.'

Verse 8 is basically a repetition of the previous verse — in both ideas and vocabulary. On that basis, modern scholars have claimed that it is the result of dittography (unintentional repetition of words — e.g., a scribal error), or of textual conflation (a composite reading of a text), or that it is a literary gloss (an expanded commentary or interpretation). Thus, numerous commentators want to eliminate verse 8 from the text.[19]

Repetition, however, for the purpose of emphasis is an essential Hebrew literary device.[20] Reiteration drives home the point of this passage: that is, Israel's grumblings are hazardous because they are ultimately directed against God Almighty! The prophets, although initially on the receiving end of the complaints, are merely the instruments of God's work — it is really against him that Israel is rebelling.

The use of the negative at the end of the verse is not denying the fact that criticism has been levelled against Moses and Aaron, but rather it 'is ironic, achieving criticism by emphasizing that murmuring against God's messenger is murmuring against God'.[21]

16:9. And Moses said to Aaron, 'Speak to all the congregation of the children of Israel, 'Come before Yahweh because he has heard your grumblings.'

Aaron continues to serve as Moses' spokesman. Originally a role given to Aaron in the dispute against Pharaoh, his public speaking was also sometimes addressed to the Hebrews (see 4:16).

'Come before Yahweh' is a formula often found in the Torah, and here it obviously refers to the Israelites approaching the glory cloud. Because the expression is later used in regard to Israel's drawing near to the sanctuary (Num. 16:17), Childs argues that it signifies the Tent of Meeting in the present verse.[22] His reconstruction is incorrect because the tabernacle was not built until after the law was given at Mount Sinai (25:1-9).

16:10. And it came to pass while Aaron was speaking to all the congregation of the children of Israel that they turned to the wilderness, and behold the glory of Yahweh appeared in the cloud.

The verb **'turned'** ('looked', NIV, NKJV) when followed by the preposition *'el* (to) means 'to turn and look'.[23] Apparently the Hebrews are acting according to the command that Aaron had conveyed to them in verse 9: they are coming before Yahweh whose theophonic presence is in the cloud leading the people through the wilderness.

'Cloud' has a preposition and a definite article attached to it, giving it the meaning **'in *the* cloud'**. It is thus referring to the very cloud that had been leading them (13:21-22; 14:19-24). For a study of the glory cloud throughout Scripture, see the work of Meredith Kline.[24]

16:11-12. Then Yahweh spoke to Moses, saying, 'I have heard the grumblings of the children of Israel. Speak to them, saying, 'At twilight you shall eat meat and in the morning you shall be satisfied with bread.' And you will know that I am Yahweh your God.'

Yahweh declares that he will make the people **'satisfied'** by supplying meat and bread for them. That is the same word the grumblers had used in verse 3 to describe their circumstances in Egypt. It is only Yahweh and his provisions that will truly satisfy.

Regarding the use of the dual form **'twilights'**, see commentary on 12:6.

The phrase, **'You will know that I am Yahweh,'** has become idiomatic in the exodus account. It is used of the Egyptians (see 7:5,17; 8:22; 14:4,18), and of the Hebrews (see 6:7). One of the major points of the entire text of Exodus is the recognition of Yahweh as God over all.

16:13. And it came to pass in the evening that quail came up and covered the camp and in the morning a layer of dew was around the camp.

Quail *(Coturnix coturnix)* is for food whenever it is mentioned in the Bible.[25] The habits of quails as we know them today fit the biblical picture. First, the bird flies mostly at night. Secondly, after migration the birds are so exhausted that they can be caught with bare hands.[26] Lastly, during migration they make use of favourable winds: in the description of the provision of quail in Numbers 11:31 it says, 'Now there went forth a wind from the LORD, and it brought quail from the sea...'

Although large flocks of quail live in the Sinai Peninsula (mainly on the Mediterranean coast), the miracle of the provision of quail in Exodus and Numbers is primarily in the timing and extent of the events. The amount of quail in and around the Hebrew camp was astounding: the birds were 'beside the camp, about a day's journey on this side and a day's journey on the other side, all around the camp, and about two cubits deep on the surface of the ground' (Num. 11:31). Psalm 78:27 concurs by relating that 'He rained meat upon them like the dust, even winged fowl like the sand of the seas.'

16:14. **And the layer of dew went up, and behold upon the surface of the desert thin flakes like frost on the earth.**

In the morning a layer of dew covers the ground. Soon the sun evaporates the dew and another layer of a substance is revealed. The exact nature of the substance is difficult to determine: the text describes it as **'thin/fine/small'**. In addition, it is called **'flaky'**, a participial form from the verb 'to scale/peel' which occurs only here in the Masoretic Text. The Septuagint did not even try to translate the latter verb, but simply inserted 'white coriander seed' (based upon the description of the substance in Num. 11:7).

Numerous attempts have been made to define scientifically the nature of the food.[27] For example, Bodenheimer remarks: 'Accordingly we find that manna production is a biological phenomenon of the dry deserts and steppes. The liquid honeydew excretion of a number of cicadas, plant lice, and scale insects speedily solidifies by rapid evaporation. From remote times the resulting sticky and often times granular masses have been collected and called manna.'[28] Such explanations are not sufficient, and they do not precisely fit the biblical descriptions. It is unwise to remove the miraculous element: manna is 'bread from

God' (Exod. 16:15), 'food from heaven' (Ps. 78:24), and the 'bread of angels' (Ps. 78:25).

16:15. When the children of Israel saw [it] they each said to his comrade, 'What is it?' For they did not know what it was. And Moses said to them, 'It is the bread which Yahweh has given to you to eat.'

When the Hebrews see the flaky substance, they ask *'mān hû"*, literally, **'What is it?'** The word *mān* is unique in Hebrew — the normal way of asking 'What?' is *māh* (used later in the verse in the phrase, **'what it was'**). *Mān* is an ancient dialectic variant found in Canaanite literature, such as in the texts at Ugarit.[29]

The term 'manna' (see 16:31) for the bread is based upon the Hebrew *mān*, 'what?' Thus, the present incident describes a popular etymology — that is, the first use of the word, and where it came from. Other similar etymologies are common in the Old Testament.[30]

16:16. 'This is the word which Yahweh commands: "Gather for yourselves each man according to what he eats; you shall take an omer for the number of persons in each tent."'

Moses now gives more detailed instructions regarding the gathering of the manna. First, the prophet says the Hebrews are to pick up manna, literally, **'a man according to his eating'**. This is precisely the command given at the Passover sacrifice: the lamb was to be divided according to what each man could eat (Exod. 12:4). The point of these two directives is that no one should hoard any food. A natural desire because of hunger would be to take much and store some of it for future use. God is forbidding hoarding: Israel must trust him daily for their sustenance.

An **'omer'** normally signifies 'a sheaf' (Lev. 23:11-15; Deut. 24:19; Ruth 2:7,15), and it can be used figuratively of food in general (Job 24:10). In this verse, 'omer' is a measurement of weight or capacity. It is one-tenth of an ephah; an ephah is one-tenth of a homer; and a homer equals 48.4 gallons. Thus, an omer is approximately half a gallon.

16:17-18. The children of Israel did so, and some gathered much and some little. And when they measured it by the omer, he who gathered much did not have too much, and he who gathered little did not have too little. Every man gathered what he could eat.

At this point, the text indicates that the Hebrews do as they are commanded. And God adequately and precisely meets the needs of the people: no one has too much or too little.

16:19. Then Moses said to them, 'Let no one leave any of it until morning.'

The Hebrew prophet lays a further stricture on the people. He uses a negative (*'al*) followed by a jussive, which in the Hebrew language constitutes a negative imperative. They are commanded not to save any of the manna from day to day. The Israelites are to gather it in the morning and use it throughout the day, but that is all. Thus they must constantly have faith that God will provide for them each and every day.

16:20. But they did not listen to Moses. And some of the people left it until morning. And worms grew [in it], and it smelled. And Moses was irate with them.

Some of the people apparently had too great a concern for the next day: what shall we eat tomorrow? So they dis-obeyed God's command by keeping some of the manna until the following morning. As a result, there was a plague on the manna. The nature of the plague is not certain, although the word used commonly refers to **'worms'**.[31] The manna thus became contaminated and smelled. This seems to be a deliberate allusion to the first plague on Egypt in which the Nile was contaminated and smelled (the same word is used in both places — see 7:18).

The verb translated **'grew'** (NIV, 'it was full of [maggots]') is problematic. Brown, Driver and Briggs understand it as meaning 'to be wormy' (p. 942). However, it may simply stem from the common root that means 'to rise/grow'.

Moses responds to the Hebrews' disbelief and disobedience with anger. There is no stronger verb in Hebrew to reflect wrath/anger than the one used here. The Hebrews are again living by sight and not by faith; Moses is therefore highly indignant.

Application

The reason that God gives manna to the children of Israel is not merely to feed them. A much greater purpose is being served. Moses later comments that 'He humbled you and let you be hungry, and fed you with manna which you did not know, nor did your fathers know, that he might make you understand that man does not live by bread alone, but man lives by everything that proceeds out of the mouth of the LORD ... in the wilderness he fed you manna which your fathers did not know, that he might humble you and that he might test you, to do good for you in the end' (Deut. 8:3,16).

The primary intent of the provision of manna was to teach God's people to depend upon God and upon his Word. Man's survival is dependent upon the Lord, and him alone. The reader should consider Jesus' response to Satan's temptation that he should turn stones into bread! (Matt. 4:4).

Manna is also a type and foreshadowing of Jesus.[32] In John 6, the crowd asks for a sign from Jesus so that they might believe, a sign like the manna in the wilderness: 'They said therefore to him, "What then do you do for a sign, that we may see, and believe you? What work do you perform? Our fathers ate the manna in the wilderness; as it is written, 'He gave them bread out of heaven to eat'" (vv. 30-31).

In response, Jesus claims that he is the true bread of heaven that has been sent by the Father to quench people's thirst and hunger: 'Jesus therefore said to them, "Truly, truly, I say to you, it is not Moses who has given you the bread out of heaven, but it is my Father who gives you the true bread out of heaven. For the bread of God is that which comes down out of heaven, and gives life to the world." They said therefore to him, "Lord, evermore give us this bread." Jesus said to them, "I am the bread of life; he who comes to me shall not hunger, and he who believes in me shall never thirst"' (vv. 32-35).

Sabbath commands (Exodus 16:21-30)

In verse 5 of the present chapter, Yahweh gave a general command to Moses regarding the gathering of the manna. There he ordered that on the sixth day of the week a double portion of manna should be collected in order to provide for the sixth and seventh days. In the paragraph now under consideration, Moses provides specific regulations relating to that law. These are the first Sabbath laws of the Bible.

16:21. And they gathered it morning by morning each according to what one could eat; but when the sun grew hot, it melted.

This verse serves as a general introduction to the next section. The Hebrews have mended their ways, and now they are obedient to the commands of God regarding the manna.

A repetitive expression for the time of gathering is employed here: literally, **'in the morning, in the morning'**. Reiteration of the preposition and the noun signifies entirety in distribution — in other words, it expresses the idea that the Israelites collected manna each and every morning.

16:22. And it came to pass on the sixth day that they gathered twice as much bread, two omers for one [person]. And all the leaders of the congregation came and they told it to Moses.

Some commentators believe that the double amount of manna on the sixth day was a surprise to Israel when the people went out to the fields.[33] Based on that discovery, they say, Moses then used the opportunity to instruct the Hebrews in the Sabbath principle. But the fact of the matter is, the Sabbath law did not simply come out of the blue. God had already explained it to Moses in verse 5. The existence of the Sabbath is assumed in the present verse; it had existed since the time of creation in Genesis 2:1-3.

16:23. And he said to them, 'This is what Yahweh says, "Tomorrow is a Sabbath, a holy Sabbath to Yahweh; bake what you will bake and boil what you will boil. Whatever is left over, you shall keep for yourselves until morning."'

On the same day as the events of verse 22 (the sixth day), Moses tells the people that the next day is to be observed as a Sabbath day. It is a **'holy'** day — that is, one that is set apart, unique and special; that, of course, reflects the account of the original creation: 'Then God blessed the seventh day and made it holy, because in it he rested from all his work which God had created and made' (Gen. 2:3).

The command concerning cooking reads literally: **'That which you will bake, bake. And that which you will boil, boil.'** In both phrases, an imperfect verbal form is followed by an imperative of the same root. This is the *idem per idem* principle which serves to provide the subject with total freedom in carrying out a command.[34]

'You shall keep [it]' is the same command that was given to the Israelites in Egypt in regard to saving the Passover lamb until the proper moment of sacrifice (12:6). These things must be done according to God's timing and laws.

Two basic interpretations have been proposed for the general command of this verse. The first is that all the manna had to be baked or boiled on the sixth day so that the Sabbath would not be profaned by cooking on it; the second view is that the Israelites were to bake and boil only the manna which they needed on the sixth day; uncooked manna would not be contaminated on the Sabbath. In other words, the law had nothing to do with cooking on the Sabbath.[35] On the basis of the *idem per idem* formula, the latter explanation appears to be the most appropriate.

16:24. So they saved it until the morning as Moses commanded, and it did not smell or have worms in it.

The Hebrews obeyed God's orders as they were given through Moses. The result is that the manna gathered on the sixth day kept overnight; it did not become contaminated or rancid, in contrast to what happened on the other six nights. If they hoarded manna on those days, it would be spoilt by morning (v. 20).

The general sense of the verb for 'save' is 'to rest': **'So they rested it until morning.'** Actually, because of the command it was the Hebrews who were to rest, not the manna.

16:25. And Moses said, 'Eat it today because today is a Sabbath to Yahweh; today you will not find it in the field.'

Verses 23-25 contain the first instances of the noun Sabbath (Hebrew, *sabat*) in the Bible. Certainly the concept existed as early as creation, yet the specific name of the day is not revealed to the reader until this time.

The definite noun translated **'today'** occurs three times. It is for emphasis, to underscore the uniqueness of the Sabbath to the people of Israel.

16:26. 'Six days you may gather it, but on the seventh day is a Sabbath; it will not be there.'

The formulation, **'Six days ... but on the seventh day'** first appears in the Bible in this verse, but it becomes idiomatic for the Sabbath laws throughout the Torah (see Exod. 20:9-11; 23:12; 31:15,17; 34:21; 35:2). This literary convention is another indicator that the central ideas and laws of the Sabbath are present in the story of the manna. It is again important to note that these concepts precede the giving of the law at Sinai.

16:27. And it came to pass on the seventh day that some of the people went out to gather, and they did not find [any].

A prepositional phrase serves as the subject of the sentence. **'From the people'** (preposition *min*) is a partitive marker referring to a part of the subsequent noun (cf., 2 Sam. 11:17; 2 Kings 9:33). The word **'some'** is a solid translation. The subject is so general, however, that one cannot determine the extent or number of the people involved in the disobedience.

Ezekiel, a sixth-century prophet of Judah, alludes to this event by saying, 'So I took them out of the land of Egypt and brought them into the wilderness. And I gave them my statutes and informed them of my ordinances, by which, if a man observes them, he will live. And also I gave them my Sabbaths to be a sign between me and them, that they might know that I am the LORD who sanctifies them. But the house of Israel rebelled against me in the wilderness. They did not walk in my statutes, and they rejected my ordinances, by which, if a man observes them, he will live; and my Sabbaths they greatly profaned' (20:10-13). Implied in the prophet's account is the idea that the scene was one of widespread violation.[36] Exactly how many people were involved in defiance is a mystery, however.

16:28. Then Yahweh said to Moses, 'How long will you refuse to keep my commands and my instructions?'

Clearly, the **'commands'** and **'instructions'** that God is speaking about are the Sabbath statutes that have just been elaborated. Again, God is testing the obedience of his people. They, however, are failing miserably.

The Lord's charge against Israel (through the covenant mediator Moses) is similar to his assault upon Pharaoh. In Exodus 10:3 the Lord said to Pharaoh, 'How long will you refuse?' The Hebrews are thus acting like the Egyptian king; that is, stubbornly disregarding the Word of God. But God has warned them. If they continue to act in disbelief and rebelliousness, then they will receive the same diseases/plagues that fell on Egypt (see 15:26).

16:29. 'See that Yahweh has given you the Sabbath; therefore he is giving you bread on the sixth day for two days; everyone shall stay in his place; no one shall go out from his place on the seventh day.'

Yahweh himself is speaking here. He announces that the Sabbath is a divine gift to the people of Israel. Thus it is right to emphasize the joyfulness of the day. It is not something that the Hebrews celebrated in Egypt — Pharaoh was an oppressor and he would give them no time for rest. Unfortunately, many of the Hebrews apparently saw the Sabbath as oppressive, and that is why they disobeyed and went in search of manna. They had got it the wrong way round (see Deut. 5:15). P. D. Miller sums up the meaning of this verse by saying, 'Here is an explicit statement in a narrative about the Sabbath that it is the gift of the Lord. In a larger way that is clearly the point that the Exodus form of the commandment means to make by reading the Sabbath into creation and identifying the Sabbath as blessed by the Lord and hallowed. That is, the Lord's blessing of the Sabbath is the providing of the Sabbath as a gift for human existence.'[37] While I would strongly disagree with his statement that the Sabbath is to be read into creation — rather than being integral to it —

yet, his emphasis upon the Sabbath as blessing is quite accurate.

16:30. So the people rested on the seventh day.

The verb **'rested'** is *šābāt*, from which derives the noun 'Sabbath'. Consequently, the opening phrase could actually read, 'So the people kept the Sabbath' (cf. Lev. 23:32).[38]

The reader should also note the assonance in the verse: the verb is *šābāt* and the word for **'seventh'** is *šēbaʿ*. Thus the section ends on a lovely and highly poetical note.

Application

Many in the church today feel that the Sabbath/Lord's Day is oppressive and burdensome. They act as if the day were one of drudgery and dull legalisms. That general misconception is unfortunate, because the Sabbath is to be a day of celebration and joy. Even Karl Barth, with whom we have little in common, recognizes the jubilant and joyful nature of the day: 'On this day he is to celebrate, rejoice and be free, to the glory of God. In this celebration, joy and freedom he will be obedient. To withdraw from it under any pretext would be disobedience.'[39] That, of course, is Jesus' point when he says, 'The Sabbath was made for man, not man for the Sabbath' (Mark 2:27). It is for humanity's well-being; it is a blessing; and it is to be a delight.

When I first began teaching, a number of my students were convicted of the necessity of keeping the Sabbath. They believed that the day should be set apart for acts of piety, necessity, mercy and rest. Their main concern was the idea of not being able to study on that day. An odd thing happened, however. When they kept the Sabbath their grades actually improved. They worked diligently the other six days of the week and they looked with eager anticipation to the Sabbath — and it became a day of joy to them. God makes a grand promise to his people about the Sabbath:

'If you keep your feet from breaking the Sabbath
and from doing as you please on my holy day,
if you call the Sabbath a delight
and the LORD's holy day honourable,
and if you honour it by not going your own way
and not doing as you please or speaking idle words,
then you will find your joy in the LORD,
and I will cause you to ride on the heights of the land
and to feast on the inheritance of your father Jacob.'
The mouth of the LORD has spoken

(Isa. 58:13-14).

Commemorating the provision of manna (Exodus 16:31-36)

The biblical author now inserts some editorial comments regarding the provision of manna throughout the remainder of the wilderness wanderings. He first gives a further description of the nature of the manna. An explanation of the length of time during which manna was eaten then follows. Finally, Moses comments upon the manna as a symbolic reminder of God's goodness to Israel in the wilderness.

16:31. And the house of Israel called its name manna; it was white like coriander seed and its taste like wafers in honey.

This editorial section opens by recounting and adding to previous material from chapter 16. First, it mentions the naming of the manna which was related earlier in verses 14-16. The main difference is that now the Hebrews are called, literally, **'the house of Israel'**. That title appears in the Bible for the first time here. But it is not out of place: the idea of 'house' being used of a group of people is not new to Exodus (see 2:1). In addition, the designation is common in the Torah (Exod. 40:38; Lev. 10:6; 17:3,8,10; Num. 20:29). So the Septuagint's translation 'the children of Israel' is misplaced.

Secondly, the verse provides another description of the manna (see verse 14). It agrees with the account of Numbers 11:7-8, but more detail is provided here.

16:32. And Moses said, 'This is the word which Yahweh commanded, "Take an omerful of it to keep throughout your generations, so that they might see the bread with which I fed you in the wilderness, when I brought you from the land of Egypt."'

Yahweh directs the Hebrews to preserve one omer of manna — the amount of a daily ration — for future generations to see. This has a didactic purpose. It is to serve as a vivid reminder, a memorial, of God's aid to the Israelites in their time of need. As Coats remarks, 'The manna stands here as a symbol of a positive relationship between God and his people during the wilderness period.'[40]

The form of the verb 'to eat' is a Hiphil causative, and thus it takes an active meaning — 'to feed' someone with something.

At the beginning of the Lord's command there is no verb; it literally says in the Masoretic Text, **'the fulness of an omer'**. The lack of a verb caused the Septuagint and Targum translators to read the noun 'fulness' rather as an imperative verbal form, 'Fill!' The latter reading makes the passage clearer in meaning.

16:33. And Moses said to Aaron, 'Take one jar and put in it an omerful of manna and place it before Yahweh to keep throughout your generations.'

The verse opens with the command (imperative form), literally, **'Take *one* jar.'** Indefinite nouns in Hebrew are normally left unmarked, but occasionally indefinite nouns can carry the adjective 'one'[41] (for further examples, see Judg. 9:53; 13:2; 1 Sam. 1:1; 7:9,12).

This is the only occurrence of the Hebrew word translated **'jar'** . The Septuagint translates it as 'vessel'. It may be related to an Aramaic word which means 'basket'. In any event, the word signifies some type of receptacle.

Moses' order does not date from the time when the manna was first given. The wording, **'place it before Yahweh'**, implies that a priesthood exists and that a sanctuary is in operation — a point that is confirmed by the next verse. Such circumstances did not exist until after the law was provided on Mount Sinai.

Repetition of the phrase, **'to be kept for the generations to come'**, from verse 32, is for emphasis. It underscores the purpose of the ritual: it is to teach future generations of Israel how God provided for his people.

16:34. As Yahweh commanded Moses, so Aaron placed it before the Testimony to keep.

Moses now dictates that his brother (later to be the high priest) set the jar of manna before **'the Testimony'**. That term is often used in the Torah of the tabernacle containing the ark of the testimony (see Exod. 38:21; Num. 1:50,53; 10:11). This reference to it has long been recognized as anachronistic, because neither the tabernacle nor the ark has yet been built. Early commentators regard the verse either as anticipatory or prophetic.[42] In reality, it is Moses simply inserting this material when he wrote the book of Exodus to show that the Israelites did fulfil the commands God gave them at the time of the provision of the manna.

This is the third time the Hebrew infinitive **'to keep'** appears, and it occurs in three verses in a row. This is for emphasis, in order to accentuate the preservation of the manna as a teaching tool for Israel's posterity.

16:35. And the children of Israel ate the manna forty years until coming to an inhabited land; they ate the manna until they came to the border of the land of Canaan.

This editorial remark takes the reader even further into the future to the point at which the manna ceased to be provided for Israel. Joshua 5:12 defines that moment: 'And the manna ceased on the day after they had eaten some of the produce of the land, so that the sons of Israel no longer had manna, but they ate some of the yield of the land of Canaan during that year.'

The period of forty years in the wilderness is historical, but also perhaps symbolical. Often the number **'forty'** signifies a period of adversity and trial (see Gen. 7:12; 1 Sam. 17:16; Matt. 4:2). The testing of Israel is a central concept of the wilderness wanderings and God's provision of manna (see 16:4).

16:36. And the omer is one tenth of an ephah.

See commentary on 16:16.

Application

This section underscores God's great and continual provision for the house of Israel. It is not a one-off provision, but 'a continual feast', to quote Matthew Henry. Manna rained from heaven for forty years, and that demonstrates, in Henry's words, 'how constant the care of providence is'. And the manna never failed, even in the light of the people's ingratitude. Despite Israel's great sins of murmuring and rebellion, 'God's special bounty', as Calvin calls it, came daily and yearly. Therefore, a memorial pot of manna was to be set in the tabernacle; it was there to witness to the magnitude, the glorious nature and the graciousness of the miracle.

The church should take great encouragement from this story. As the apostle Paul comments, 'These things happened to them as an example, and they were written for our instruction, upon whom the ends of the ages have come' (1 Cor. 10:11). We must always remember and believe that God is providentially caring for his church, supplying her with great bounty! And, therefore, we need to trust in him at all times and in all circumstances.

The incident at Massah and Meribah (Exodus 17:1-7)

Now occurs a most severe test for the people of Israel. The people are travelling in stages through the desert. They arrive at Rephidim and there is no water. How do they respond to the hardship? We are now introduced to the fourth instance of grumbling in the wilderness (the first three are 14:11-12; 15:24; 16:2).[43]

17:1. And the whole congregation of the children of Israel journeyed from the wilderness of Sin, place by place, according to the command of Yahweh. And they camped in Rephidim. And there was no water for the people to drink.

The Hebrews depart from the area in which manna and quail are first given to them, that is, the Wilderness of Sin. They travel, literally, **'according to their goings out'**. That is all one word in Hebrew, and it derives from a verb normally denoting source, origin, or beginning.[44] The vein that yields silver (Job 28:1), the spring that gives rise to water (2 Chron. 32:30; Ps. 107:33-35) and the bud from which the flower develops (Job 38:27) are each called by this Hebrew word. The term also signifies the place of a journey's commencement. Simply put, it denotes a starting-point, or place of departure.[45]

The directions to and locations of these encampments are given to the Hebrews, literally, **'by the mouth of Yahweh'**. God is the one directing the people through the desert, and he is taking them from one oasis to another.

On the significance of the verb 'to camp', see the commentary on 14:9. The siting of the camp at Rephidim is uncertain.[46]

The problem at Rephidim is lack of water.[47] It is a more severe problem than at Marah. At Marah there was water, and God made it sweet. At Rephidim water must appear, apparently, *ex nihilo*.

17:2. So the people quarrelled with Moses and they said, 'Give us water to drink and we will drink.' And Moses said to them, 'Why are you quarrelling with me? Why are you testing Yahweh?'

The response of the people to their circumstances is more combative than mere grumbling. The word **'quarrelled'** is a strong word meaning 'to strive', or to find fault with a measure of hostility. The intensity is further emphasized by the stark demand of the Hebrews, the imperative: **'Give us water to drink!'**[48]

The prophet answers the rebels in much the same way as he responded to the third case of grumbling (see 16:7). When Israel contended with Moses they were really testing the Lord who had placed Moses in a position of authority. It was ultimately a lack of faith in Yahweh that led the people to act in such a manner.

The second occurrence of the verb 'to quarrel' ends with a *nun paragogicum*. This 'usually expresses a marked emphasis' and certainty, although it can also signify that something is by way of contrast.[49] In any event, its appearance in this verse demonstrates Moses' strong reaction to the accusation made by the Hebrews.

17:3. But the people were thirsty for water there. So the people grumbled against Moses. And they said, 'Why did you bring us up out of Egypt to kill us and our children and our livestock with thirst?'

The language of Israel's response is angry and hostile.
They accuse Moses of bringing them out to the wilderness
to die. It is the second time they have charged him with
this crime (see 16:3).

The spoken complaint reflects the oneness and self-
centredness of the people. It is reported in the first person
singular and reads, literally, **'Why did you bring us up
out of Egypt? To kill me, and my children and my
livestock?'** Numerous versions, such as the Septuagint,
the Syriac and the Vulgate, translate the endings as first-
person plurals — and, indeed, every English translation
does the same.

17:4. Then Moses cried out to Yahweh, saying, 'What shall I
do for this people? They are almost ready to stone me.'

The opposition of the rebels to Moses' authority is reaching
fever pitch and mounting towards a climax. Moses himself
discerns that the people are close to murdering him: he
says, literally, **'Yet a little while and they will stone me.'**
The first part of that statement in the Hebrew is a durative
phrase that conveys a sense of impending action and
urgency (see Hosea 1:4; Jer. 51:33). It is not hyperbole in
any sense, but it demonstrates clear and present danger.

The prophet's response is to pray to the Lord. He
petitions the God of the Hebrews for an answer to the
problem.

17:5. And Yahweh said to Moses, 'Cross before the people,
and take with you some of the elders of Israel, and your rod
with which you struck the Nile. Take it in your hand and go.'

Yahweh's solution to the prophet's dilemma is constructed
on three imperatives. First, Moses is commanded to **'pass
on by'** the Hebrews. That verb carries the idea of going
ahead of the people into the wilderness. Second, the
prophet is told to **'take'** some of the elders of Israel with

him.[50] They are to serve as witnesses to the subsequent event.[51] Finally, Moses is instructed to **'take'** the rod that had been a tool of God's miraculous power during the plague cycles in Egypt.

Yahweh makes mention of the first plague that came upon Egypt. The probable reason for the comment is to draw a contrast. The very rod that had struck the Nile river to deprive Egypt of water (7:14-25) now becomes a source of benefit to the people of Israel by providing water for them.

17:6. 'Behold, I will stand before you there upon the rock at Horeb. And you will strike on the rock, and water will come forth from it so that the people may drink.' And Moses did so before the eyes of the elders of Israel.

God meets Israel's needs, and he does so miraculously and abundantly. Moses is to go to **'Horeb'**, to the place where God had revealed himself to the prophet at the burning bush. Horeb is an alternative name for Mount Sinai, where the Hebrews will soon receive the law from Yahweh (see commentary on 3:1,12).

Yahweh announces that he **'will stand'** on the rock at Horeb. Some commentators argue this is mere anthropo-morphic language, using human imagery to describe the presence of God.[52] Others see a theophany in which the pillar of cloud descends upon the rock.[53] Either way, God is at Horeb in a special, unique way in order to provide for his people.

A natural explanation of water spewing from rocks, such as that given by Cassuto, is unwarranted.[54] The point of the story is to demonstrate that if need be God will go to great and miraculous lengths to sustain the Hebrews.

17:7. And he called the name of the place Massah and Meribah because of the quarrel of the children of Israel and because they tested Yahweh, saying, 'Is Yahweh among us or not?'

In good Semitic fashion, Moses names the place of the miracle according to the incident that occurred there. These etymologies are based upon assonance. **'Massah'** means 'test', and it is a derivative of the verb 'to test' in verse 2. **'Meribah'** means 'quarrel', and it derives from the verb 'to quarrel' also in verse 2.[55] The purpose of naming the site in this way was so that the people of Israel should never forget how foolishly and shamefully they had acted here.

The author drives home the point of the etymology by employing a chiastic structure:

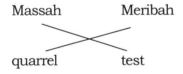

Massah   Meribah

quarrel   test

Application

Many authors have suggested that the events at Massah/Meribah serve as paradigms or pointers to certain New Testament stories. Some of these proposals have been good, while others have been less convincing. For example, the claim that the water ceremony in John 7:37-39 is a re-enactment of the wilderness water miracle seems to be stretching parallels too far.[56] Also, the idea that the Lord's Prayer is based upon the Massah/Meribah tradition is a bit strained.[57]

On the other hand, when Satan tempts Jesus to throw himself off the temple to see if God would be faithful and truly save him as he promised (Matt. 4:5-7), Jesus answers by quoting Deuteronomy 6:16: 'You shall not put the LORD your God to the test, as you tested him at Massah.' Jesus is being tempted to commit the same sin into which Israel fell when they were tested in the wilderness. Jesus, however, does not fail, as Israel failed, but remains true, obedient and faithful to God.

The apostle Paul also provides us with a fuller meaning and understanding of the Massah/Meribah occurrence, when he says, 'For I do not want you to be unaware, brethren, that our fathers were all under the cloud, and all passed through the sea; and all were baptized into Moses in the cloud and in the sea; and all ate the same spiritual food; and all drank the same spiritual drink, for they were drinking from a spiritual rock which followed them; and the rock was the Messiah' (1 Cor. 10:1-4). The identification of the Messiah with a rock is not an anomaly in the Old Testament. It is a term that is frequently used of God (see Gen. 49:24; Deut. 32:4,15,18,30-31). And, thus, Paul '… connects an episode from the history of Israel with the current conditions in Corinth. Christ was present in the wilderness as he is present with the church today. God's rejection of those Israelites who tested and tried him is a relevant lesson and reminder for those Corinthians who dabble in idolatry.'[58] Israel is the church in the Old Testament. And we should learn from our forefathers, and not act the way they did at Massah/Meribah.

Attempts to use Moses at Massah/Meribah as a model for ministry today are not very successful.[59] That is not the point of the story, and many of these studies easily slip into allegorical teaching.

8. Preparation for Sinai

Exodus 17:8 - 18:27

War with Amalek (Exodus 17:8-16)

This section has a lot in common with the previous incident (17:1-7). Both accounts are based at Rephidim; a great test or period of suffering occurs in both stories; the rod of God plays a significant role in each; Yahweh intervenes to save his people both times; and there are similar-sounding words (i.e. examples of assonance) in the two episodes (cf. 17:2,7,15). The major difference is that up to this point the adversity experienced by Israel after leaving Egypt has been of an inanimate nature. Now the people are confronted with human power and military might. This episode describes the first fight against another nation since the Hebrews left Egypt.

17:8. Then the Amalekites came and they fought with Israel at Rephidim.

As if Israel does not already have enough problems at Rephidim (17:1), now they are attacked there by a pagan, warring nation.[1] The Amalekites were a semi-nomadic people who lived in the desert lands to the south of Palestine (e.g., Gen. 14:7). Some analysts believe that they were fighting over control of the Kadesh Oasis, a most important caravan centre.[2] The exact location of the battle is unknown, however. Probably the most that can be said is that the Amalekites attacked Israel because they feared encroachment on their control of oases and caravan routes, in general.[3]

Their method of attack is described in Deuteronomy 25:17-18: 'Remember what Amalek did to you along the way when you came out from Egypt, how he met you along the way and attacked among you all the stragglers at your rear when you were faint and weary.'

17:9. And Moses said to Joshua, 'Choose men for us, and go forth to fight against the Amalekites. Tomorrow I will stand upon the top of the hill, and the rod of God will be in my hand.'

Israel does not respond by fleeing — as they did in Egypt — but they make their own necessary defence against the aggressor. In the escape from Egypt, the people merely stood and watched Yahweh stunningly defeat the Egyptians; now they must help to defend themselves.

The man **'Joshua'** is mentioned for the first time in Scripture, as he is appointed field commander to choose capable warriors to drive back the Amalekites. We later learn that he was the son of Nun (33:11), and the assistant to, and successor of, Moses (24:13; Josh. 1:1-3). It was he who later led Israel in the conquest of Canaan.

Moses was advanced in years, and so he could not lead the military attack. He would do his part, however, by placing himself on top of a hill at the battlefield so as to be seen by Israel. There he would hold the staff of God, as he said, **'in my hand'** — that powerful instrument that had channelled God's power to bring plagues on Egypt and to produce water from the rock at Rephidim.

In the original a question exists regarding whether the word **'tomorrow'** should be attached to the activity of Joshua (first clause) or to the work of Moses (second clause).[4] Perhaps it refers to both.

17:10. So Joshua did as Moses said to him — to fight against the Amalekites. And Moses, Aaron and Hur went up to the top of the hill.

As in the case of Joshua in verse 9, so too the figure of Hur is first introduced here. He was later to become an important judicial figure in early Israel (24:14). Perhaps he was from the tribe of Judah and was the grandfather of Bezalel, the leader in the construction of the tabernacle (31:2; 35:30; 38:22). Jewish tradition also claims that he was either the husband or the son of Miriam, the sister of Moses.[5]

17:11. And whenever Moses held up his hand, Israel prevailed; whenever he lowered his hand, then the Amalekites prevailed.

The battle begins. Whenever Moses holds up **'his hand'** Israel dominates, but when he rests **'his hand'** the Amalekites sway the battle. Much ink has been spilled regarding Moses' part and activity in the conflict. Sarna, for instance, argues it is 'highly plausible' that 'Moses held up a standard bearing some conspicuous symbol that signified the presence of God in the Israelite camp'.[6] Confirmation of this position rests in the name Moses gives to the battle site in verse 15: 'Yahweh is my banner.' Others insist we are witnessing an act of prayer — when Moses' hands are raised for divine intervention, God responds. There is absolutely nothing in the text to support this idea. Still others believe Moses is acting as a cult-magician, employing magical powers much like those of the magicians of Egypt. Coats remarks, 'By quasi-magical ritual, he determines the proceedings of the battle.'[7]

The answer is quite simple. Moses has God's rod in his hand — see verse 9 in which 'hand' is also singular. The rod is the mediating instrument of God's power.[8] It is God who is fighting for Israel, and he who is to be glorified. And the reason Israel does not prevail when the rod is lowered is to show the people that God contributes more to their victory than do sword and shield.

17:12. When Moses' hands [became] heavy, they took a stone and they set it under him and he sat upon it. And Aaron and Hur held his hands up, one on one side and one on the other. And his hands were steady until the setting of the sun.

The problem for the aged prophet was that **'the hands of Moses'** were **'heavy'**. This is a noun clause in Hebrew (it has no verb) and its purpose is 'to emphasize very strongly the unconditional relation between the subject and predicate'.[9] If Israel was to be victorious, Moses needed help.

With the aid of Aaron and Hur, Moses, in a sitting position, was able to keep his hands **'steady'** until the going down of the sun. The basic meaning of the word 'steady' is 'faithful/trustworthy/true'.[10] It is normally used in moral contexts, and this is the only time in Scripture that it relates to a physical activity.

17:13. So Joshua overcame Amalek and his people by the edge of the sword.

Joshua's defeat of the Amalekites was not one of total destruction or annihilation. The verb **'overcame'** has the basic sense of 'to weaken/disable' (cf. Isa. 14:12).[11] The use of this verb has an ironic twist to it. A possible word-play exists between the verb (*hālaš*) and the noun used in Deuteronomy 25:18 to describe the Hebrew stragglers/weak ones (*hănnĕhĕšālîm*) being picked off by the Amalekite army.[12] Thus Joshua made weak and disabled those who preyed upon the weak and disabled!

17:14. Then Yahweh said to Moses, 'Write this memorial in the book, and put it in the ears of Joshua, that I will surely blot out the remembrance of Amalek from under the sun.'

Because of the hostility of Amalek, Yahweh commands (imperative mood) Moses to record **'a memorial in the book'**.[13] The term reflects a historical record of what God promises. The pledge is to be kept orally and in writing from generation to generation.

The content of the memorial inscription is directly stated: **'I will completely blot out the memory of Amalek.'** The statement is intensive, because the infinitive absolute of the verb is followed by an imperfective form of the same verb. It literally reads, 'Blotting out, I will blot out.' In addition, it should be noted that the word **'memory'** is related to 'memorial' from earlier in the verse. The point is to contrast the eternality of God's command and justice with the eventual demise of the people of Amalek (see 1 Sam. 15:1-33).

17:15. And Moses built an altar, and he called its name 'Yahweh is my standard.'

On account of the great deliverance at Rephidim, Moses erects an altar to Yahweh and he names it *Yahweh nissi*, that is, **'Yahweh is my standard.'** Similar memorials are known elsewhere in the Old Testament: for instance, Jacob constructs an altar at Shechem, and he calls it 'El the God of Israel' (Gen. 33:20). These altars were not for sacrifice, but were erected in commemoration of the event that had taken place at the site.

The Hebrew term often translated 'banner' is really a **'standard'** or signal-pole.[14] In antiquity, a standard was a rallying-point. Often it bore an emblem, symbol, or banner on its top. A standard was normally raised on a hill or other high place to be seen by all (see Num. 21:4-9). It was an object of focus and hope for the people.

Moses' appearance on top of the hill with the rod of God in his hand acted much like a standard.[15] The rod on the hill served as a symbol of Yahweh's power. Yahweh was thus seen to be the standard beneath which Israel rallied. The standard as a figure of the divine is known from other places in the Old Testament. In Isaiah 11:10, the Messiah, the 'root of Jesse', is one who 'will stand as a standard for the people'.

17:16. And he said, 'Because a hand was against the throne of Yahweh, Yahweh will make war against Amalek from generation to generation.'

The difficulty in interpreting this verse has been recognized by commentators for a long time. My concern is not to analyse each and every proposal — Childs has already done that masterfully.[16] I will generally present the problems, and then explain what I think to be the best solutions.

The first part of the verse is fragmentary, and it appears to have a poetical form. It literally says, **'Because a hand upon *kēs yāh...*'** The meaning of *kēs yāh* is much in dispute. The Septuagint translates it as 'a secret hand' — which is a weak attempt. Some want to see a scribal error, and believe the word *kēs* should be *nēs* (standard/banner) in line with verse 15. The Vulgate and other translations view it as a scribal omission of a syllable and assume the word should be *kîssē'*, meaning 'throne'. The latter is probably correct.

The **yāh** is the abbreviated form of Yahweh seen previously in 15:2. See commentary on that verse.

The preposition **'upon/to'** in the clause is probably being used in an oppositional sense, meaning 'against' (see Exod. 20:3). Thus the entire phrase would read, **'Because a hand was against the throne of Yahweh'**. In other words, the Amalekites assaulted the rule and sovereignty of the Hebrew God.

As a result, Yahweh will do battle against Amalek for generations to come. And that provides the setting for what follows in Scripture regarding the relationship of Israel and Amalek (see 1 Sam. 15; 30).

Application

The medieval writer Dante wrote a book called *The Inferno*. In it, the Roman poet Virgil leads Dante through hell and its different compartments. In Canto III, Dante is introduced to the souls of the dead who in life were neither for good or evil but only for themselves — their only banner was 'me'. They race round and round in a black haze pursuing a wavering banner on a standard. Dante relates the scene: 'I saw a banner there upon the mist. Circling and circling, it seemed to scorn all pause. So it ran on, and still behind it pressed a never-ending rout of souls in pain... These wretches, never born and never dead, ran naked in swarms of wasps and hornets that goaded them the more they fled, and made their faces stream with bloody gouts [drops] of pus and tears that dribbled to their feet to be swallowed there by loathsome worms and maggots.' These dead ran after a standard to call their own, a banner to give them identity, meaning and significance. In *The Inferno,* the dead could never catch the banner.

Christians, like the church of old, are to proclaim, 'The Lord is my Banner.' He is the ensign on the standard around which we are to rally, and which is to lead us into battle. It is the emblem of whom we serve!

> Onward Christian soldiers,
> Marching as to war,
> With the cross of Jesus
> Going on before:
> Christ, the royal Master,
> Leads against the foe;
> Forward into battle,
> See his banners go.

Onward Christian soldiers,
Marching as to war,
With the cross of Jesus
Going on before.

Jethro and Moses (Exodus 18:1-12)

This section presents an antithesis, or contrast, to the preceding block of material. In it we see one of the leaders of a neighbouring people not seeking to destroy Israel, as had the Amalekites. Instead here is one who honours the unique and wonderful redemption that God had accomplished for his people.

18:1. And Jethro, the priest of Midian, the father-in-law of Moses, heard all that God had done for Moses and for Israel his people, that Yahweh had brought out Israel from Egypt.

The last mention of Jethro was in 4:18, where he gave Moses leave to return to Egypt. Because it has been so long since Jethro has been referred to in the text, the author details his status, as a reminder to the reader: he was **'the priest of Midian and the father-in-law of Moses'** (see 3:1).[17] Thus Moses is taking us back to a situation and relationship that preceded all the events which took place in Egypt.

Jethro had heard about Yahweh's redemption of Israel out of Egypt. He probably received reports in the common manner from caravans travelling through his land into and out of Egypt. In addition, Zipporah and her sons would have brought news to Jethro because they had originally accompanied Moses on his journey to the land of the pharaohs (see 4:20).

18:2-3. And Jethro, the father-in-law of Moses, took Zippo-rah, the wife of Moses, after he had sent her back, and her two sons, of whom the name of one was Gershom, for he said, 'I was an alien in a foreign land.'

Now we read about an episode about which nothing further is known. Apparently Moses had sent his family back from Egypt to live with Jethro. The cause of the separation is uncertain. It may have been related to the incident concerning the circumcision of his son described in 4:24-26. That was the last time that Moses' family has been mentioned up to this point. The incident at the inn was a distressing one, and it may be that his family went no farther into Egyptian territory. It has also been fre-quently proposed that once matters began heating up in Egypt with the plagues, then Moses sent his family away for their protection.

Some Rabbinical writings, such as *Mekilta*, understand the sending away of Zipporah as a divorce. The verb 'send back' in rare instances can mean the judicial separation of a marriage (see Deut. 24:1). Yet Jethro refers to Zipporah as Moses' 'wife' in verse 6. 'Send back' seems to carry its basic, common meaning here; in other words, Moses sent her back to her father for safe-keeping.

Moses' two sons had accompanied Zipporah on her return to Midian. The author, here and in the next verse, provides the names of the children and the meaning of their names. The names are given because they apply to the recent and present circumstances of Moses and Israel. The naming of Gershom is a word-for-word duplication of 2:22, in which Gershom was first named by his father (see commentary on that verse). The name is a word-play. **'Gershom'** means 'a sojourner/stranger there'.

The verbal form used in the naming of Gershom is a perfective, and it reads, **'I was an alien in a foreign land.'** It is likely this is a reference to Egypt, from where Moses had recently fled with Israel.

18:4. And the name of the other was Eliezer, for [he said],
'The God of my father was my help, and he delivered me
from the sword of Pharaoh.'

The name of the second son was **'Eliezer'**, which means
'God is help.' His name reflects God's deliverance of his
people from the foreign land of verse 3 — that is, Egypt.
Moses explains that God is his helper.[18]

The phrase **'the sword of Pharaoh'** is unique and
curious. It may perhaps be a reference to Egyptian literature. In numerous inscriptions from the New Kingdom, the
reigning pharaoh is accorded the title 'lord of the sword'.[19]
This is particularly true of Rameses II, who may well have
been the pharaoh of the exodus.[20] The sword is a metaphor for military prowess, power and victory. It is from that
dazzling force that Yahweh has delivered Israel.

18:5. And Jethro, Moses' father-in-law, and his sons, and his
wife came to Moses, to the wilderness, where he was
camping at the mountain of God.

Jethro brings Moses' family to meet him at **'the mountain
of God'**. In Exodus 3:1, the 'mountain of God' is identified
as Horeb, another name for Mount Sinai. It is here that
God called Moses at the burning bush. Camping and
worshipping 'at this mountain' was also the sign and
fulfilment of the promise God had given that he would be
with Moses (see 3:12).

The miraculous event of bringing water from the rock
near Rephidim occurred at Horeb (17:6) and the war with
Amalek also took place in the vicinity of the mountain
(17:8). Finally, this was to be the site where Israel received
the law of Yahweh (19:2ff.).

18:6. And he said to Moses, 'I, Jethro, your father-in-law, am
coming to you with your wife and her two sons with her.'

In the light of verse 5, translators have had difficulty understanding this verse. It begins, literally, **'And he said to Moses, '"I, your father-in-law Jethro, am coming to you.'"'** How could Jethro be speaking these words to Moses? The Septuagint and Syriac alter the reading of the verse to: 'And it was said to Moses, "Behold, your father-in-law Jethro, is coming to you."' The two changes made are, first, to read the verb **'said'** passively rather than actively,[21] and, secondly, to substitute *hinneh* ('Behold') in place of *'ni* ('I'). These modifications signify that a third party, a messenger, came to Moses announcing the imminent arrival of his family.

The problem is that the Masoretic Text makes perfect sense as it stands, and is in no need of emendation. It is clear from verse 7 that a messenger is employed — but, as any good messenger does, he speaks the exact words of the patriarch who sent the message. The herald thus speaks in the first person. He is a mere instrument, or tool, of the sender.

18:7. So Moses went out to meet his father-in-law, and he bowed down and he kissed him. And they asked each other concerning their welfare. Then they entered the tent.

The meeting between Moses and Jethro takes priority over the return of Moses' family. That is because Jethro is the one with the highest station, even above that of Moses. The formal courtesies that Moses gives to Jethro underscore the homage due to the elder, the one of greater authority. First, Moses travels to meet his father-in-law on the way, an act of humility and obeisance (see Gen. 33:3). And, secondly, Moses greets Jethro by bowing before him and kissing him, also common acts when meeting a person of higher status (e.g., 2 Sam. 14:33).

Other formal civilities of the ancient Near East then occur. Literally, they **'asked each of his comrade as to peace/welfare'**. This is a Hebrew idiom of greeting, that is, finding out how the other person has been faring in life (see its use in Judg. 18:15; 1 Sam. 10:4; 17:22; 25:5). And, finally, after the formalities, the two men retire to a tent for more serious discussions.

18:8. And Moses recounted to his father-in-law all that Yahweh had done to Pharaoh and to Egypt for Israel's sake, all the hardship they had found on the way, and how Yahweh had delivered them.

This verse opens the general discussion that the two men had in the tent. It begins with the testimony of Moses. The prophet first tells Jethro about what Yahweh had done in and to Egypt, i.e., the events of the plagues and the Red Sea. Then he describes the various troubles and difficulties Israel had faced in leaving Egypt and travelling through the wilderness — lack of water at Marah, grumbling over food in the Wilderness of Sin, the rebellion over the water shortage at Massah/Meribah, and the battle against the Amalekites. Finally, he declares how Yahweh had delivered Israel from all their trials and tribulations.

Moses gives all the glory to Yahweh. He talks to Jethro about **'everything Yahweh did'** and **'how Yahweh saved them'**. The prophet takes no honour to himself.

18:9. And Jethro was delighted about all the good which Yahweh had done for Israel when he delivered them from the hand of the Egyptians.

Jethro is greatly moved by the testimony of Moses. And he displays a similar enthusiasm and excitement to his son-in-law; in fact, he uses similar vocabulary to that used in Moses' recitation in the previous verse.

The opening verb, translated **'delighted'**, is rare (it comes from *hdh*, see Job 3:6). The Septuagint translates it as if it derives from the verbal root *hrd*, which means 'to tremble/shudder'. The Jewish *Midrash B. Sanhedrin 94b* renders the verb as 'He felt cuts in his body.'[22] No matter how one views it, the word reflects a heightened response on the part of Jethro.

18:10. So Jethro said, 'Blessed is Yahweh, who delivered you from the hand of the Egyptians and from the hand of Pharaoh, who delivered the people from under the hand of the Egyptians!'

The next two verses constitute Jethro's confession. He begins his benediction with, literally, **'Blessed be Yahweh.'** A blessing beginning this way becomes a recognized formula in Israel's history.[23] In addition, this is by no means the only blessing upon God and Israel invoked by non-Israelites (see Gen. 26:28-29; Josh. 2:9-11; 1 Kings 5:2). It is also important to note that Jethro does not employ a generic name applying to any deity, but he specifically names **'Yahweh'** as the blessed one. Here is a Midianite calling on the personal name of the God of the Hebrews!

The Septuagint, apparently sensing an example of dittography, does not include the second half of the verse in its translation. In agreement, the *Biblia Hebraica Stuttgartensia* notes a lacuna at the end of verse 11, and thus places the second half of verse 10 at the end of verse 11. All this is unnecessary literary gymnastics. What we have here is a poetical confession, in which the second line basically repeats the first line for emphasis (the essence of Hebrew poetry).[24] It is an incomplete synonymous parallelism, looking like this:

a	b	c
Blessed be Yahweh	who delivered you (plural)	from the hand of the Egyptians and from the hand of Pharaoh

b	c
who delivered the	from under the
people	hand of the
	Egyptians.

8:11. 'Now I know that Yahweh is greater than all the gods because they acted arrogantly against Israel.'

'Now I know' is an expression commonly used in the Old Testament (e.g. 1 Kings 17:24; 2 Kings 5:15). In the majority of its appearances the formula is used of a person being convinced of a truth by an event. It reflects conviction on the part of the recipient. Whether or not it signifies the conversion of Jethro to follow the Hebrew God is uncertain: that may have happened earlier, in which case he now has greater belief in the Lord or firmer conviction. It does appear, however, that at some point Jethro became a devotee of Yahweh.[25]

The second half of the verse is difficult. It literally reads, **'because of the way in which they acted arrogantly against them'**. Who is meant by **'they'**? Some argue it is a reference to the Egyptians of verse 10.[26] On the other hand, it is more likely that it represents the **'gods'** of the earlier part of the verse 11. Indeed, the two halves of the verse are tied together by a word that serves to introduce a causal clause (**'because'**). Thus, the entire verse signals another mockery of the gods of Egypt — it is they who acted presumptuously and arrogantly against the people of God. This is a confirmation of Exodus 12:12.

18:12. Then Jethro, the father-in-law of Moses, took a whole burnt offering and other offerings before God; and Aaron and all the elders of Israel came to eat food with the father-in-law of Moses before God.

Jethro offers sacrifices to God as expressions of joy, thankfulness and devotion. The first sacrifice is the **'burnt offering'**. This type of animal offering had existed since the time of Noah, when the patriarch sacrificed victims immediately after the Flood (Gen. 8:20). It was later used in the temple/tabernacle morning and evening as a symbol of unceasing communion with God (Exod. 29:42). The Hebrew word literally means 'that which ascends', implying that the offering goes up heavenward to the great God. The sacrifice 'makes its meaning plain enough, impressing on the thoughtful worshipper the desire of God for 'truth in the inward parts', and for a disciplined devotion. It depicts a general self-dedication which is worked out in careful and painstaking detail.'[27]

The other **'sacrifices'** refer to an extremely ancient type of sacrifice, of which we first read in the Scriptures in Genesis 31:54 and 46:1. The word reflects a class of sacrifices. However, normally the rite included the eating of the flesh of the victim at a feast held in honour of God. Often it was an offering of thanksgiving.

After the ritual of sacrifice, **'Aaron and all the elders of Israel'** had a meal with Jethro. It may be that the meal consisted of the remains of the sacrificial animals: the term **'bread'** used here in the original is often a synecdoche for food in general.

The content of the verse may actually 'portray the making of a covenant between the Israelites and the Midianite Jethro'.[28] The constituent parts of the scene find parallels with sacrificial events that are part of covenant-making (see Gen. 31:54, in particular). The sacrificial meal shared by Jethro and the Israelite leaders is the strongest point in favour of this interpretation.

Application

What a wonderful family conversation we are witnessing! Moses and Jethro are not talking about the weather, sheep-herding, or the latest caravan gossip or news. No, but they are talking about the wondrous works of God. Moses is telling Jethro of the marvellous deeds of Yahweh — it is Moses' testimony, his sharing of the good news with his father-in-law. How profitable is this type of conversation! Each of us ought to consider the manner in which we deal with our families — what do we talk about around the dinner table? In what do we rejoice when we hear of it? I believe Moses' evangelistic efforts put many of us to shame.

Jethro's response to the good news is also astounding. Whereas the Israelites murmured and grumbled throughout their wanderings, here is a Midianite rejoicing over God's goodness to Israel! The faith of the Gentile is putting to shame the faith of the Hebrew. What Jesus says about the Roman centurion in Matthew 8:10 could be said about Jethro: 'Truly I say to you, I have not found such great faith with anyone in Israel.'

Judging the people (Exodus 18:13-27)

The purpose of this paragraph is to show the foundation of the judicial system in Israel. It is a self-contained narrative regarding Moses' appointment, at the behest of Jethro, of judges for the people. The story is essentially repeated in Deuteronomy 1:9-18, and that passage should be consulted.

The date of this material is a matter of controversy. Many scholars want to date it after the giving of the law at Sinai and thus see its present position as a retrojection. On the other hand, the passage does bear marks of great antiquity; Sarna comments on the salient point that 'so important an Israelite institution as the judiciary is ascribed to the initiative and advice of a Midianite priest. This extraordinary fact testifies to the reliability of the tradition and to its antiquity. In light of the hostility that later characterized the relationships between the Midianites and the Israelites, it is hardly likely that anyone would invent such a story.'[29] The fact that judges should have been appointed prior to the giving of the law at Sinai is not a problem — as we have frequently seen, Israel was not a lawless society prior to Sinai. Therefore, the people were in need of a judicial administration.

18:13. And on the next day, Moses sat to judge the people. And the people stood near Moses from morning until evening.

This verse provides the general setting for the entire passage. First, it gives a chronological connection with the events recorded in the previous verses: **'And it came to pass on the morrow.'** The timing is important because it indicates that Jethro was still present and the Israelites had not departed from Horeb. At that time Moses **'sat'** (the same word as in 17:12) to serve as judge over the disputations of the Hebrews.

Moses was acting alone in judicial authority and, therefore, the people **'stood by/beside'** him (a locational preposition is used). Apparently crowds of people approached him in order to have their cases heard by him. The activity of the prophet is described in terms of two all-inclusive opposites: he judged the people **'from the morning until the evening'**.[30] The figure of speech is used to highlight the great number of cases waiting to be dealt with by Moses.

18:14. When the father-in-law of Moses saw all that he was doing for the people, he said, 'What is this thing that you are doing for the people? Why are you sitting alone, and all the people standing near you from morning until evening?'

After watching the proceedings all day long, Jethro asks Moses two questions. The first one is rhetorical: Jethro knows exactly what Moses has been doing, but now he wants his son-in-law to acknowledge his activity. The second question is an accusation. But what is it that he is accusing Moses of? 'It is important to note that Jethro does not accuse Moses of misappropriation of power; Moses clearly stands in a legal office. Nor does Jethro introduce Moses to legal responsibility. The text presupposes that Moses carries a legitimate juridical position.'[31] The problem is that Moses is doing too much **'alone'**. He is carrying too great a burden on his own. He has no assistance.

18:15. And Moses said to his father-in-law, 'Because the people come to me to enquire of God.'

Moses' response is straightforward: the Hebrews come to him **'to enquire of God'**. That verb is often used of the act of dispensing oracles. In other words, when a person desires to know the will of a god, or what might happen in the future, he or she would seek answers from a deity. Oracular activity was quite common in the ancient Near East, and it is sometimes referred to in the Bible using the word 'enquire' (see Gen. 25:22; 1 Sam. 9:9; 2 Kings 22:18).[32] A commentator might conclude that Moses is thus acting as a seer, or diviner, for the Hebrew people.

The problem with this understanding of the passage is the fact that the context of the people's enquiry is judicial. They went to receive answers to their legal disputations (18:16). And, so, the word 'enquire' has taken on a technical, legal meaning within the context of our story, and it has nothing to do with divination.

18:16. 'Whenever they have a dispute, they come to me, and I judge between a man and his neighbour. And I make known the decrees of God and his laws.'

The verse opens, literally, **'when a matter is to them'**. The noun is normally translated 'thing/word/matter', but here it obviously signifies a dispute, or an affair that needs to be dealt with. The disagreement is then brought to Moses.[33] He responds in two ways. First, he acts as the adjudicator, or the judge who decides what is right. Secondly, he is the law-giver: **'I make known'** (a Hiphil causative) the precepts of God.

Because of Moses' position as law-giver, some scholars argue that the events recorded in Exodus 18 must have occurred after the provision of the law at Sinai.[34] This is a *non sequitur*. The fact of the matter is that many laws preceded the giving of the law at Mount Sinai, such as the Sabbath statutes of Exodus 16 and the Passover commands of Exodus 12.

18:17. And the father-in-law of Moses said to him, 'The thing you are doing is not good.'

Jethro passes judgement on Moses' activity. He speaks directly and plainly. His speech opens with the words *lō' tôb*, **'not good'** (cf. Gen. 2:18). This is emphatic: 'When expressing absolute denial, the Bible always uses *lō'* followed by an additional word.'[35] When *lō'* precedes any part of the sentence other than the verb, it means the word or expression thus singled out is being 'strongly emphasized'.[36] In speaking to Moses, Jethro is not vacillating or wavering in his opinion. To him, what Moses is doing is wrong.

18:18. 'You are certainly wearing down, both you and this people who are with you, because the thing is too heavy for you. You are not able to do it alone.'

The reason for Jethro's judgement that what Moses is doing is 'not good' is now stated. And it is given in the strongest and most forceful terms. His point is accentuated by the use of an infinitive absolute followed by an imperfective of the same verb: literally, **'Fading you will fade.'** The verb means 'to sink/languish/drop down/ wither' . It is used of the drooping of a leaf (Isa. 1:30; Ps. 1:3). In the present context, it refers to exhaustion, wearing down and discouragement.

The two verbs are followed by a double use of an emphatic particle: **'Indeed you! Indeed this people!'** The negative effects of the present circumstances, will, first of all, have an impact upon the prophet who is an old man and unable to **'do it alone'**. The Hebrew people will also be worn down and frustrated as they wait all day to have their cases heard.

The entire situation is simply **'too heavy'** for Moses.[37] The word for 'heavy' is *kābēd*, which as we have noted elsewhere, is a key term in the book of Exodus, having been used earlier of Pharaoh's heart (8:15,32; 9:34; 10:1), of the plagues (8:24; 9:3,18, 24; 10:14) and of Moses' arms (17:12).

18:19. 'Now hear my voice, and I will advise you. May God be with you! You be for the people a representative before God, and you bring the disputes to God.'

Jethro now wants Moses' attention (he uses the imperative **'hear!'**) so that he may advise him. But before he gives his advice, Jethro utters a benediction in the form of a jussive clause: **'May God be with you!'** The content of Jethro's advice is the need for the establishment of a new order of judicial hierarchy. He begins, in this verse and the next, to define the nature of Moses' responsibilities in the new order. First, Moses must act as the people's **'representative before God'**. The Hebrew word is normally used as a preposition meaning 'in front of', and rarely as a substantive meaning 'front' (only twice in Scripture). In the present context it is figurative, signifying 'the one in front of God'. He is to serve first and foremost as the covenant mediator between Israel and Yahweh.

Secondly, Moses, as mediator, is to bring various cases before God to receive decisions. Obviously, this duty does not involve every single dispute, but rather ones that are intricate and difficult (see 18:22). The workload and caseload falling on Moses are to be eased.

18:20. 'And you must teach them the statutes and the laws, and make known to them the way in which they should walk, and the work they should do.'

Jethro's job description for Moses has a pedagogic aspect: he is to be a teacher/instructor of the Word of God. The word translated **'teach'** is probably related to a verb that means 'to enlighten/shine'. However, it also carries a sense of gravity and warning.[38]

The content of Moses' teaching is to include **'the decrees and the laws'**. This is certainly a reference to verse 16, which defines these laws as originating with the Creator. He is also to **'make known to them the way they should walk'** — that is, 'live'. Thus, Moses' didactic task is not merely 'religious' instruction, but he is to teach the people how to function in all areas of life. He is to present them with a world- and life-view based upon God's Word.

18:21. 'And you shall select men of character from all the people who fear God, men of truth, haters of dishonest gain; and you shall set them as leaders over thousands, leaders over hundreds, leaders over fifties and leaders over tens.'

Jethro tells Moses that he has a further duty. He is to **'select'** able men from among the people. The verb used means 'to see/behold'. In this passage it probably signifies that Moses is to look for such men (the verb is also used that way in Genesis 41:33).

Moses' father-in-law then describes the qualifications of the men that Moses is to search for. First, they are to be **'men of character'** — that is, men of integrity and virtue. The term is frequently applied in military contexts to 'men of strength', but here it implies 'one of sterling character'.[39] Secondly, they are to be ones who **'fear God'**, a term in Hebrew that means a reverence that leads to obedience. Thirdly, the ones chosen are to be **'men of truth'**. And, finally, they ought to hate **'unjust/dishonest gain'**; in other words, they are to be incorruptible.

The judicial hierarchy is to be set up on the plan of a military administration (see 1 Sam. 22:7-8; 2 Sam. 18:1; 2 Chron. 1:2).[40] This structure is not surprising because the entire account of Israel's wilderness journey is written in terms of a military itinerary (see Num. 33:1-49).[41]

18:22. 'And they will judge the people at all times. And every great matter will be brought to you, and they shall judge every small matter. And it will be lighter for you, and they will bear it with you.'

Jethro now explains to Moses the function and duty of the men whom he should choose: **'They will judge the people.'** They will do the same job that Moses has been doing. They are to share with him the status of the office of judge. There is, however, to be one difference between them: the judges are to care for the common, normal, everyday disputes and matters, while cases of major importance (literally, **'large'** matters) are to be brought to Moses.

The position of judge is not a temporary one. The text says it will be **'at all times/continually/permanently'** (see the use of that phrase in Ps. 34:1; Lev. 16:2; Prov. 8:30). The position of judge remained in existence throughout the history of the nation of Israel.

The purpose of the shared judicial duty was so that Moses' burden and load would be less. Jethro expresses this with a Hiphil imperative: **'Make light!'** The verb used here is the antonym of the verb meaning 'to be heavy' used in verse 18. Jethro is urging Moses to act on his advice, and he does so in no uncertain terms.

18:23. 'If you do this thing, and God commands you, then you will be able to stand and also all this people will go to their place in peace.'

Here is a conditional 'if … then' clause. If Moses implements the changes suggested by Jethro, then specific consequences will follow. First, Moses **'will be able to stand'**. This statement seems to have both figurative and literal qualities. It means, on the one hand, that Moses will be able to stand up to the number of cases brought to him. On the other hand, the word 'stand' is purposely

contrasted with 'sit' in verse 13: Moses' strength is preserved so that he may *stand* before the people.

Secondly, Jethro says, **'All the people will go to their
place in peace.'** This clause implies that the court system
will function properly and efficiently. The people will not be
waiting all day for their disputes to be decided. Thus no
social disorder or unrest will result from such a judicial
system.

There is one caveat attached to the implementation of
this administration. It must have divine approval and
sanction. Childs expresses the opinion that what Jethro is
really saying is that God is commanding that such an
institution be established.[42] That is probably incorrect
because the conditional clause 'if...' still applies to God's
commands in the sentence structure.

18:24. And Moses listened to the voice of his father-in-law,
and he did all that he said.

The prophet accepted the advice of Jethro as he **'listened
to the voice of his father-in-law'**. Back in verse 19
Jethro had said to him, 'Now listen to my voice,' and
Moses was obedient.

18:25-26. And Moses chose men of character from all Israel.
And he made them heads over the people, leaders of thousands, leaders of hundreds, leaders of fifties and leaders of
tens. And they judged the people at all times. But they
brought the difficult disputes to Moses, and every small
dispute they judged themselves.

These two verses are the detailed outworking of the
instructions given by Jethro that Moses carried out. They
are a repetition of Jethro's words from verses 21-22,
almost verbatim. There are a few slight changes, such as
the use of the word **'difficult/hard'** in place of 'large'. The
alteration is significant, probably indicating that Moses not

only took the major, important cases, but he also dealt with any disputes that were particularly vexing and complex.

18:27. Then Moses sent his father-in-law away, and he went to [what belonged to him], to his land.

Here we read of the departure of Jethro. It stands in parallel with his arrival in verse 1 of the chapter.

Application

Ligon Duncan has commented that, 'In the words of wise counsel from Jethro (in Ex. 18) we discover that: to establish justice and righteousness amongst the people "men who fear God" are needed.'[43] The church in the Old Testament could not run properly or effectively without being led by men of sound judgement, great reverence and personal holiness. The same is true of the church today: only when church leaders, such as pastors, elders and deacons, are righteous and reverent can God's people expect to flourish.

The Word of God being taught to the church is central and the key to its sanctification. However, it is not enough. Discipline, through judges or elders, must be applied in the church situation — only then will holiness and righteousness prevail in the church.

End of volume 1

Notes

Preface
1. John Calvin, *Commentaries on the Epistle of Paul the Apostle to the Romans,* ed. H. Beveridge (Grand Rapids: Baker, 1993 reprint), p.xxiii.

Introductory matters
1. The idea of 'seed' signifying offspring or posterity is verified in ancient Near-Eastern documents. In the Merneptah Stela from Egypt, for instance, Israel is mentioned with the statement, 'Their seed is not.'
2. See D. Garrett, *Rethinking Genesis* (Grand Rapids: Baker, 1991); I. M. Kikiwada and A. Quinn, *Before Abraham Was: A Provocative Challenge to the Documentary Hypothesis* (Nashville: Abingdon, 1985); R. N. Whybray, *The Making of the Pentateuch* (Sheffield: JSOT Press, 1987); and G. J. Wenham, *Genesis 1-15.* Word Biblical Commentary (Waco: Word, 1987).
3. D. B. Redford, 'An Egyptological Perspective on the Exodus Narrative,' in *Egypt, Israel, Sinai: Archaeological and Historical Relationships in the Biblical Period,* ed. A. F. Rainey (Tel Aviv: Tel Aviv University Press, 1987), p.138.
4. T. E. Peet, *Egypt and the Old Testament* (Liverpool: University Press of Liverpool, 1923), p.93.
5. John D. Currid, 'The Egyptian Setting of the Serpent Confrontation in Exodus 7,8-13,' *BZ* 39.2 (1995): 224.
6. John D. Currid, 'The Rod of Moses,' *Buried History* 33:4 (1997): 107-14.
7. John D. Currid, *Ancient Egypt and the Old Testament* (Grand Rapids: Baker, 1997), p.155.
8. See, for example, J. K. Hoffmeier, 'The Arm of God versus the Arm of Pharaoh in the Exodus Narratives,' *Biblica* 67 (1986): 378-87; C. R. Krahmalkov, 'Exodus Itinerary Confirmed by Egyptian Evidence,' *BAR* 20:5 (1994): 54-62; S. Noegel, 'Moses and Magic: Notes on the Book of Exodus,' *JANES* 24 (1996): 45-59; G. A. Rendsburg, 'The Egyptian Sun-God Ra in the Pentateuch,' *Henoch* 10 (1988): 3-15; Z. Zevit, 'Three Ways to Look at the Ten Plagues,' *BR* 6:3 (1990): 16-23, 42; and many others.

9. J. H. Sailhamer, *The Pentateuch as Narrative* (Grand Rapids: Zondervan, 1992), p.23.

10. See, for instance, K. A. Kitchen, *The Bible in Its World: The Bible and Archaeology Today* (Downers Grove, InterVarsity, 1977), pp.75-9; Kitchen, *Ancient Orient and Old Testament* (London/Chicago: Tyndale/InterVarsity, 1966), pp.61-9; J. Bright, *A History of Israel* (Philadelphia: Westminster, 1972), pp.127-30.

11. Unless, of course, one identifies the *'apiru* and the Hebrews as one and the same people. The Egyptian text Papyrus Leiden 348 describes the *"'apiru* who drag stone for the great pylon of the structure "Rameses II-Beloved-of-Truth"' (see R. A. Caminos, *Late-Egyptian Miscellanies*, Providence: Brown University, 1954, p.491). One of the major problems with the identification is that the *'apiru* included many more groups than just the Hebrews, for they were spread over a vast area in antiquity.

12. Kitchen, *The Bible in Its World*, pp.76-7.

13. M. Beitak, *Tell el-Dab'a*, vol. 2 (Vienna: Oesterreichische Akademie der Wissenschaften, 1975), pp.28-43.

14. *ANET*, pp.376-8.

15. See F. Yurco, '3,200-Year-Old Picture of Israelites Found in Egypt,' *BAR* 16:5 (1990): 20-38.

16. Sarna, *Exodus*, p.xiv.

17. James K. Hoffmeier, *Israel and Egypt: The Evidence for the Authenticity of the Exodus Traditions* (Oxford: Oxford University Press, 1997).

18. Especially, see R. S. Hess, 'Early Israel in Canaan: A Survey of Recent Evidence and Interpretations,' *PEQ* 125 (1993): 126-42.

19. An English summary of this view may be found in A. Alt, *Essays in Old Testament History and Religion* (Oxford: Blackwell, 1966), pp.135-69.

20. G. Mendenhall, 'The Hebrew Conquest of Palestine,' *BA* 25 (1962): 66-77.

21. R. B. Dillard and T. Longman, *An Introduction to the Old Testament* (Grand Rapids: Zondervan, 1994), p.59.

22. J. J. Bimson, *Redating the Exodus and Conquest* (Sheffield: JSOT, 1978).

23. Bryant G. Wood, 'Did the Israelites Conquer Jericho? A New Look at the Archaeological Evidence,' *BAR* (1990): 44-58.

24. See, for example, B. Halpern, 'Radical Exodus Redating Fatally Flawed,' *BAR* 13:6 (1987): 56-61.

25. *Ibid.*, p.60.

26. J. Bimson and D. Livingston, 'Redating the Exodus,' *BAR* 13:5 (1987): 40-53, 66-8.

27. B. Waltke, 'The Date of the Conquest,' *WTJ* 52 (1990): 181-200. Quoted in Dillard and Longman, *An Introduction to the Old Testament*, p.58.

28. N. M. Sarna, *Exploring Exodus: The Heritage of Biblical Israel* (New York: Schocken, 1986), p.103.

29. John D. Currid, *Ancient Egypt and the Old Testament* (Grand Rapids: Baker, 1997), pp.121-41.

30. For a discussion of each theory, see I. Beit-Arieh, 'The Route through Sinai: Why the Israelites Fleeing Egypt Went South,' *BAR* 14.3 (1988): 28-36. See also B. J. Beitzel, *The Moody Atlas of Bible Lands* (Chicago: Moody, 1985), pp.85-91.

31. A. H. Gardiner, 'The Ancient Military Road between Egypt and Palestine,' *JEA* 6 (1920): 99-116; T. Dothan, *Deir el-Balah* (Jerusalem: Hebrew University, 1978); T. Dothan, 'Gaza Sands Yield Lost Outpost of the Egyptian Empire,' *National Geographic* 162.6 (1982): 738-69.

32. See M. Bietak, *Tell el-Dab'a*, vol. 2 (Vienna: Oesterreichische Akademie der Wissenschaften, 1975); Bretak, *Avaris and Piramesse* (Oxford: British Academy, 1979); Bretak, 'Avaris and Piramesse,' *Proceedings of the British Academy* 65 (1979): 225-89; E. P. Uphill, 'Pithom and Raamses: Their Location and Significance,' *JNES* 27 (1968): 291-316 and 28 (1969): 15-39.

33. *ANET*, p.259.

34. A. Sneh, T. Weissbrod and I. Perath, 'Evidence for an Ancient Egyptian Frontier Canal,' *American Scientist* 63 (1975): 542-8; and W. H. Shea, 'A Date for the Recently Discovered Eastern Canal of Egypt,' *BASOR* 226 (1977): 31-8.

35. D. B. Redford, 'Pi-hahiroth,' *ABD* 5:371.

36. See B. Batto, 'The Reed Sea: *Requiescat in Pace*,' *JBL* 102:1 (1983): 27-35; Batto, 'Red Sea or Reed Sea?' *BAR* 10:4 (1984): 57-63.

37. I. Beit-Arieh, 'Serabit el-Khadim: New Metallurgical and Chronological Aspects,' *Levant* 17 (1985): 89-116.

38. Beit-Arieh, 'The Route through Sinai,' p.36.

39. See Beit-Arieh, 'Route through Sinai,' pp.28-37, for an adequate survey of the leading proposed locations of Mount Sinai. Recent announcements of the discovery of Mount Sinai in Saudi Arabia (including treasures at the base of a mountain) seem to me to be questionable at best and spurious at worst.

40. Y. Aharoni, *The Land of the Bible* (Philadelphia: Westminster, 1979), p.183.

41. The identification of Ezion-Geber with Tell el-Kheleifeh has been disproved. See G. Pratico, 'Where is Ezion-Geber? A Reappraisal of the Site Archaeologist Nelson Glueck Identified as King Solomon's Red Sea Port,' *BAR* 12:5 (1986): 24-35; Pratico, *Nelson Glueck's 1938-1940 Excavations at Tell el-Kheleifeh: A Reappraisal* (Atlanta: Scholars, 1993).

42. C. R. Krahmalkov, 'Exodus Itinerary Confirmed by Egyptian Evidence,' *BAR* 20:5 (1994): 54-62.

Chapter 1 — Suffering in Egypt

1. U. Cassuto, *A Commentary on the book of Exodus* (Jerusalem: Magnes Press, 1967), p.8.
2. Some commentators want to translate **'leave the country'** as 'gain ascendancy over the country'. This rendering implies that the Hebrews are a threat to take over Egypt rather than flee from it. Contextually, the translation 'leave the country' is correct because Israel does 'leave the country', and that is the irony. See the discussion of Robert B. Lawton, 'Irony in the Early Exodus,' *ZAW* 97:3 (1985): 414.
3. *Preliminary and Interim Report on the Hebrew Old Testament Text Project*, vol. 1 (New York: United Bible Societies, 1979), p.88.
4. D. B. Redford, 'Exodus 1:11,' *VT* 13 (1963): 401-18; and my response to him in John D. Currid, *Ancient Egypt and the Old Testament* (Grand Rapids: Baker, 1997).
5. See W. F. Albright, *JAOS* 74 (1954): 222-33.
6. For a detailed study of the women's roles in this account, see J. Cheryl Exum, '"You Shall Let Every Daughter Live": A Study of Exodus 1:8-2:10,' *Semeia* 28 (1983): 63-82.
7. This is what Shalom M. Paul calls 'deceptive disobedience'. See his 'Exodus 1:21: "To Found a Family" A Biblical and Akkadian Idiom,' *Maarav* 8 (1992): 139.
8. Renita J. Weems argues that the 'midwives do not lie, they simply do not tell the whole truth'. See her 'The Hebrew Women are Not Like the Egyptian Women,' *Semeia* 59 (1992): 25-34.
9. Nina Shea, *In the Lion's Den* (Nashville: Broadman and Holman, 1997), p.1.

Chapter 2 — God raises a deliverer

1. For a classic study of the birth narrative of Moses, see B .S. Childs, 'The Birth of Moses,' *JBL* 84 (1965): 109-22.
2. N. Sarna says that the parallel with the Genesis creation narrative 'suggests that the birth of Moses is intended to be understood as the dawn of a new creative era'. *The JPS Torah Commentary: Exodus* (Philadelphia: JPS, 1991), p.9.
3. D. B. Redford demonstrates that in the ancient Near East a 'common literary motif used of gods and humans alike is the story of the hero cast away in infancy'. See his 'Literary Motif of the Exposed Child,' *Numen* 14 (1967): 209-28. It should be noted that the prevailing view in scholarship is that the birth episode of Moses is not influenced by Egyptian writings.
4. See G. W. Coats, 'II Samuel 12:1-7a,' *Interpretation* 40:2 (1986): 170-74.
5. M. Greenburg, *Understanding Exodus* (New York: Behrman House, 1969), p.44.
6. *Ibid.*, p.45. That interpretation is based on the one other occurrence of the phrase, 'and he saw that there was no man', in

Isaiah 59:16. In that passage, God is said to have rescued Israel because no one else would help her.

7. *Ibid.*

8. Cassuto, *A Commentary on the book of Exodus,* p.30.

9. *Ibid.,* p.25.

10. *BDB,* p.384.

11. W. Von Soden, *The Ancient Orient* (Grand Rapids: Eerdmans, 1985; English translation, 1994), p.72.

12. For a discussion of the unity of Exodus 3, see E. J. Young, 'The Call of Moses,' *WTJ* 29-30 (1967): 117-35, 1-23.

13. N. Wyatt (in 'The Significance of the Burning Bush,' *VT* 36, 1986: 361-5), suggests that the burning bush is an archetype of the temple in Jerusalem, the wilderness is a symbol of Babylon and Moses represents exilic man. To say that such a reconstruction is far-fetched is an understatement.

14. Cassuto, *A Commentary on the Book of Exodus,* p.32.

15. B. K. Waltke and M. O'Connor, *An Introduction to Biblical Hebrew Syntax* (Winona Lake, IN: Eisenbrauns, 1990), p.567.

16. Sarna, *Exodus,* p.15.

17. See Sarna's excellent discussion in *Exodus,* p.268.

18. J. G. Janzen, 'Resurrection and Hermeneutics: On Exodus 3.6 in Mark 12.26,' *JSNT* 23 (1985): 43-58.

19. T. Muraoka, *Emphatic Words and Structures in Biblical Hebrew* (Jerusalem: Magnes, 1985), p.84.

20. P. K. McCarter comments that it is 'a stereotyped phrase referring to the raising of livestock and bee-keeping, staple economies of the central Israelite hills' ('Exodus' in *Harper's Bible Commentary,* ed. J. L. Mays, San Francisco: Harper and Row, 1988, col. 135b).

21. One need only consider the many offering-lists of the *Papyrus Harris* that include considerable portions of both products. See, J. H. Breasted, *ARE IV,* pp.155-6, 159, 176, 197. P. D. Stern argues that 'the religious context for the ubiquitous biblical phrase of milk and honey' is really Canaanite — see his 'The Origin and Significance of "The Land Flowing with Milk and Honey,"' *VT* 42 (1992): 554-7.

22. Moses' character of humility is underscored in Numbers 12:3. One has to be careful, however, not to project that passage into the context of Exodus 3. The times and circumstances are very different.

23. The title 'Jehovah' is a misnomer. It is a combination of the consonants of YHWH with the vowels of Adonai. That mixture was then anglicized to form the name Jehovah.

24. YHWH appears in the imperfect and, thus, it is sometimes translated in the future: 'I will be who I will be.' The imperfect in Hebrew actually can appear in any tense, past, present, or

future. It is rather to be understood as uncompleted action. And that fits our story. God is ever-being and ever-acting.

25. W. A. VanGemeren, ed., *Dictionary of Old Testament Theology and Exegesis*, vol. III (Grand Rapids: Zondervan, 1997), p.455.

26. See J. K. Hoffmeier, 'The Arm of God versus the Arm of Pharaoh in the Exodus Narratives,' *Biblica* 67 (1986): 378-87; and D. R. Seely, 'The Image of the Hand of God in the Exodus Traditions,' (Ph.D. dissertation, University of Michigan, 1990).

27. See the work of G. W. Coats, 'Despoiling the Egyptians,' *VT* 18 (1968): 450-57.

28. John D. Currid, 'The Rod of Moses,' *Buried History,* 33:4 (1997): 107-14.

29. See A. Gardiner, *Egyptian Grammar,* 3rd ed. (Oxford: Oxford University Press, 1982), p.510; R. J. Williams, 'Egypt and Israel,' in *The Legacy of Egypt,* ed. J. R. Harris (Oxford: Clarendon, 1971), p.263.

30. See L. Keimer, *Histories de Serpents dans l'Egypte ancienne et moderne* (memories, Institut d'Egypte 50, 1947), pp.16-17, figs. 14-21.

31. See the translation in W. K. Simpson, ed. *The Literature of Ancient Egypt* (New Haven: Yale University Press, 1973), pp.15-30.

32. E. Hulse, 'The Nature of Biblical "Leprosy" and the Use of Alternative Medical Terms in Modern Translations of the Bible,' *PEQ* 107 (1975): 87-105; J. F. A. Sawyer, 'A Note on the Etymology of Sara'at,' *VT* 26 (1976): 241-5.

33. P. Jouon, *Grammaire de l'hebreu biblique,* 2nd ed. (Rome: Pontifical Biblical Institute, 1923), p.287.

34. See the discussion of J. Tigay, '"Heavy of Mouth" and "Heavy of Tongue": On Moses' Speech Difficulty,' *BASOR* 231 (1978): 57-67.

35. S. Noegel, 'Moses and Magic: Notes on the Book of Exodus,' *JANES* 24 (1996): 54-5.

36. Other examples of this formula are Exodus 16:23; 1 Samuel 23:13; 2 Samuel 15:20; etc.

37. Cassuto, *A Commentary on the Book of Exodus,* p.51.

38. Sarna, *Exodus, p.22.*

39. G. K. Beale, 'An Exegetical and Theological Consideration of the Hardening of Pharaoh's Heart in Exodus 4-14 and Romans 9,' *Trinity Journal* 5 (1984): 129-54.

40. *ANET,* p.54.

41. The link between Israel as God's first-born and Jesus as God's first-born is explored in P. Bretscher, 'Exodus 4:22-23 and the Voice from Heaven,' *JBL* 87 (1968): 301-11.

42. The preposition here is probably a *lamed* of specification. See Waltke and O'Connor, *An Introduction to Biblical Hebrew Syntax,* p.206.

43. Verses 24-26 are the most difficult to interpret in the entire book of Exodus, and they have received various interpretations. For a sampling of them, see the following works: G. W. Ashby, 'The Bloody Bridegroom, the Interpretation of Exodus 4:24-26,' *Expository Times* 106 (1995): 203-5; W. J. Dumbrell, 'Exodus 4:24-26: A Textual Re-Examination,' *Harvard Theological Review* 65 (1972): 285-90; L. H. Fink, 'The Incident at the Lodging House,' *Jewish Bible Quarterly* 21 (1993): 236-41; S. Frolov, 'The Hero as Bloody Bridegroom: On the Meaning and Origin of Exodus 4,26,' *Biblica* 77 (1996): 520-23; C. Houtman, 'Exodus 4:24-26 and Its Interpretation,' *Journal of Northwest Semitic Languages* 11 (1983): 81-105; H. Kosmala, 'The Bloody Husband,' *VT* 12 (1962): 14-28; S. Kunin, 'The Bridegroom of Blood: A Structural Analysis,' *JSOT* 70 (1996): 3-16.

Chapter 3 — The Opening Foray

1. According to *Midrash*, the elders lose their courage and they flee one by one as they near the Egyptian palace (see Exod. R. 5:17).
2. See K. Kitchen, *The Bible in its World* (Downers Grove: Inter-Varsity Press, 1977), p.78.
3. Cassuto, *A Commentary on the Book of Exodus*, p.67.
4. Kitchen, *The Bible In Its World*, p.77. For an important recent study of the conditions of working in Egypt, see L. and B. Lesko, 'Pharaoh's Workers: How the Israelites Lived in Egypt,' *BAR* 25:1 (1999): 36-45.
5. Cassuto, *A Commentary on the Book of Exodus*, p.71.
6. Gesenius, *Hebrew Grammar*, 2nd English ed. (Oxford: Clarendon Press, 1910), p.298.
7. See G. A. Rendsburg, 'The Egyptian Sun-God Ra in the Pentateuch,' *Henoch* 10 (1988): 3-15.
8. See the discussion in Cassuto, *A Commentary on the Book of Exodus*, p.76.
9. *ANET*, p.3.
10. This does not mean that the name Yahweh was never used by the patriarchs, but they did not fully appreciate its significance. J. Motyer comments, 'It was the character expressed by the name that was withheld from the patriarchs and not the name itself' (*The Revelation of the Divine Name*, Leicester: Theological Students Fellowship, 1959, pp.15-16).

Some scholars employ verbal gymnastics to understand this verse. G. E. Whitney, for example, argues that the negative of the verse is really 'a form of hyperbolic verbal irony intended to intensify the contrast between what is present in the mind of the audience and what ought to be present' ('Alternative Interpretations of *Lo'* in Exodus 6:3 and Jeremiah 7:22,' *WTJ* 48 (1986): 151-9). Compare the more balanced approaches taken by

S. Glisson, 'Exodus 6:3 in Pentateuchal Criticism,' *Restoration Quarterly* 28:3 (1986): 135-43; and W. R. Garr, 'The Grammar and Interpretation of Exodus 6:3,' *JBL* 111 (1992): 385-408.

11. *BDB*, p.486.

12. O. P. Robertson, *The Christ of the Covenants* (Grand Rapids: Baker, 1980), p.46.

13. See D. M. Fouts, 'A Defense of the Hyperbolic Interpretation of Large Numbers in the Old Testament,' *JETS* 40:3 (1997): 377-87.

14. G. Galil, 'The Sons of Judah and the Sons of Aaron in Biblical Historiography,' *VT* 35 (1985): 488-95.

15. Scribes attempted to correct the text by adding a *nun* between the first and second consonants of the Hebrew name Moses. It would then be vocalized as Manasseh. See the discussion in E. Tov, *Textual Criticism of the Hebrew Bible* (Minneapolis: Fortress, 1992), p.57.

16. Currid, *Ancient Egypt and the Old Testament,* p.122.

Chapter 4 — God's judgement upon Egypt

1. For a view of how the source critic views the plague section of Exodus, see D. J. McCarthy, 'Moses' Dealings with Pharaoh: Ex 7,8-10,27,' *CBQ* 27 (1965): 336-47.

2. T. E. Fretheim, 'The Plagues as Ecological Signs of Historical Disaster,' *JBL* 110 (1991): 385-96.

3. Much of this material is taken from Currid, *Ancient Egypt and the Old Testament,* pp.83-103.

4. Cassuto, *A Commentary on the Book of Exodus,* p.94.

5. Currid, *Ancient Egypt and the Old Testament,* pp.86-7.

6. For an expanded discussion, see J. Currid, 'The Egyptian Setting of the Serpent Confrontation,' *BZ* (1995): 203-24.

7. J. Vergote, *Joseph en Egypte* (Louvain: Publications Universitaires, 1959), p.67.

8. J. Davis, *Moses and the Gods of Egypt* (Grand Rapids: Baker, 1971), pp.90-91.

9. S. Noegel, 'Moses and Magic: Notes on the Book of Exodus,' *JANES* 24 (1996): 49-50.

10. For an important study of the formation of the Nile river, see W. C. Hayes, 'Most Ancient Egypt. Chapter I. The Formation of the Land,' *JNES* 23 (1964): 74-114.

11. J. G. Griffiths, 'Hecataeus and Herodotus on "A Gift of the River,"' *JNES* 25 (1966): 57-61.

12. Bulk of the translation by J. L. Foster, 'Thought Couplets in Khety's "Hymn to the Inundation,"' *JNES* 34:1 (1975): 1-29. For a general discussion of various hymns to the Nile, see R. T. R. Clark, 'Some Hymns to the Nile,' *University of Birmingham Historical Journal* 5 (1955): 1-30.

13. For a detailed study of all three terms, see Beale, 'An Exegetical and Theological Consideration of the Hardening of Pharaoh's Heart in Exodus 4-14 and Romans 9,' pp.129-54.

14. See the discussion of C. J. Collins in *The New International Dictionary of Old Testament Theology and Exegesis 3*, pp.577-87.

15. Currid, *Ancient Egypt and the Old Testament*, pp.96-103.

16. Cassuto, *A Commentary on the Book of Exodus*, p.97.

17. Waltke and O'Connor, *An Introduction to Biblical Hebrew Syntax*, p.401.

18. *ANET*, pp.372-3.

19. G. Hort, 'The Plagues of Egypt,' *ZAW* 69 (1957): 84-103; 70 (1958): 48-59.

20. Cassuto, *A Commentary on the Book of Exodus*, p.99.

21. Other interpretations abound. C. Houtman argues that wood and stone refer to the buildings of Egypt, that the water kept in them turned to blood. See his 'On the Meaning of *UBA'ESIM UBA'ABANIM* in Exodus VII.19,' *VT* 36 (1986): 347-52. Houtman also surveys other ingenious proposals for interpreting the passage.

22. See the discussion of Tov, *Textual Criticism of the Hebrew Bible*, pp.4-5, 52-3.

23. G. A. F. Knight, *Theology as Narration* (Grand Rapids: Eerdmans, 1976), p.62.

24. See, for instance, Genesis 15:18 in which the Nile is referred to as the 'river' of Egypt.

25. Cassuto, *A Commentary on the Book of Exodus*, p.102.

26. See J. I. Durham, *Exodus* (Waco: Word, 1987), pp.89-110.

27. The Septuagint adds 'for me' to the monarch's request (cf. Exod. 8:24).

28. On the emphatic use of the *lamed*, see Waltke and O'Connor, *Biblical Hebrew Syntax*, p.211.

29. *BDB*, p.787.

30. Knight, *Theology as Narration*, pp.62-4. A scarab is defined 'an ancient Egyptian gem cut in the form of a beetle and engraved with symbols on its flat side, used as a signet etc.' (*Oxford English Reference Dictionary*, OUP, 1996, p.1292).

31. D. B. Redford, 'Exodus I 11,' *VT* 13 (1963): 401-18.

32. See the discussion in J. H. Hayes and J. M. Miller, *Israelite and Judaean History* (Philadelphia: Westminster, 1977), pp.156ff.

33. The use of 'redemption' as a direct object appears to be out of place. Scholars have attempted to emend the Hebrew text for that very reason: see, for example, G. I. Davies, 'The Hebrew Text of Exodus VIII 19 (Evv.23) An Emendation,' *VT* 24 (1974): 489-92. Such tinkering with the text is unnecessary. Cf., A. A. Macintosh, 'Exodus VIII 19, Distinct Redemption and the Hebrew Roots *hdp* and *ddp*,' *VT* 21 (1971): 548-55.

34. For the use of 'ransom' in a sense of deliverance, see Ps. 111:9; 130:7; Isa. 50:2.

35. In late Hebrew, that verb is a technical term used of a girl who would not acknowledge a marriage contract.

36. J. K. Hoffmeier, 'The Arm of God versus the Arm of Pharaoh in the Exodus Narratives,' *Biblica* 67 (1986): 378-87.

37. G. A. F. Knight, *Nile and Jordan* (London: J. Clarke, 1921), p.160.

38. Currid, *Ancient Egypt and the Old Testament*, p.111.

39. Cassuto, *A Commentary on the Book of Exodus*, p.111.

40. Waltke and O'Connor, *An Introduction to Biblical Hebrew Syntax*, p.215.

41. The consistency of the dust as powdery is part of the meaning of the Hebrew word for 'fine dust' (see Ezek. 26:10; Nahum 1:3; Deut. 28:24).

42. Sarna, *Exodus*, p.45.

43. Cassuto, *A Commentary on the Book of Exodus*, p.113.

44. See Beale, 'An Exegetical and Theological Consideration of the Hardening of Pharaoh's Heart in Exodus 4-14 and Romans 9,' pp.129-54.

45. Beale, 'An Exegetical and Theological Consideration,' p.149.

46. Cassuto, *A Commentary on the Book of Exodus*, p.117.

47. M. Futato, *'drb,'* in the *New International Dictionary of Old Testament Theology and Exegesis*, vol. 1, p.738, incorrectly cites Ps. 69:47-48.

48. *BDB*, p.544.

49. Cassuto, *A Commentary on the Book of Exodus*, p.119.

50. For the importance of the number seven in Egyptian magic and in Hebrew literature, see S. B. Noegel, 'The Significance of the Seventh Plague,' *Biblica* 76 (1995): 532-9.

51. Cassuto, *A Commentary on the Book of Exodus*, p.120.

52. *BDB*, p.759. See 1 Samuel 6:6 for this verb again being used in the context of God mocking the Egyptians.

53. *ARE* 4: 456.

54. Waltke and O'Connor, *An Introduction to Biblical Hebrew Syntax*, p.447.

55. G. A. Rendsburg, 'The Egyptian Sun-God Ra in the Pentateuch,' *Henoch* 10 (1988): 3-15; and G. A. Rendsburg, 'Bilingual Wordplay in the Bible,' *VT* 38: 3 (1988): 354-7.

56. R. Weiss in a convincing argument says that part of the verse should be translated, 'Go and serve Yahweh because Yahweh you have been seeking.' See his 'A Note on *hta* in Ex 10,11,' *ZAW* 76:2 (1964): 188. For disagreement with that translation, see G. R. Driver, 'Forgotten Hebrew Idioms,' *ZAW* 78:1 (1966): 1-7.

57. Although the Hebrew of 10:24 does not mention the Hebrew women, the NIV includes them in its translation.

58. W. A. VanGemeren, ed. *Dictionary of Old Testament Theology and Exegesis, vol. II*, p.501.

Chapter 5 — The tenth plague: Passover

1. *BDB*, p.478.

2. A few recent studies have suggested that the despoiling of the Egyptians points to the fact that the Hebrews really left Egypt surreptitiously; that is, they left Egypt without Pharaoh's consent or knowledge. See G. W. Coats, 'Despoiling the Egyptians,' *VT* 18 (1968): 450-57; and N. L. Collins, 'Evidence in the Septuagint of a Tradition in which the Israelites Left Egypt without Pharaoh's Consent,' *CBQ* 56 (1994): 442-8.

3. Cassuto, *A Commentary on the Book of Exodus*, p.133.

4. F. C. Fensham ('The Dog in EX. XI 7,' *VT* 16, 1966: 504-7) says that 'the eager movement of the dog's tongue may point to the eagerness to eat the flesh of the transgressor or victim' (p.506).

5. Currid, *Ancient Egypt and the Old Testament*, p.113.

6. For recent resources on verses 1-14 of this section, see the bibliography of P. Weimar, 'Zum Problem der Entstehungsgeschichte von Ex 12,1-14,' *ZAW* 107 (1995): 1-17; P. Weimar, 'Ex 12,1-14 und die priesterschriftliche Geschichtsdarstellung,' *ZAW* 107 (1995): 196-214. For works on verses 21-27, see S. Bar-On, 'Zur literarkritischen Analyse von Ex 12, 21-27,' *ZAW* 107 (1995): 18-30.

7. A common understanding of this chapter by the source critic is expressed by W. Johnstone in 'The Two Theological Versions of the Passover Pericope in Exodus,' in *Text as Pretext*, ed. R. Carroll (Sheffield: JSOT, 1992). He says the Passover passage of Exodus 12-13 'has passed through two final processes of theological redaction which I have termed the "D-version" and the "P-edition"' (p.160).

8. Sarna, *Exodus*, p.54.

9. *Ibid.*, p.54.

10. *Ibid,* p.55. Sarna argues that the animal must be a year old or younger (see Exod. 22:29; Lev. 22:27).

11. Cassuto, *A Commentary on the Book of Exodus*, p.139.

12. *BDB*, p.342. In noun form, as it is in verse 11, it only appears in the Old Testament in relation to the exodus event.

13. H. L. Bosman, 'פסח,' in the *New International Dictionary of Old Testament Theology and Exegesis*, vol. 3, pp.642-4.

14. Waltke and O'Connor, *An Introduction to Biblical Hebrew Syntax*, p.197.

15. The rainbow in Genesis 9:13 is a sign. It is a pointer to the reality of a covenant between God and the earth. The rainbow is not the covenant, nor does it cause the covenant; it merely represents it.

16. *BDB*, p.290.

17. J. Wellhausen, *Prolegomena to the History of Ancient Israel* (Edinburgh: A. and C. Black, 1885), pp.83ff., argues that the Passover and the Feast of Unleavened Bread were originally separate feasts. A redactor brought two different sources together to make one celebration in Exodus 12. Wellhausen further propounded the view that both feasts are of great antiquity. H. G. May ('The Relation of the Passover to the Festival of Unleavened Cakes,' *JBL* 55, 1936: 65-82), is in general agreement with Wellhausen. More recent studies, however, even question the antiquity of the two festivals: see J. Van Seters, 'The Place of the Yahvist in the History of Passover and Massot,' *ZAW* 95 (1983): 167-82.

18. Gesenius, *Hebrew Grammar*, p.478.

19. Sarna, *Exodus*, p.59.

20. Gesenius, *Hebrew Grammar*, p.312.

21. Waltke and O'Connor, *Biblical Hebrew Syntax*, p.198.

22. A feminine noun that appears in only two places in the entire Old Testament, here and in the previous verse (v. 19).

23. Here is the severe apodictic negative in Hebrew: *lo'* followed by an imperfective verb.

24. *BDB*, p.706.

25. Sarna, *Exodus*, p.60.

26. Gesenius, *Hebrew Grammar*, p.480.

27. Cassuto, *A Commentary on the Book of Exodus*, p.145.

28. B. S. Childs, *The Book of Exodus* (Philadelphia: Westminster, 1974), p.201.

29. S. R. Driver, *A Treatise on the Use of Tenses in Hebrew*, 3rd ed. (Oxford: Clarendon, 1892), pp.35-6.

30. Gesenius, *Hebrew Grammar*, p.314.

31. K. A. Kitchen, 'Exodus,' in *ABD* 2: 700-708; K. A. Kitchen, 'Exodus,' in *Zondervan Pictorial Encyclopedia* 2: 429; Y. Aharoni, *The Land of the Bible* (Philadelphia: Westminster, 1967), p.179; and B. Beitzel, *The Moody Atlas of Bible Lands* (Chicago: Moody, 1985), p.86.

32. E. L. Bleiberg, 'The Location of Pithom and Succoth,' *Ancient World* 6 (1983): 21-7.

33. *BDB*, p.150.

34. A. Lucas, 'The Number of Israelites at the Exodus,' *PEQ* 76 (1944):164-8.

35. D. M. Fouts, 'A Defense of the Hyperbolic Interpretation of Large Numbers in the Old Testament,' *JETS* 40: 3 (1997): 377-87.

36. G. Mendenhall, 'The Census Lists of Numbers 1 and 26,' *JBL* 77 (1958): 52-66.

37. For analysis of the apparent discrepancy, see H. W. Hoehner, 'The Duration of the Egyptian Bondage,' *Bibliotheca Sacra* 126 (1969): 306-16; P. J. Ray, 'The Duration of the Israelite Sojourn

in Egypt,' *Andrews University Seminary Studies* 24:3 (1986): 231-48; and J. R. Riggs, 'The Length of Israel's Sojourn in Egypt,' *Grace Theological Journal* 12 (1971): 18-35.

38. The 'day' mentioned here is no doubt a reference to the Passover. See H. Hosch, 'Exodus 12:41: A Translational Problem,' *Hebrew Studies* 24 (1983): 11-15.

39. Gesenius, *Hebrew Grammar*, p.380.

40. R. de Vaux, *Studies in Old Testament Sacrifice* (Cardiff: University of Wales, 1964), pp.9-10.

41. Sarna, *Exodus*, p.64.

42. G. A. Barton, 'A Bone of Him Shall Not be Broken,' John 19:36,' *JBL* 49 (1930): 12-18.

43. M. Noth, *Exodus* (Philadelphia: Westminster Press, 1962), pp.100-101.

44. L. Morris, *The Gospel According to John* (Grand Rapids: Eerdmans, 1971), p.823.

45. A. H. Konkel, '*rwg*', in *NIDOTTE*, vol. 1, p.837.

46. Waltke and O'Connor, *An Introduction to Biblical Hebrew Syntax*, p.594.

47. Gesenius, *Hebrew Grammar*, p.466.

48. Waltke and O'Connor, *An Introduction to Biblical Hebrew Syntax*, p.108.

49. I. Mendelsohn, 'On the Preferential Status of the Eldest Son,' *BASOR* 156 (1959): 38-40. See, also, R. de Vaux, *Ancient Israel: Its Life and Institutions* (London: Darton, Longman Todd, 1965), pp.443-4.

50. Sarna, *Exodus*, p.65.

51. The most detailed study of the vocabulary of this section is M. Caloz, 'Exode, XIII, 3-16 et son rapport au Deutéronome,' *RB* 75 (1968): 5-62.

52. Gesenius, *Hebrew Grammar*, p.346.

53. Waltke and O'Connor, *An Introduction to Biblical Hebrew Syntax*, p.593.

54. Sarna, *Exodus*, p.65.

55. *ANET*, p.320.

56. For a study of the formula 'to your forefathers', see J. L. Townsend, 'Fulfillment of the Land Promise in the Old Testament,' *Bibliotheca Sacra* 142 (1985): 320-37.

57. Regarding the instruction of parents to children in Hebraic society, see W. Brueggemann, 'Passion and Perspective: Two Dimensions of Education in the Bible,' *Theology Today* 42 (1985): 172-80; and R. Martin-Achard, 'La mémoire de Dieu, devoir et grâce, selon l'Ancien Testament: quelques remarques à propos de la catéchèse,' *Etudes Théologiques et Religieuses* 63 (1988): 183-97.

58. Gesenius, *Hebrew Grammar*, p.447.

59. For detailed studies, see A. F. Segal, 'Covenant in Rabbinic Writings,' *Studies in Religion* 14:1 (1985): 53-62; E. A. Speiser, 'TWTPT,' *JQR* 48 (1957/8): 208-17; and Sarna, *Exodus*, pp.270-73.
60. Waltke and O'Connor, *An Introduction to Biblical Hebrew Syntax*, p.186.
61. Sarna, *Exodus*, p.67. See the discussion of J. J. Davis, *Moses and the Gods of Egypt* (Grand Rapids: Baker, 1971), p.154.
62. E. Nielsen, 'Ass and Ox in the Old Testament,' *Studia Orientalia J. Pedersen ... dicta* (Munksgaard, 1953), pp.263ff. Noted in Childs, *The Book of Exodus*, p.207.
63. Waltke and O'Connor, *An Introduction to Biblical Hebrew Syntax*, p.626.

Chapter 6 — Salvation at the sea

1. Cassuto, *A Commentary on the Book of Exodus*, p.158.
2. A. Gardiner, 'The Ancient Military Road between Egypt and Palestine,' *JEA* 6 (1920): 99-116; T. Dothan, *Deir el-Balah* (Jerusalem: Hebrew University, 1978); T. Dothan, 'Gaza Sands Yield Lost Outpost of the Egyptian Empire,' *National Geographic* 162.6 (1982): 738-69.
3. W. A. Ward, 'The Semitic Biconsonantal Root *sp* and the Common Origin of Egyptian *cuf* and Hebrew *sup*: 'Marsh(-Plant),' *VT* 24 (1974): 339-49.
4. B. Beitzel, *Moody Atlas of Bible Lands* (Chicago: Moody, 1985), p.90.
5. B. Batto, 'The Reed Sea: *Requiescat in Pace*,' *JBL* 102.1 (1983): 27-35; B. Batto, 'Red Sea or Reed Sea?' *BAR* 10.4 (1984): 57-63.
6. Currid, *Ancient Egypt and the Old Testament*, pp.134-6.
7. *ANET*, p.259.
8. For a full-scale discussion of theophany in the Old Testament, see J. J. Niehaus, *God at Sinai: Covenant and Theophany in the Bible and Ancient Near East* (Grand Rapids: Zondervan, 1995).
9. M. G. Kline, *Kingdom Prologue* (South Hamilton: Gordon-Conwell Seminary, 1986); also see his *Images of the Spirit* (Grand Rapids: Baker, 1980).
10. *Ibid.*, p.38.
11. W. H. Grispen, *Exodus* (Grand Rapids: Zondervan, 1982), p.51.
12. For a study of the so-called history of traditions problem in the Red Sea event, see Brevard S. Childs, 'A Traditio-Historical Study of the Reed Sea Tradition,' *VT* 20 (1970): 406-18.
13. E. D. Oren, 'Migdol: A New Fortress on the Edge of the Eastern Nile Delta,' *BASOR* 256 (1984): 7-44.
14. Gardiner, 'Ancient Military Road,' pp.107-9.
15. W. F. Albright, 'Baal-Zephon,' in *Festschrift Alfred Bertholet zum 80. Geburtstag*, ed. W. Baumgartner et al. (Tübingen: Mohr,

1950), pp.1-14; N. Sarna, *Exploring Exodus: The Heritage of Biblical Israel* (New York: Schocken, 1986), p.109.

16. G. I. Davies, *The Way of the Wilderness* (Cambridge: Cambridge University Press, 1979), p.82; J. Simons, *The Geographical and Topographical Texts of the Old Testament* (Leiden: Brill, 1959), pp.247-8.

17. A. Servin, 'La Tradition judéo-chrétienne de l'exode,' *Bulletin de l'Institut d'Egypte* 31 (1948-49): 315-55.

18. D. B. Redford, 'Pi-hahiroth,' *ABD* 5:371.

19. W. H. Shea, 'A Date for the Recently Discovered Eastern Canal of Egypt,' *BASOR* 226 (1977): 31-8.

20. Currid, *Ancient Egypt and the Old Testament*, pp.130-35.

21. Waltke and O'Connor, *An Introduction to Biblical Hebrew Syntax*, pp.211-12.

22. *BDB*, p.922.

23. A. H. Gardiner, *Late-Egyptian Miscellanies* (Brussels: Fondation égyptologique de la reine Elisabeth, 1937), pp.132-7.

24. *BDB*, p.939.

25. *BDB*, p.1026.

26. B. A. Mastin, 'Was the *SALIS* the Third Man in the Chariot?' in J. A. Emerton, ed., *Studies in the Historical Books of the Old Testament*, *SVT* 30 (1979): 125-54.

27. Sarna, *Exodus*, p.72.

28. I. Finkelstein, *The Archaeology of the Israelite Settlement* (Jerusalem: Israel Exploration Society, 1988); I. Finkelstein, 'Searching for Israelite Origins,' *BAR* 14.5 (1988): 34-45, 58.

29. A. R. Schulman, 'Egyptian Representations of Horsemen and Riding in the New Kingdom,' *JNES* 16 (1957): 263-71; A. R. Schulman, 'Chariots, Chariotry, and the Hyksos,' *JSSEA* 10 (1979): 105-53.

30. *BDB*, p.673.

31. H. Frankfort, *Kingship and the Gods* (Chicago: University of Chicago Press, 1948), pp.7-9.

32. Gesenius, *Hebrew Grammar*, p.483.

33. G. W. Coats, *Rebellion in the Wilderness* (Nashville: Abingdon, 1968). For an in-depth study of the complaint scene at the Red Sea, see M. Vervenne, 'The Protest Motif in the Sea Narrative,' *Ephemerides Theologicae Lovanienses* 63 (1987): 257-71.

34. Currid, *Ancient Egypt and the Old Testament*, p.145.

35. Waltke and O'Connor, *An Introduction to Biblical Hebrew Syntax*, p.567.

36. *BDB*, p.426.

37. For a study of the heavenly war imagery of Exodus 14:13-31 and parallels in Egyptian literature, see M. Weinfeld, 'Divine Intervention in War in Ancient Israel and in the Ancient Near East,' in *History, Historiography, and Interpretation*, eds. H.

Tadmor and M. Weinfeld (Jerusalem: Magnes Press, 1984), pp.121-47.

38. *BDB*, p.386.

39. S. R. Driver, *A Treatise on the Use of the Tenses in Hebrew* (Oxford: Clarendon, 1892), pp.35-6.

40. Verse 20 has a difficult textual problem. For various proposals, see Childs, *The Book of Exodus*, p.218; and R. Althann, 'Unrecognized Poetic Fragments in Exodus,' *JNSL* 11 (1983): 9-27. It is best to take the Masoretic Text at face value. Some, however, argue that the root of the verb 'to bring light' means 'to cast a spell'. See E. A. Speiser, 'An Angelic Curse: Exodus 14:20,' *JAOS* 80 (1960): 198-200.

41. According to Rabbinic exegesis, verses 19-21 each contain seventy-two letters. For a kabbalistic or mystical explanation of this phenomenon, see T. Schrire, 'Samaritan Amulets, 'Yat' and Exodus 14:20,' *IEJ* 22:2-3 (1972): 153-5.

42. *BDB*, p.237.

43. *BDB*, p.964.

44. M. Barlian, *The Significance of the Concept of Dry Land from Genesis to Joshua* (Th.M. Dissertation, Reformed Theological Seminary, 1995), pp.42-61.

45. See, most recently, D. Nof and N. Paldor, 'Are There Oceanographic Explanations for the Israelites' Crossing of the Red Sea?,' *Bulletin of the American Meteorological Society* 73:3 (1992): 305-14; and S. Segert, 'Crossing the Waters: Moses and Hamilcar,' *JNES* 53 (1994): 195-203.

46. R. W. Dalman, *The Theology of Israel's Sea Crossing* (Th.D. Dissertation, Concordia Seminary, 1990).

47. The Westcar Papyrus is incomplete and it dates to the Hyksos period before Dynasty 18 (which began *c.* 1550 B.C.). Its composition, however, appears to be as early as Dynasty 12 (*c.* 1991-1783 B.C.). See W. K. Simpson, ed., *The Literature of Ancient Egypt* (New Haven: Yale University Press, 1973), pp.15-30.

48. Much of this discussion is found in Currid, *Ancient Egypt and the Old Testament*, p.84.

49. *BDB*, p.327.

50. *BDB*, p.243.

51. J. H. Stek, 'What Happened to the Chariot Wheels of Exod. 14:25?,' *JBL* 105:2 (1986): 293-4.

52. *BDB*, p.624.

53. Waltke and O'Connor, *An Introduction to Biblical Hebrew Syntax*, p.400.

54. Cassuto, *A Commentary on the Book of Exodus*, p.170.

55. Childs, *The Book of Exodus*, p.217.

56. W. A. Gage, *The Gospel of Genesis* (Winona Lake, Ind: Carpenter Books, 1984), pp.20-21.

57. *Ibid.,* p.20.

58. Currid, *Ancient Egypt and the Old Testament*, pp.113-17.

59. D. Bridge, *Signs and Wonders Today* (Leicester: IVP, 1985), p.17.

60. Intriguing studies that compare Exodus 15 with other victory hymns are J. S. Kselman, 'Psalm 77 and the Book of Exodus,' *JANES* 15 (1983): 51-8; and A. J. Hauser, 'Two Songs of Victory: A Comparison of Exodus 15 and Judges 5,' in *Directions in Biblical Hebrew Poetry*, ed. E. R. Follis (Sheffield: JSOT Press, 1987), pp.265-84.

61. For structural analysis, see R. D. Patterson, 'The Song of Redemption,' *WTJ* 57 (1995): 453-61; G. W. Coats, 'The Song of the Sea,' *CBQ* 31 (1969): 1-17; R. L. Giese, 'Strophic Hebrew Verse as Free Verse,' *JSOT* 61 (1994): 29-38; and M. Howell, 'Exodus 15, 1b-18, A Poetic Analysis,' *Ephemerides Theologicae Lovanienses* 65 (1989): 5-42.

62. For studies dealing with the literary phrases of the song, see P. C. Craigie, 'The Poetry of Ugarit and Israel,' *TB* 22 (1971): 3-31; B. Gosse, 'Le texte d'Exode 15,1-21 dans la rédaction biblique,' *BZ* 37:2 (1993): 264-71; and G. Fischer, 'Das Schilfmeerlied Exodus 15 in seinem Kontext,' *Biblica* 77:1 (1996): 32-47.

63. Waltke and O'Connor, *An Introduction to Biblical Hebrew Syntax*, pp.14-15.

64. For examples, see W. W. Hallo, ed. *The Context of Scripture*, vol. 1 (Leiden: Brill, 1997), pp.470ff.

65. I. Rabinowitz, "*az* followed by Imperfect Verb-Form in Preterite Contexts: A Redactional Device in Biblical Hebrew,' *VT* 34 (1984): 53-62. See the discussion of Waltke and O'Connor, *An Introduction to Biblical Hebrew Syntax*, pp.513-14.

66. F. M. Cross and D. N. Freedman, 'The Song of Miriam,' *JNES* 14 (1955): 243-4; S. B. Parker, 'Exodus XV 2 Again,' *VT* 21 (1971): 373-9; and M. L. Barre, '"My Strength and My Song" in Exodus 15:2,' *CBQ* 54 (1992): 623-37.

67. S. E. Loewenstamm, 'The Lord is My Strength and My Glory,' *VT* 19 (1969): 464-70; and cf., E. M. Good, 'Exodus XV 2,' *VT* 20 (1970): 358-9.

68. Sarna, *Exodus*, p.77.

69. Gesenius, *Hebrew Grammar*, pp.157-8.

70. R. J. Williams, 'Energic Verbal Forms in Hebrew,' in *Studies on the Ancient Palestinian World*, ed. J. W. Wevers and D. B. Redford (Toronto: University of Toronto, 1972), pp.75-85.

71. T. Longman and D. Reid, *God Is a Warrior* (Grand Rapids: Zondervan, 1995), p.32.

72. P. C. Craigie makes the interesting assertion that Hebrew *sls* 'may be a nominal adoption of Egyptian *srs*, "to have command

of [a corps]"'. See his 'An Egyptian Expression in the Song of the Sea (Exodus XV 4),' *VT* 20 (1970): 83-6.

73. Friedrich Delitzsch, *Babel and Bible* (New York: Putnam, 1903); and cf., H. May, 'Some Cosmic Connotations of *Mayim Rabbim*, 'Many Waters',' *JBL* 74 (1955): 9-21.

74. See the case made against it by A. Heidel, *The Babylonian Genesis* (Chicago: University of Chicago, 1951), pp.99-101.

75. To see how it has infiltrated other areas of study, consider R. A. Muller, *The Study of Theology* (Grand Rapids: Zondervan, 1991), p.76.

76. Gesenius, *Hebrew Grammar*, p.258, decries this conclusion by saying the old endings are being 'artificially used', and they are actually revivals of old forms.

77. For disagreement with this point, see W. L. Moran, 'The Hebrew Language in Its Northwest Semitic Background,' in *The Bible and the Ancient Near East*, ed. G. E. Wright (Garden City, NY: Doubleday, 1961), p.60.

78. *BDB*, p.354.

79. A. Wolters (in 'Not Rescue but Destruction: Re-reading Exodus 15:8,' *CBQ* 52, 1990: 223-40) argues that this verse is not talking about the deliverance of Israel but only of the destruction of Egypt. It is not a particularly convincing thesis.

80. Cross and Freedman, 'The Song of Miriam,' p.246. They argue that this means the Israelites are chased by the Egyptians across a storm-tossed sea in boats, rather than across dry land through the midst of the sea. For further analysis, see F. Cross, *Canaanite Myth and Hebrew Epic* (Cambridge, MA: Harvard University Press, 1973), pp.131-2. A good response to this bad theory is L. Grabbe, 'Comparative Philology and Exodus 15,8: Did the Egyptians Die in a Storm?,' *SJOT* 7:1 (1993): 263-9.

81. Gesenius, *Hebrew Grammar*, p.484, n. 1.

82. Cassuto, *A Commentary on the Book of Exodus*, p.175.

83. Cross and Freedman, 'The Song of Miriam,' pp.246-7.

84. See H. D. Hummel, 'Enclitic *Mem* in Early Northwest Semitic, Especially Hebrew,' *JBL* 76 (1957): 85-107.

85. The concept of the majesty of God as the unifying theme of Exodus 15 is agreed upon by many commentators. See, for instance, D. N. Freedman, '"Who Is Like Thee Among the Gods?" The Religion of Early Israel,' in *Ancient Israelite Religion*, ed. P. D. Miller, P. D. Hanson, and S. D. McBride (Philadelphia: Fortress, 1987), pp.315-35.

86. Cross and Freedman, 'The Song of Miriam,' p.247; cf., P. D. Miller, 'Two Critical Notes on Psalm 68 and Deuteronomy 33,' *HTR* 57 (1964): 240ff.

87. R. K. Ritner, *The Mechanics of Ancient Egyptian Magical Practice* (Chicago: Studies of Ancient Oriental Civilization, OI, 54, 1993), p.103.

88. Driver, *A Treatise on the Use of the Tenses in Hebrew*, pp.35-6.

89. Gesenius, *Hebrew Grammar*, p.315.

90. M. Dahood, *Psalms I* (Garden City, NY: Doubleday, 1966), p.106; Cross and Freedman, 'The Song of Miriam,' pp.247-8.

91. J. Allegro, 'Uses of the Semitic Demonstrative Element $\underline{Z}$ in Hebrew,' *VT* 5 (1955): 309-12.

92. Waltke and O'Connor, *An Introduction to Biblical Hebrew Syntax*, pp.516-17.

93. Gesenius, *Hebrew Grammar*, p.251.

94. Waltke and O'Connor, *An Introduction to Biblical Hebrew Syntax*, p.261.

95. Gesenius, *Hebrew Grammar*, p.428.

96. Cross and Freedman, 'The Song of Miriam,' p.249.

97. M. Dahood, '"Nada" "To Hurl" in Ex. 15,16,' *Biblica* 43 (1962): 248-9.

98. W. F. Albright (in *Yahweh and the Gods of Canaan*, Garden City, NY: Doubleday, 1968, p.26, n.59), says Exodus 15:17 'is itself an equally clear reflection of passages in the Baal Epic'.

99. Cross and Freedman, 'The Song of Miriam,' p.250.

100. The kingship of Yahweh is examined in detail by J. Gray, 'The Hebrew Conception of the Kingship of God: Its Origin and Development,' *VT* 6 (1956): 268-85; J. Gray, 'Kingship of God in the Prophets and Psalms,' *VT* 11 (1961): 1-29.

101. Some authors argue that she is so important that her song is the primary one and the Song of Moses, in reality, is a response to it. See J. G. Janzen, 'Song of Moses, Song of Miriam: Who is Seconding Whom?,' *CBQ* 54 (1992): 211-20; cf. P. Trible, 'Bringing Miriam Out of the Shadows,' *BR* 5 (1989): 14-25, 34. Such a reconstruction is totally unconvincing.

102. Sarna, *Exodus*, p.83; and C. H. Gordon, 'Fratriarchy in the Old Testament,' *JBL* 54 (1935): 223-31.

103. C. L. Meyers, 'A Terracotta at the Harvard Semitic Museum and Disc-holding Female Figurines Reconsidered,' *IEJ* 37 (1987): 116-22.

104. E. Poethig, *The Victory Song Tradition of the Women of Israel* (Dissertation at Union Theological Seminary, New York, 1985).

105. B. W. Anderson, 'The Song of Miriam Poetically and Theologically Considered,' in *Directions in Biblical Hebrew Poetry*, ed. E. R. Follis (Sheffield: JSOT Press, 1987), pp.285-96, incorrectly says it is actually being sung to the women of Israel.

106. W. H. Bennett, *Exodus* (New Century Bible; Edinburgh: Clark, 1908), p.137; and Cassuto, *A Commentary on the Book of Exodus*, p.182.

107. In the Dead Sea scrolls, a fragment of a larger Song of Miriam has been discovered. There is no evidence that it reflects

a date of composition during Old Testament times. See G. J. Brooke, 'A Long-Lost Song of Miriam,' *BAR* 20:3 (1994): 62-5.
108. W. Hendriksen, *More Than Conquerors* (Grand Rapids: Baker, 1965 ed.), p.159.

Chapter 7 — Grumblings in the desert

1. Coats, *Rebellion in the Wilderness*, p.249.
2. For a study on how the passage has been interpreted throughout the history of Judaism and church history, see B. P. Robinson, 'Symbolism in Exod. 15:22-27 (Marah and Elim),' *RB* 94 (1987): 376-88. Many have understood the passage in an allegorical sense: for instance, the twelve springs of verse 27 symbolize the twelve apostles of Christ, and the seventy date palm trees are the seventy disciples chosen by Christ in Luke 10:1.
3. This is an early theory. See S. R. Driver, 'Shur,' in *Hastings Dictionary of the Bible*, vol. IV (New York: Scribner's, 1902), p.510.
4. J. Fichtner, 'Die Etymologische Aetiologie in den Namengebungen der Geschichtlichen Bucher des Altne Testaments,' *VT* 6 (1956): 388.
5. Numerous suggestions have been made. See, for example, J. Simons, *The Geographical and Topographical Texts of the Old Testament* (Leiden: Brill, 1959), pp.251-2.
6. Cassuto, *A Commentary on the Book of Exodus*, p.184.
7. J. Hempel, 'Ich bin der Herr, dein Arzt: Ex. 15, 26,' *Theologische Literaturzeitung* 82 (1957): cols 809-26.
8. Simons, *Geographical and Topographical Texts*, p.252.
9. For a source-critical analysis of Exodus 16, see E. Ruprecht, 'Stellung und Bedeutung der Erzhlung vom Mannawunder (Ex. 16) im Aufbau der Priesterschrift,' *ZAW* 86:3 (1974): 269-307.
10. I. Beit-Arieh, 'Serabit el-Khadim: New Metallurgical and Chronological Aspects,' *Levant* 17 (1985): 89-116.
11. W. M. F. Petrie, *Researches in Sinai* (London: Murray, 1906), p.169.
12. K. A. Kitchen, 'Wilderness,' in *Illustrated Bible Dictionary*, ed. J. D. Douglas, 3 vols. (Leicester: Inter-Varsity, 1980): 3:1644-5.
13. Childs, *The Book of Exodus*, p.284.
14. The word *lehem* can have the wider meaning of food, but here it should retain its narrower meaning. The subsequent context demands such a reading.
15. *BDB*, p.566.
16. W. A. M. Beuken, 'Exodus 16:5,23: A Rule regarding the Keeping of the Sabbath?,' *JSOT* 32 (1985): 3-14, unconvincingly argues against this interpretation.

17. A type of sabbath appears in Babylonia. See W. G. Lambert, 'A New Look at the Babylonian Background of Genesis,' *JTS* 16 (1965): 296-7.

18. For this idea of anxiety in the wilderness, see the sermon by K. D. Sakenfeld, 'Bread of Heaven,' *The Princeton Seminary Bulletin* 7:1 (1986): 20-24.

19. For an argument for the integrity of the Masoretic Text throughout this passage, see P. W. Ferris, 'The Manna Narrative of Exodus 16:1-10,' *JETS* 18:3 (1975): 191-9.

20. R. Althann ('Unrecognized Poetic Fragments in Exodus,' *JNSL* 11, 1983: 9-27) would therefore understand this verse to be poetic.

21. G. E. Whitney, 'Alternative Interpretations of *LO* in Exodus 6:3 and Jeremiah 7:22,' *WTJ* 48 (1986): 154.

22. Childs, *The Book of Exodus*, p.287.

23. *BDB*, p.815.

24. M. G. Kline, *Images of the Spirit* (Grand Rapids: Baker, 1980).

25. V. Moller-Christensen and K. E. Jordt Jorgensen, *Encyclopedia of Bible Creatures* (Philadelphia: Fortress, 1965): 171-4.

26. E. Orni and E. Efrat, *Geography of Israel*, 3rd ed. (Philadelphia: Jewish Publication Society of America, 1973), pp.189-90.

27. For an overview, see P. Maiberger, *Das Manna: Eine literarische, etymologische, und naturkundliche Untersuchung* (Wiesbaden: Harrassowitz, 1983).

28. F. S. Bodenheimer, 'The Manna of Sinai,' *BA* 10 (1947): 1-6.

29. F. C. Fensham, *Exodus* (Nijkerk: Callenbach, 1970), p.96; Sarna, *Exodus*, p.89. The word is also found in late Aramaic and late Syriac texts; see *BDB*, p.577.

30. See, for instance, Genesis 3:20.

31. *BDB*, p.1069. Cassuto (*A Commentary on the Book of Exodus*, p.197) and others suggest that the insects could be ants. However, that proposal is based upon modern scientific considerations and not on philological grounds.

32. Much has been written about this point. See, for example, E. M. Yamauchi, 'The 'Daily Bread' Motif in Antiquity,' *WTJ* 28 (1966): 145-56; W. A. Meeks, 'The Man from Heaven in Johannine Sectarianism,' *JBL* 91 (1972): 44-72; and especially, P. J. Borgen, *Bread From Heaven: An Exegetical Study of the Concept of Manna in the Gospel of John and the Writings of Philo* (Leiden: Brill, 1965). G. Vermes ('He is the Bread: Targum Neofiti Exodus 16:15,' *Neotestamentica et Semitica*, eds. E. Ellis and M. Wilcox, Edinburgh: Clark, 1969, pp.256-63), proposes that verse 15 may actually say, 'He is the bread', in reference to Moses; the manna in the New Testament, of course, is identified with Jesus. So Moses is a pointer to Jesus.

33. See discussion in Childs, *The Book of Exodus*, p.290.

34. Another example of *idem per idem* is Exodus 33:19b, in which God says, 'I will be gracious to whom I will be gracious, and I will show compassion on whom I will show compassion.' Although no imperative is involved, the principle acts in the same way: God is free to bestow his mercy on whomever he desires.

35. For detailed discussion, see Beuken, 'Exodus 16: 5,23: A Rule Regarding the Keeping of the Sabbath,' pp.7-11.

36. Sarna, *Exodus*, p.90.

37. P. D. Miller, 'The Human Sabbath: A Study in Deuteronomic Theology,' *The Princeton Seminary Bulletin* 6:2 (1985): 81-97.

38. Childs, *The Book of Exodus*, p.274.

39. Karl Barth, *Church Dogmatics* III:4 (Edinburgh: Clark, 1961), p.50.

40. G. W. Coats, *Exodus 1-18* (Grand Rapids: Eerdmans, 1998), p.133.

41. Waltke and O'Connor, *An Introduction to Biblical Hebrew Syntax*, p.251.

42. Childs, *The Book of Exodus*, p.291.

43. A parallel passage appears in Numbers 20:2-13. Clearly, it is a different incident but it has much in common with the present chapter. See G. W. Coats, *Saga, Legend, Tale, Novella, Fable: Narrative Forms in Old Testament Literature* (Sheffield: JSOT Press, 1985), pp.68-9. For a general study of Exodus 17:1-7, see S. Lehming, 'Massa und Meriba,' *ZAW* 73 (1961):71-7.

44. *TDOT* 6: 225-50.

45. Currid, *Ancient Egypt and the Old Testament*, pp.123-5.

46. See the suggestion, however, of Simons, *Geographical and Topographical Texts*, p.253.

47. At the close of the verse is a rare genitive of the subject after an infinitive: it says 'for the drinking of the people' (see Gesenius, *Hebrew Grammar*, p.354).

48. The imperative is a plural. The Samaritan Pentateuch and other manuscripts change it to a singular, thus corresponding to the threat to the individual Moses. However, the plural may reflect not only Moses, but the leadership of Israel, including even Yahweh.

49. Gesenius, *Hebrew Grammar*, p.128.

50. The *min* preposition is partitive, that is, referring to only part of the noun following it.

51. The group called elders is first mentioned in 3:16.

52. Sarna, *Exodus*, p.94.

53. Cassuto, *A Commentary on the Book of Exodus*, p.202.

54. *Ibid.*, p.202.

55. These are not aetiologies as Coats would have us believe. Aetiology is normally understood to be stories made up to explain names of sites already in existence. See his *Exodus 1-18*, p.137.

56. It has been thoroughly presented by B. H. Grigsby, 'If Any Man Thirsts: Observations on the Rabbinic Background of John 7:37-39,' *Biblica* 67:1 (1986): 101-8.
57. See C. B. Houk, 'Peirasmos, the Lord's Prayer, and the Massah Tradition,' *SJT* 19 (1966): 216-25.
58. S. J. Kistemaker, *New Testament Commentary: Exposition of the First Epistle to the Corinthians* (Grand Rapids: Baker, 1993), p.325.
59. See D. E. Wingeier, 'Tapping the Rock: A Model for Ministry,' *Asia Journal of Theology* 3 (1989): 558-63.

Chapter 8 — Preparation for Sinai
1. For a contextual study of the present passage, see B. P. Robinson, 'Israel and Amalek: The Context of Exodus 17.8-16,' *JSOT* 32 (1985): 15-22.
2. S. Mowinckel, 'Kadesj, Sinai, og Jahve,' *Norsk Geografisk Tidsskrift* 11 (1942): 13-15.
3. Sarna, *Exploring Exodus*, pp.120-26.
4. The Masoretes place the *'atnah* — an accent that marks the end of the first half of the verse — before the word 'tomorrow'.
5. Josephus, *Antiquities*, Loeb Classical Library (Cambridge, MA: Harvard University, 1978), p.345.
6. Sarna, *Exodus*, p.95.
7. Coats, *Genesis 1-18*, p.141.
8. Currid, 'The Rod of Moses,' pp.107-14.
9. Gesenius, *Hebrew Grammar*, p.452.
10. This is one of the points that leads G. W. Coats to conclude that the story 'maintains no consistent point of tension, but rather relies on relatively disjointed notations in order to emphasize, not the battle as an event in God's dealings with his people, but the stamina and faithfulness of Moses to his task'. See his 'Moses Versus Amalek,' *VT Supplement* 28 (1975): 29-41. I would differ with Coats at this juncture. The fact that Moses employs the rod of God and then names the event after Yahweh demonstrates the centrality of God in the story.
11. *BDB*, p.325.
12. Cassuto, *A Commentary on the Book of Exodus*, p.206.
13. The article attached to the word 'book' is generic: it speaks of a particular book that will be written, not one already in existence. See Waltke and O'Connor, *An Introduction to Biblical Hebrew Syntax*, p.245, n. 13.
14. See discussion in Currid, *Ancient Egypt and the Old Testament*, pp.149-54; and C. Houtman, 'YHWH is My Banner — A 'Hand' on the 'Throne' of YH,' in *New Avenues in the Study of the Old Testament*, ed. A. S. Van Der Woude (Leiden: Brill, 1989), pp.110-20.

15. D. M. Beegle, *Moses, the Servant of Yahweh* (Grand Rapids: Eerdmans, 1972), p.190.

16. Childs, *The Book of Exodus*, pp.311-12.

17. For a discussion of the identity of Jethro, see A. Chiu, 'Who is Moses' Father-in-law?' *East Asia Journal of Theology* 4:1 (1986): 62-7.

18. Attached to 'my helper' there is a *beth* preposition. It serves as a *beth* of identity (see Exod. 6:3).

19. Breasted, *ARE II*, p.342.

20. Breasted, *ARE III*, pp.197-200.

21. A similar emendation seems necessary in Genesis 48:1-2.

22. Cassuto, *A Commentary on the Book of Exodus*, p.215.

23. See W. S. Towner, '"Blessed be YHWH" and "Blessed Art Thou, YHWH": The Modulation of a Biblical Formula,' *CBQ* 30 (1968): 386-99.

24. R. Althann, 'Unrecognized Poetic Fragments in Exodus,' *JNSL* 9 (1983): 9-27.

25. *Contra* Coats, *Exodus 1-18*, p.146.

26. Fensham, *Exodus*, p.108.

27. F. D. Kidner, *Sacrifice in the Old Testament* (London: Tyndale Press, 1952), pp.14-15; see, also, R. de Vaux, *Studies in Old Testament Sacrifice* (Cardiff: University of Wales Press, 1964).

28. A. Cody, 'Exodus 18,12: Jethro Accepts a Covenant with the Israelites,' *Biblica* 49:2 (1968): 165. See, in addition, Y. Avishur, 'Treaty Terminology in the Moses-Jethro Story (Exodus 18:1-12),' *Aula Orientalis* 6 (1988): 139-47, who compares Exodus 18 with the treaty between Solomon and Hiram in 1 Kings 5.

29. Sarna, *Exodus*, p.100.

30. For an analysis of Israel's early judicial system, see R. R. Wilson, 'Israel's Judicial System in the Pre-exilic Period,' *JQR* 74 (1983): 229-48. Wilson unfortunately takes the unwarranted position that Exodus 18:13-27 is a late text, and it is merely a retrojection of a later judicial system.

31. Coats, *Exodus 1-18*, pp.146-7.

32. For a treatment of divination practices in Egypt, see R. K. Ritner, *The Mechanics of Ancient Egyptian Magical Practice*, Studies in Ancient Oriental Civilization (Chicago: Oriental Institute, 1992); and Currid, *Ancient Egypt and the Old Testament*, pp.219-28.

33. The Septuagint translates the word 'brought' as a plural, thus referring to the disputants. However, the Masoretic Text makes perfect sense in the singular as indicating the affair or dispute.

34. J. Van Seters, 'Etiology in the Moses Tradition: The Case of Exodus 18,' *HAR* 9 (1985): 355-61.

35. Y. Hoffman, 'Did Amos Regard Himself as a *nabi*?', *VT* 27 (1977): 209-10. Z. Zevit, 'Expressing Denial in Biblical Hebrew

and Mishnaic Hebrew, and in Amos,' *VT* 29 (1979): 505-8, disagrees with Hoffman's conclusions.

36. Waltke and O'Connor, *An Introduction to Biblical Hebrew Syntax*, p.567.

37. The *min* of comparison is used here — see Gesenius, *Hebrew Grammar*, p.430.

38. *BDB*, p.264.

39. *NIDOTTE*, vol. II, p.118.

40. R. Knierim, 'Exodus 18 und die Neuordnung der Mosaischen Gerichtsbarkeit,' *ZAW* 73 (1961): 146-71.

41. Currid, *Ancient Egypt and the Old Testament*, pp.121-3.

42. Childs, *The Book of Exodus*, p.331.

43. Ligon Duncan, 'Grace and Responsibility,' *Tabletalk* 22:4 (1998): 44.

A wide range of excellent books on spiritual subjects is available from Evangelical Press. Please write to us for your free catalogue or contact us by e-mail.

Evangelical Press
Faverdale North Industrial Estate, Darlington, DL3 0PH, England

Evangelical Press USA
P. O. Box 84, Auburn, MA 01501, USA

e-mail: sales@evangelical-press.org

web: www.evangelical-press.org